PAPWA:

IN THE GRIP OF A CHAMPION

PAPWA:

IN THE GRIP OF A CHAMPION

Derrick Hubbard

PAPWA: IN THE GRIP OF A CHAMPION

iUniverse books may be ordered through booksellers or by contacting:

iUniverse
1663 Liberty Drive
Bloomington, IN 47403
www.iuniverse.com
844-349-9409

ISBN: 978-1-6632-1726-4 (sc)
ISBN: 978-1-6632-1725-7 (e)

Library of Congress Control Number: 2021901488

Print information available on the last page.

iUniverse rev. date: 01/22/2021

ONE

As he lined up to strike the ball, the boy adjusted his body this way and that, emulating the more seasoned golfers he surreptitiously watched as they practised their swings on the golf course nearby. Already he'd learned that if he swung his hips as he struck, the ball would travel further. With his short stature and skinny frame, he needed all the ballast he could muster. He bent his knees into the shot. Satisfied with his stance, the boy glanced down at his hands on the club: his right hand above the left. He didn't pay much attention to their placement. In his mind, it was just as other players gripped their clubs and of no consequence. Besides, it was what felt most comfortable. The club was not a club – not a true club at least. Fashioned from the limb of a tree by his father, it was little more than a stick. The ball was a lucky find. So far he had two.

The boy sniffed the air for wind, but there was not a hint of the slightest breeze. There *was* the faint but foetid stench emanating from the river, the stronger, nearer smell of wood-smoke and paraffin for boiling water and cooking food and even though it was so early, the mouth-watering scent of crushed garlic and ginger and other spices sizzling in ghee.

Riverside's residents were rousing from sleep. A dog barked and others joined in, whining at the cold dawn. A man howled at the dogs to stop and was berated by another. Women's voices added to the din, muttering in Hindi, Tamil, Gujarati, Urdu and Telugu. A flock of yellow-billed Myna birds soared overhead, chirping and growling at one another as they passed. The boy heard nothing, saw nothing;

smelled nothing. No birds nor dogs nor human voices disturbed his concentration. Neither was he aware of anyone watching him. He looked to the sky one last time, searching for the sun, but the morning was still new: the sky grey and cloudy like a dirty pearl on a rich woman's ring.

Deftly, the boy took the shot. The ball landed in the tin can buried in the dirt yard.

Aware now of being watched, the boy sought out his lone spectator, a thin, dark-skinned man dressed in pyjama pants and a thick cardigan against the chill, though his feet, like the boy's, were bare.

"Look, Pa! Hole in one!"

"Very well, Papwa, now try from farther away."

"Yes, Pa," the boy mock grumbled as he shuffled further from his target. He knew this was his father's way, to encourage him to try harder, to stretch himself. It was better than any well-intentioned compliment other fathers would give their sons, this belief that his boy could exceed his best. Always.

The boy lined up his shot again. The ball clinked into the tin.

"Yes! Hole in one!"

The father shook his head proudly and with some disbelief. He laughed as his son scampered like a monkey to retrieve his ball from the tin can, but as the boy lined up to putt once more, standing even further away this time, it was with a grown-up concentration that tightened his chest.

The father watched the scene replay itself for the next few minutes: the way the boy sniffed the wind and sought out hints of the sun's ascent; the concentration that furrowed his brow. He saw his son's frustration when he missed the tin and encouraged him to try again. When the ball found its target, he reminded his son to play from even farther away.

Minutes passed and the responsibilities of the day began to encroach, even for a seven-year-old boy with no school to attend.

"Come, Son, time for a roti and a cup of tea, then we need to get to the beach, else the fish will be gone by the time we get there."

"Just a little more, Pa!" The boy smiled engagingly and the father relented.

"Five more minutes," he said, waggling a hand.

The father knew he should be sterner, but he was a sports-lover too. Soccer, not golf was his sport. On Saturdays he played for a local team.

"Five more minutes, then we need to go inside, right? Ma is waiting."

Quickly and without bothering with his run-through this time, the boy putted the ball.

"Hole in one!"

Smiling, the father saw that the sun had come out, bathing his son in its burgeoning glow.

TWO

Breakfast consisted of slices of yesterday's *pattha*, a fried snack made from the spinach-like leaves of the *madumbi* plant, served with roti, homemade mango *achar* and lime pickle. The mangoes and *pattha-leaves* had been gleaned from the surrounding area. Like most families in Riverside the Sewgolums kept a vegetable garden, but even with Pa's green fingers it was inadequate to sustain two adults and five children. Situated close to where the Umgeni River flows into the Indian Ocean, Riverside provided certain opportunities for impoverished families to supplement their diet with fish – particularly shad and barracuda and sometimes sardines, and the pickings from the trees and shrubs that grew unchecked in the area. With few exceptions, the families living there *were* impoverished and had long learned to be grateful for whatever extras they could lay their hands on.

In the early 1930s, poverty was not limited to Riverside. South Africa, along with most of the developed world, was in the throes of what had already become known as the Great Depression. In South Africa the protracted economic downturn had caused the demand for exports to plunge, while a drought from 1932 to 1933 further exacerbated the strained economy. Manufacturing declined to adjust to the diminished demand and this, coupled with a reduction in agricultural income, had resulted in widespread unemployment.

With so many men out of work, Pa had come to value his job as a grass-cutter for the Durban Corporation. Yes, the municipality had long been notorious for the meagre wages it paid its workers. Wages so inadequate that people still spoke about the time – more than sixty years ago – that the entire Magazine Barracks, that in those days housed most of the Corporation's Indian workers, had once sent a petition begging for better pay. Perhaps people remembered it so well, Pa thought, because the request had not been granted. As it was, he had to resort to his trusty fishing pole every chance he could – with one of his three sons: Mohan, Papwa or Harilal, in tow, sometimes all three, to give his wife, Parvathy, a respite from the rambunctious boys.

Luckily for him, fishing was not only a vital solution for a household where finances were stretched thin, it was also a welcome distraction from the crowded shack in the teeming settlement where inadequate sanitation and poor nutrition led to a number of health problems such as dysentery and diarrhoea amongst the people who lived there. Privacy and personal space were unheard of luxuries, particularly living as they did as part of the joint family system, with shared living space, though they at least had their own wood-and-iron dwelling behind the big-house. Sitting at the shore with a fishing pole in one hand, Pa could breathe deeply, savouring the briny air.

As for Papwa, he loved being outside; loved feeling the warmth of the sun on his skin and the light sting of the breeze blowing off the water. During those alone times with Pa, the two could just be, and often sat in silence. Even if they walked farther away from home and joined the bustle of men fishing from the North Pier, Pa would keep to himself, allowing the hullabaloo to follow around him. He was soft-spoken, Pa, a man who kept to himself, spoke little. But when they were alone, once the silence had been exhausted, Papwa would ask his father all the pressing questions a young boy needed to have answered.

"But why can't we play there, Pa?" Papwa would ask, pointing in the direction of the golf course at the sea's edge.

His father thought the boy too old for such questions; he'd expect it from his youngest son, maybe, someone who hadn't yet learned how things were. Politics was a dirty business. No need to think about such things.

"Just because, Papwa," Pa said with a sigh. "It's the way it's always been."

"You don't like golf, then, Pa?"

"Our people don't play golf, Papwa."

"But why, Pa? Why don't *our* people play golf?"

Looking at his son, the furrowed brow and inquisitive expression in his eyes as he tried to understand, Pa relented. "Some of our people like to play golf my boy. Did I ever tell you the story of Bambata Boodhan?" Without waiting for a reply, he continued. "Bambata was a Hindu man like us, born in Durban and all. He started out carrying the bags of the European players at the club where he worked. When that prince from England came here – this was before you were born right – Bambata carried his bags even, but Bambata? He was more than a caddie boy, I tell you!"

Caddie boy? Papwa frowned at the unknown term, but did not want to interrupt his father.

"He learned to play the game and he was good, very good; beat many of the Union's best players. He was so good that he went to take part in competitions overseas and all."

"Did he win the competitions, Pa?" Papwa asked, his eyes wide and gleaming, as a grin spread across his face.

Pa smiled, not wanting to disillusion his son. He'd heard that the dismal Scottish weather – the cold and the rain – hadn't agreed with the player, who was accustomed to Durban's tropical climate, and he'd fared badly.

"So what happened to Bambata, Pa? If he's famous, he must be rich!"

Pa didn't know what had become of the player whom one Scottish newspaper had referred to as "little Ramnath Boodhan Bambata, the Coloured player from Durban" when he'd played in the British Open at Muirfield. Someone said he'd died a few years ago, but he wasn't sure. For all he knew, Bambata was still caddying somewhere. He doubted he'd become rich, but did not tell the boy this. Sometimes a boy needed to have dreams, aspirations. "Oh he's very wealthy my boy, he lives in a big house with many, many servants. Maybe one day if you continue to practise, you'll play just as well and will be just as rich as he!"

"No, Pa. When I'm big I'll be better than Bambata, you'll see! I'll make lots of money and buy you and Ma a big house – bigger than Bambata's house. One day Pa, you'll see!"

Papwa abandoned his fishing pole and picked up the "club" that accompanied him everywhere he went. Aiming at shells, he began practising his swing.

"What about the fishing, Papwa?" his father asked, shaking his head.

Papwa swung at the shells for a few minutes, hitting them far into the surf with a satisfying noise before returning to his father's side.

Handing the fishing pole to his son, Pa said: "One day the whole Natal will know your name, son. Just keep on practising and remember to always try harder. Don't take the easy shots and you'll go far!"

The boy seemed so convinced of his future success that the father felt bad for raising his hopes like that. There was never enough money for the necessities of life and even if his son had all the expensive equipment he needed to play golf, where would he play? Even Bambata had only been allowed to play on the greens of the Durban golf club where he'd worked, first as a caddie and then as a coach, due to the special consideration shown him by its management. He had been unable to play in competitions in the Union thanks to the colour bar and other discriminatory laws that disallowed Indians from competing in the white man's competitions. When Bambata failed to make a name for himself at the British Open, there'd been many who'd taken pleasure in his lack of success. Thinking about Bambata and the obstacles he'd faced in pursuing the sport he loved, Pa sighed. There'd be time enough for the boy to learn what it meant to be a poor Indian boy living in South Africa, but Papwa was young still and it was always good to have dreams.

Sometimes Pa wondered what dreams his own grandfather must have nurtured when he'd left his home in India in search of a better life. He knew what had brought his grandfather to Natal. Everyone spoke of the terrible poverty in India in those days, a poverty exacerbated by famine and the punishing taxes imposed by the nation's British rulers. Trying to pay those taxes had caused many a family to lose its land. Once a man lost his land and the living that land provided, he had very few choices. The glass and paper and textile factories – forced to compete against duty-free British imports – were disgorging workers at the time, workers who had no recourse to eking a living from the land. It was really no wonder, he admitted, that so many Indian men – and women – had chosen to hire themselves out for years at a stretch, travelling by boat to unwelcoming places until they were thousands of miles away from their homes and families ... using the only thing they had left to trade: the sweat of their brow.

Yes, Pa knew that not everyone had made the choice. He'd heard about young men and women in India being tricked by unscrupulous agents – promised one thing and receiving another bill of goods when they landed. There were days he worried whether his grandfather had willingly made the journey to Natal. If he had, and he chose to believe that he had, why on earth had he stayed?

It always came down to the British – the British Raj that ruled India and the British colonial government of Natal. Everyone knew that Indians had only been brought to Natal to satisfy the European farmers' need for a cheap and reliable source of labour. It was said that while content to work for short periods, the native Zulu could not be compelled to leave their land and established way of living during the early days of the sugar industry. So the Natal farmers, aware of how farmers in Mauritius had benefitted from the importation of indentured workers from India, inveigled upon their government for the same. Before long, the two governments reached an accord and in so doing changed the lives of more than one hundred and fifty thousand Indians from Agra, Bihar, Madras, Mysore and Oudh, those who would go on to exchange one set of colonial rulers for another. Moreover, the practice of bringing over these indentured labourers would continue to impact the lives of their descendants for generations to come – long after the final ship arrived in Durban Harbour in 1911. The cessation of the trade, sixty years after it had begun, came about only once the Indian government took a firm stand, refusing to send any more of its people to be mistreated in the newly established Union of South Africa into which Natal had been incorporated. Pa accepted that he and his family were the living proof of the iniquities inherent in the system as they battled for survival in a land that had only recently deigned to accept them as citizens.

From the stories his father had told, Pa knew that his grandfather had been amongst the first batch of Indians who'd made the long journey across the seas – arriving on the Natal shore in 1860 where they were met not by an immigration agent as promised, but by hordes of Europeans curious to see the spectacle. Once landed, the new immigrants had been taken to half-built barracks by policemen armed with bayonets and guns and there they remained until days later they were assigned to work on the sugar plantations or other farms, for the railways or for the Durban Corporation. A lucky few were taken on as special servants and granted work as coachmen, cooks, waiters or orderlies. They were allotted numbers as a means of identification and renamed "Coolie" – those immigrants, who'd never been meant to stay.

The deal had been to sign up for a period of three years, work out their contracts and leave. Three years became five. Five years of working for a few shillings a month. If workers agreed to another five years with the same masters, they were promised free passage home, or a small grant of Crown land if they chose to stay. Masters, yes, for they were treated like slaves. Old men still spoke about it. Yes, they were paid those shillings, with money deducted for missing work and for other infractions. Yes, they were provided with food, clothing and a place to sleep. True, they'd not been bought and sold, but they were not free, not really. They were not allowed to leave their employees' premises without a signed pass and curfew laws meant immediate arrest for any "persons of colour" found on the streets after a certain time at night without that pass.

Sugar – so sweet you could almost taste it. Life on the plantations was anything but sweet. His own father had followed in *his* father's footsteps, but when the chance had come for his son to work for the Corporation, he'd pushed him in that direction. The cane-fields were snakes and rats and long hours under a blazing sun. The cane-fields were "Coolie lines" of corrugated iron and mud without any space for an uncluttered thought. The cane-fields were sleep disturbed by the clang of the sirdar's bell; trudging to work while the sun rose. The cane-fields were the flay of a whip; the flog of a hunting crop.

On days when the sun burned his back and it took all he had not to swoon from the heat or the humidity or the hunger that never quite receded, Pa would consider how much better off he had it compared to his father and grandfather before. On days when there wasn't enough money to go around, no matter how he juggled it, on days when the sun turned their tin home into a furnace, he thought about his father and his grandfather and their cramped shacks in the "Coolie lines". On those days he wondered whether there was ever any way to escape one's karma.

Yes, let the boy dream, he thought. Perhaps by the time his son was old enough, the world would be ready for him – ready for a Hindu boy who believed that if he practised and played well, he would find a way out of the shantytown into which he had been born. Pa hoped so. It was a dream in which he too wanted to believe.

THREE

"Look Pa!"

Papwa's shout woke his father. He couldn't believe that he'd allowed himself to fall asleep with the fishing pole in his hand, but these days he was always tired, a fatigue he felt deep in his bones. With a near-sightless wife and seven mouths to feed, he knew that he could not succumb to weakness. A man's duty was to fend for his family. He'd taught his sons that.

"Pa!"

The boy's excited shouts wiped away the last remnants of sleep.

As usual, Papwa had abandoned his own pole and was practising his driving. His father had learnt that word, "driving" eager to learn as much as possible about the game that so engrossed his son. It was the least he could do. He'd taught his other sons to play soccer. They liked cricket too. On warm evenings when the sun was late to set, the boys of the neighbourhood would get together in the streets for an impromptu game of cricket. The fathers would gather around, watching the game, offering advice and conferring amongst themselves. Not all the neighbourhood boys played, no. His Papwa was not interested in cricket. He was not interested in soccer. It was always and only golf. He and that bloody stick were inseparable.

Pa tracked the ball's progress. It went far. Farther than he'd seen his son hit a ball before. Almost as far as the long drives he and the boy saw being executed by the players at the club whom they watched from the beach. Since the first time he'd seen Papwa strike the ball in their backyard, he'd watched his son, waiting for him to lose interest. The boy's devotion to the game never wavered. It had been months now.

He often found himself wishing that he could teach his son more about the game. Practical things, like how to stand or hold the stick. The boy had been so grateful when he'd fashioned that stick for him. His boys were good boys, yes. They received so little, yet they swelled their father's heart with pride at their appreciation for the small things he could provide. Still, a father wanted to be able to teach his sons. His own father had been too busy to teach him much, his body too battered after long hours in the fields, but they'd had their fishing and their stories of the old days in an India his father had not known – third-hand stories passed down from his father's father.

Shick!

The ball flew into the air again. The boy was practising on the sand, against the surf. He treasured that ball so much; he couldn't bear to lose it in the water. Pa remembered the day the other ball was lost. Papwa had hit it so far away that he'd been unable to find it. He'd been so distraught that his father and brothers had tried to help him. Eventually someone had pointed out that he had another. All this made the boy treasure the ball he'd managed to keep even more. Every night before bed, Pa noted how Papwa polished the ball with an old rag he kept for that express purpose.

Funny how Papwa's panicked reaction to losing that ball had reminded him of the European men who commanded the golf course. If you went close enough, you could hear them swearing at the caddies when balls went missing – lost in the bushes or trapped in one of the obstacles that hampered the course. More so than the players' actions, whenever balls went missing on the course, it was the caddies' reactions that interested the father most: "Sorry sir, very sorry sir!" These apologies would rise into the air and reach the boy and his father hidden in the bushes. If they were too far away to hear, they could still discern the apology from the hunched shoulders of the caddies as their bodies tensed for blows that fortunately did not come, and the furious bobbing of their heads on too narrow necks.

The caddies were just boys, Pa noted, and were already servile. As a man, he'd learned to master the art of apologising.

"Sorry sir, very sorry sir!"

"What you said, Pa?"

Pa shook his head. He hadn't realised he'd been saying the words out loud. He walked closer to his son; put a hand on his shoulder, stilling him. The little boy's body was always in motion, falling into his familiar putting stance or dancing to a film tune only he could hear. He was always smiling, his son. So-so grateful, so-so happy; Pa wished it would be a long time before he realised just how little he had to be grateful for. He hoped it would be years yet before his son became practised in the art of servility.

Casting his thoughts aside, he concentrated on the boy's progress. "You hit the ball really far this time, son."

Papwa beamed then lowered his gaze. Along with always striving to do his best and avoiding complacency, he'd learned humility – one of his mother's lessons.

"How do you do it, son? How do you know where to hit the ball, where it will land?"

The boy shrugged. "I just know, Pa. I don't know how I do it. It's just like the men we see," he said, veering his chin in the direction of the golf course. "They too know. They just know. Like me.'

"Remember, you can't go there," Pa warned. "Not without me. Don't go too close. Don't you go looking for trouble now!"

Papwa stared at his father in disbelief. He knew better than to approach the men at the club. His father had said nothing about wandering the course early in the morning before the players arrived, though. Certain mornings he would see the boys playing – boys who looked like him, only older. At those times the urge to ask whether he could play with them was strongest, but he did not have the courage. In any case, he was too young to play with the big boys. They'd probably laugh at him if he asked; chase him off the course.

"No Pa, I know where I can go," the boy said, "and where I cannot. You don't worry Pa."

The boy's answer saddened his father. Again he thought that a father should be able to teach his son not only how to fear, but more importantly, how to be brave.

FOUR

"*Arré*, you should see the boy play, my brother! I can't understand it; the way he hits that ball so flipping far ..."

Pa was always in a more garrulous mood after a successful Saturday morning soccer match. One of his teammates lived nearby and they were talking outside the house before parting ways. By now, everyone in the area had seen Papwa with his club; he seldom left home without it, though he was certainly not one to show off. He practised his longer drives in the dunes behind their home, or on the beach. Again, he couldn't take the chance of his ball falling into the wrong hands. Or maybe he concentrated better when he was alone, his father thought.

"It's good for boys to play sport," Pa's friend agreed. "But I don't understand this golf business. Wouldn't you rather he played cricket like the other boys? Or soccer? Chip off the old block and all!"

"No, Daya, the boy's really good at golf. I can't get him interested in the other games."

His friend slapped him on the back. "Why you don't take him to the course, brother? Mr Arumugan from Magazine Barracks is the caddie master there. I know his cousin. Maybe he can help the boy with the rules and whatnot. They take on young boys as caddies, you know, and it's so close by. You should take him. He will surely love it."

"He's too young to work," Pa said sharply. "He's only a boy. Maybe when he's older . . ."

Pa imagined taking Papwa to the course and trying to persuade this Mr Arumugan to take his son on, not as a caddie, but as a protégé. Surely someone with the title of caddie master would be able to help with the boy's game? *Arré*, what would the man ask him? Would a demonstration be enough to convince others of his son's skill? Pa knew that he did not have the words to convince anyone of anything. For his son, he'd try, but he knew that if this caddie master was another Indian man, he'd have no power to help the boy either. Besides, a caddie master was probably a man who adhered to the rules – rules that did not include a poor, dark-skinned Indian boy playing on a white man's course.

No, he knew he would not be taking the boy to the course. What was the use of raising his hopes when he would only be disappointed? Pa's throat clenched with another truth: he would not be able to bear it if his son were to be chased away, like a dog. *No Indian Players Allowed.* Although no such sign existed, it was all but implied. In so many ways, Durban really was the last outpost of the British Empire.

His father had spoken about how things had been when Aja had first arrived in Natal, but theirs was not a political family – not overly so. He remembered sitting at his father's feet as a young boy, listening as the men of the "lines" discussed a new tax the government had introduced in order to compel indentured workers to accept new contracts. His father's second five-year contract had been coming to an end and eventually he'd accepted another five-year term in order to avoid paying the three-pound tax the family could not afford. Three contracts he had served – fifteen years of his life. He'd died used up, a young man with the body and bones of a man much older. That was politics for you: decisions made by rich men, by which the poor had to live or die. Even MK Gandhi, whom his father had admired and whom he for the most part admired too, had been a rich man – a lawyer from a wealthy family from Gujarat.

It had only taken one trip to Natal for the well-born, London-educated lawyer to know what it meant to be regarded as nothing more than a Coolie. While travelling from Durban to Pretoria by train, one of Mr Gandhi's fellow passengers in the first-class carriage had taken exception to travelling in the same compartment as a Coolie. When Mr Gandhi refused to move to the third-class carriage, he'd been ejected from the train.

Pa had grown up with this story; it was one all Indians living in the Union knew, but no, he was not a political man. Yet there was no getting away from politics. Several of his teammates at the soccer club spoke about politics all the time, trying to involve others in their business. It had been these teammates who'd informed him of DF Malan's announcement that Indians were considered an "alien element" within the Union. The government changed its tune later, conceding that the Indian community (or certain members of the Indian community at least) formed part of the permanent population of South Africa. Malan had even signed an agreement with the government of India, promising to raise the Indians' standards of living in line with Western standards. In the same agreement, however, Malan had proposed a plan to send Indians – most of whom had lost all ties to the land of their parents and their parents' parents – "back" to India. That was just the way the Europeans treated those they regarded as their social inferiors, Pa remembered someone saying. No, one didn't need to be political to know such things. As for Malan's promises to raise the living standards of Indians in South Africa? Well, those had been mere pie-crusts.

"I heard you speaking to Daya earlier," his wife murmured. The children were finally asleep. It was late and the man was weary, but given the close quarters in which the family lived, this was the only time the couple had to themselves.

"Yes?"

For a moment she was silent, as if weighing her words. Normally, his wife was a quiet woman, docile and respectful towards her husband. She was someone who valued the old ways and aspired to the *Mahabharata's* teachings that said that a righteous woman treated her husband with the same affection she showed her child – even if he was poor, sick, weak or weary. Righteousness was his wife's highest pursuit. She observed all the rituals and maintained a religious home with the requisite lamp and shrine to the family's deities. She fasted regularly, including once a year on *Karwa Chauth* when she fasted for the entire day so that he would prosper and enjoy a long and healthy life. It was only when it came to the welfare of her sons and daughters that she was vocal.

"You were speaking about the boy's games," she said after a while.

"Yes, Mummy, what about it?"

"It's not good that he's always playing with that stick."

"He's only a boy, Mummy. Boys play games."

"You encourage him," she nudged. "What is the use of filling his head with all those dreams when nothing can come of it?"

"You should see him play, Parvathy. I'm telling you. I've not seen anything like it, the way he hits that little ball so far. Much, much better than some of the European men we see playing. If you could see it for yourself ..." He stopped himself. His wife's eyesight had deteriorated over the years and now she was nearly blind. Perhaps if she *had* seen it with her own eyes, she'd know that the boy's abilities were out of the ordinary, remarkable. Even with his limited knowledge of golf, he could see so. Rationally, he knew that no practical good could come from it, but for now he was not ready to admit this to himself, to his wife – and especially not to his son. Why should he kill his dreams? Childhood was so brief, he'd grow up soon enough and realise for himself the ways of the world.

"I believe you," his wife said, eventually. "I can tell he loves this golf game. He's never without that stick of his, I know that much." She smiled ruefully. "But what's the use of encouraging him? Better he spends his time fishing, or learning something useful. Maybe if we could send him to school. He's such a clever boy ..."

Sighing, he took his wife's hand in his. It was a hard thing when a man could only afford to educate one of his sons, but that's how it had always been. The eldest son went to school and when he got a better-paying job, he helped to support his family until it was time for him to take a family of his own. Even then, familial ties were strong. It was common for several generations to live together – much cheaper too. Money was always hard to come by.

"Maybe we can find the money to send him to school," his wife prodded.

He would never say so, but such conversation irritated him, especially when he was tired, his body exhausted by the morning's soccer game, the long walk home, the hot sun, too little food, too little sleep. He could not understand why Parvathy was being so adamant. Neither he nor she had attended school. True, he sometimes wondered whether his life would have panned out differently had he had any schooling, but he suspected not. When he himself had been a boy, there'd been a few schools for Indians – built and funded by the community. Yet education had not been a priority in his family. There'd been too many other concerns: putting food on the table, making sure the children didn't walk around in rags. As soon as he and his brothers were old enough, they'd been sent out to work. That's just the way it was and how it would be – for his sons and their sons too, probably.

Besides, what difference would an education make when the government's so-called civilized labour policy put Europeans first in line for jobs? Look how many railway workers had lost their jobs – nearly three thousand Indian dismissed just like that, his teammates had told him. Government was interested in helping the poor, yes, but it was poor Europeans they were interested in helping, and those lousy Afrikaners. But-of-course all this meant was that the Indians living in Riverside and other areas remained poor, their future hopeless unless they already came from families with money.

FIVE

Were his steps slower, Pa wondered, or did they merely seem so? The walk he'd completed countless times before today seemed interminable, exacerbated by the cold morning mist that shrouded the landscape, turning it into something other-worldly. The sea was a dull green-grey, the sand a dirty brown while the bleached skeletons of uprooted trees appeared ghostly in the gloom. He wished he could sit down for a while, but he didn't want to frighten his son.

Remembering the boy and his responsibilities as a parent, he squinted to see where Papwa was. His eyes adjusted to the distance and there was his son – yards away, drib-dribbling the ball along the uneven terrain. This was how it had been going for the past year: more days spent fishing than not ever since the Corporation had cut his hours. The boy accompanied him often now that Mohan, his big-boy, had been taken on by the Corporation too and stopped that caddie-caddying business at the golf club. Papwa would race ahead, tracking back to his father only to urge him to catch up or to confirm whether he'd seen a particularly spectacular shot.

"You see that, Pa? You see that?"

"I see you, boy! I see it."

He no longer needed to encourage the boy to try harder. Since Papwa had no one to play golf with, he competed with himself, trying to best his last "most-amazing" drive. When the boy had first flirted with playing, he'd been interested in accuracy: hitting the ball into the tin. Now distance was his passion, striking the ball with a ferocity that belied his slim frame.

The hand-carved wooden club that had accompanied his middle-son everywhere a few years previously had been replaced with a five-iron, another auspicious find. Despite his warnings, Papwa could not resist the temptations of the golf course and would inch ever closer to watch the players. He'd found the five-iron abandoned in the thick mangrove abutting the course during one of his evening forays. When Papwa had arrived home – out of breath and mad with excitement – his father had been only too happy to cut the club down to better fit his boy.

Papwa finding that golf club had been one of the few good things to come out of the past year, Pa thought. It had been a year more difficult than most, what with his cut hours and all, not to mention the pains in his chest of which he'd told no one. A man had to be strong: a good example to his sons.

"You can be whatever you want to be," he used to tell his children. "You can do whatever you want to do. Believe in yourself. Believe in your dreams. If you work hard, they will come true."

Of all of them, Papwa was the one who'd taken the words to heart. Pa found the boy's faith in himself and his talents bewildering, but could never bring himself to say so. There were days when he wished he hadn't filled his son's head with impossible dreams and half-true stories.

And then there were days that he honestly thought that the boy's talents were a waste. Not to say that he ever doubted that Papwa's talents were extraordinary, but he feared that they were as much of a curse for him as they'd be a blessing for someone else, someone in a position to exploit them. Yes, it would have been better for all of them if the boy had been talented at something else, something more practical, like fixing bicycles or building houses. Then again, what did he know? He was a stupid man. But he was not so stupid as to think the boy would have an easy go of it, not in the Union of South Africa and not under this "fusion" government of that man Hertzog and the two-faced Smuts.

The past year alone had seen the introduction of a slew of laws aimed at diminishing the rights of South African Indians. These included acts preventing Indians from holding seats on regulatory boards; prohibiting Indians from employing whites; and one especially foul law, the Immigration Amendment Act that stripped children born outside of the Union of the rights – as they were – accorded to other

South African Indians, effectively depriving them of citizenship. Pa knew that these were but a few of the new anti-Indian laws, following so closely on the heels of the Slums Act which had raised such uproar a few years ago. That Act had caused many Indians to lose their homes under the pretence of improving living conditions for the very people it had dispossessed. So many people had been forced to move far away from their families, friends and neighbours. One of his very own cousins had been forced to move from one of the areas the government considered a slum. That had been the start of it in his mind and so it happened that the man who'd prided himself on being apolitical was finding politics something he could no longer pretend affected other people. If it had happened to his cousin, who'd lived in his home ever since he was born, what was stopping it from happening to him?

Perhaps it *was* his son's talent that had forced him see what the future held for the boy – for all his children. He found himself wondering again why his grandfather had chosen to stay in Natal. Would life in India really have been that hard if he'd returned? At least he'd have been wanted there. Was it dharma, this inheritance – each day punctuated by the needs of the day and no looking beyond it to the next? He hoped his sons and daughters would have better than he'd had, than his father and his grandfather, but what if their inheritance was an inheritance of futility?

He looked to the boy ahead, his torso twisting in delight at another successful drive. Papwa was so young. He deserved this time to play, to be a boy. Yes, it was good for the boy to play at being a big-time golfer, but that was it, only play. Golf would not provide the family with a living. Nor would it sustain the boy's wife and children when he was grown and married. Bearing this in mind, he called to his son: "No more games, Papwa! We don't have all day."

Papwa scrambled to the rock where he knew his father would join him. Before he sat down, he carefully placed the ball and club directly in front of where he'd sit so he could keep an eye on them. No matter how his attention wavered, no matter how much he'd prefer to be playing instead, the boy always sat down to fish. He knew he too had to help feed the family.

SIX

At first the day passed like all the others they'd spent together on the beach. The fish were slow to bite, but Papwa and his father persisted. Around noon they each ate a plain *roti* Ma had wrapped in paper and packed in the fishing pail. After their meal, Pa fell asleep and Papwa was free to wander the dunes and perfect his play.

"Shucks, you really hit the ball far that time!"

Papwa looked up, surprised at being disturbed. He'd crossed to the far side of the beach, away from Pa lest his drives interrupt his father's sleep. The interloper was not his father, but a boy he'd never seen before – a white boy. Europeans seldom came to this stretch of the beach, which, being so close to Riverside, was regarded as a Coolie beach.

The boy bounded closer. He was younger than he'd looked from the distance.

"I said: you really hit that ball far," he said again.

Papwa forced his gaze up. He'd become so good at blocking out distractions. He tried to ignore him, pretending not to hear him, but the boy was persistent.

"Can you teach me to play?"

Papwa shrugged. He was a friendly child if one who kept to himself. The boy was younger than he was. It would be rude to ignore him. Except ... he found himself tongue-tied, self-conscious. This was not the kind of boy he was used to dealing with; this was not a boy like him.

The boy strode even closer. "Can you speak English?" he asked.

"I can speak English."

"Who taught you to play like that? You're really good."

Papwa shrugged again. "I taught myself."

"So can you teach me? Please. No one else wants to. My father thinks I'm too young – but you're young too."

Papwa sighed, remembering how desperate he'd been when he'd first wanted to learn. "Do you know how to hold the stick?"

"No."

"This is how," Papwa demonstrated, placing one hand on top of the other as he gripped the club.

"No, no, it's not a cricket bat!" Papwa tried to rectify the boy's stance by adjusting his hands. Then, aware of his curtness, he apologised. "Sorry. Hold it like this."

"Hey, boy, what you think you're doing?"

A large, red-faced man, trailed by a black dog, came stomping towards the pair.

"I said, what do you think you're doing?"

Papwa wasn't sure whether the man was talking to the boy or to him, so he did not answer.

"I came to watch him play, Dad."

"Get away from him! Don't you know these people are dirty? Do you want to catch a disease? And you, boy!" His glare settled upon Papwa. "Don't you know your place? What were you doing here with my son?"

Words of explanation caught in Papwa's throat. Like how the boy had approached him, or that this was the beach where he practised his swing every day, or that it was here that he and his father caught shad and barracuda if they were lucky.

"You should see him play, Dad," the boy began.

"What does that rubbish know about golf?"

Papwa looked at the man, looked to the man's son and then looked at the man again. Down the beach, behind the man, he spotted his own father shuffling towards them. Sensing Pa's approach, the dog bounded towards him with an energy it had not previously shown. It began barking incessantly once it neared him. Pa slowed, then stopped altogether. He remained standing stock-still, waiting for the man to call his dog off. It advanced towards the thin, frail man, snapping and baring its teeth.

"You should teach your son to know his place, Coolie." The white man spat a wad of green phlegm at the sand.

"With all respect, sir, my son was minding his own business when your son came to bother him."

The man looked at Papwa's father, incredulous with rage. "Do you know where you are, who you're speaking to? Who do you think you are? *You* don't get to speak to me like that."

Papwa waited for Pa to give the man a piece of his mind, but his father acted as if he had not heard the man and instead looked him straight in the eye, waiting. The two adults stared at each other silently, until eventually the man grabbed the boy and turned away, muttering all the while about "Coolies who don't know their place."

"Why was that man so angry?" Papwa asked.

"Some men are just that way," Pa replied, wondering for the umpteenth time why the boy had to ask such questions. Did he really not know how the world worked?

"That boy thought I was good, Pa. He wanted me to show him how to play. I was going to show him, but then his father came."

"You *are* good, my child. The best I've ever seen. One day, I tell you, one day I'll take you in there," he said, pointing at the golf course. "One day you'll see. We'll walk right up to the caddie master and show him what you can do. He'll be so impressed that he'll take us to see the manager of the club!"

"Yes, Pa." Papwa's eyes shone.

"One day you'll be someone, Papwa. One day you'll show them all!" The father found himself once more breaking his promise to himself, the promise to stop raising his son's hopes. But no, he could not allow his son to give up on his dreams, for those were his dreams too – the dreams that every father had for his son – dreams of fulfilment and success.

SEVEN

Whatever dreams Pa might have had for Papwa and for the rest of his family ended with his death in 1938. Heart attack, people said: his heart not strong enough to power even his so-so thin body. He had not lived to see his fortieth year.

Papwa observed the proceedings at the crematorium in a dreamlike state – aware that things were happening around him, but feeling apart from it all. He watched as the priest sprinkled water on the body that had housed Pa's soul. He watched as Mohan, his *bhai*, circled the pyre three times, a clay pot containing water on his left shoulder, a burning torch behind his back. At the end of every revolution, one of his uncles knocked a hole in the pot, allowing the water to flow out. Finally, *Bhai* dropped the pot and, without looking, lit the fire and led the procession away. Not many men had come to mourn Pa's death: a handful of neighbours, some colleagues and members of the soccer club, all dressed in dull, white clothing.

As they left the grounds, malodorous smoke swiftly overpowered the strong incense and milder-scented *ghee* that had filled Papwa's nostrils earlier. The noxious smell reminded Papwa of a story Pa used to tell about when Indians first came to Natal. Ruling authorities refused to allow cremation to take place then, even though this rite was preferred by most Hindus since fire helps to release souls from their earthly bounds. Bodies of Hindu men who'd been devout in life were placed in the ground – in a cemetery near a butcher's shop. Pigs, used to eating the waste discarded by the butchery, would root out those bodies that had not been buried deeply enough, feasting on their flesh.

Now Papwa could not think why Pa had told them those stories. He hated that those pigs were what he thought about as the fire consumed his father's flesh and bones, turning it to ash. As the smoke went up his nostrils and he tasted it on his tongue, he was grateful for the fire. In a few days' time, he and his family would have to collect the ashes and scatter them in the sea that Pa had so loved and trusted. Life came from the sea and so it was returned.

Only then did the boy realise that he would never again go fishing with his father, never again enjoy those moments of quiet contemplation or unbridled conversation. He would never again impress his father with the flight of a ball. The weight of his loss cannoned into his chest, but tears were shameful and he could not allow himself to cry.

The morning after his father's funeral, Papwa found himself once more walking to the beach. This time, the fishing pole and pail did not accompany him. Tomorrow he would think about fish. Today he merely wanted to feel close to his father. More than that, he needed to hit his ball on the sea sand. He thrashed the ball longer and harder, no longer reined in by his father's presence. Finally spent, he began walking home when a familiar voice called out to him from the golfing greens.

"Hey, boy, do you want to carry today? We're one short. Someone will take you on if you want." It was Fishy, one of the neighbourhood boys and a friend of *Bhai's* from when he used to work at the golf club.

No one remembered whether it was Papwa's interest in golf or the proximity of the golf course to their home that had inspired Mohan to offer his services at Beachwood. Perhaps Pa had encouraged him, hoping to pave the way for his younger son. On most days the greens might have been off limits to a boy eager to learn to play the game of golf, but many young Indian men from the area and beyond could find work – as waiters, bartenders or caddies – at the prestigious club.

With Pa gone, Papwa knew that he would be required to help *Bhai* support the family. Fishing would help to feed them, but he needed to bring money into the home too. His older sisters could not be expected to work outside of the family home. They assisted Ma with tasks of a domestic nature. Everyone had to earn their keep and ten-year-old Papwa was no exception. There was nothing unusual about a boy his age going out to work but-of-course. *Bhai* had been only a few years older than Papwa was now when he'd started at Beachwood.

"What you're standing there for, boy? You going to carry or what?" Fishy asked, breathing through his nostrils, his mouth agape. Papwa could see how the other boy had earned his nickname. He'd landed too many fish to have any doubt about that!

EIGHT

"Can you caddie a bag, boy?"

Papwa looked around, convinced that the man could not be talking to him. Could he not see how ill at ease he was? How old did the man think he was? Papwa was certain that his knees were knocking together and there was nothing he could do to keep them straight.

Long ago, when he'd first mulled over the meaning of the words "caddie boy", *Bhai* had told him that a caddie was the one who carried the clubs and bag of another on the course. He'd pointed them out to Papwa the next time they prowled the perimeter of the golf course. Some of the caddies were grown men, but *Bhai* said it made no difference.

"I'm talking to you, boy. Can you caddie my bag?" There was no one standing next to him, Papwa realised. All the caddies had been allocated to other players.

"Yes, sir, I can caddie a bag," Papwa replied, his voice sounding foreign to his ears.

"Good," the man said, handing Papwa his bag. "Meet me at the first tee at half-past nine."

"Come, we'll show you where's the caddie master's office," one of the boys offered, introducing himself as Jayendra. "Master's strict, but not so bad. He'll want to know your name and so forth before you can start."

"You're Mohan's brother, right?" Fishy asked.

"Yes, he's my *bhai* and all," Papwa confirmed.

"We've seen you on the beach. Mohan says you can play. It helps if you can play; just don't go telling the *goras* how to play and you'll be fine," Fishy said.

"Never tell them how to play," the third boy, who'd been silent until then, agreed. His name was Gopaul.

Fishy steered him into the cramped office. "Morning, Master," he said to the man sitting behind a shining desk that bore only a notebook and pencil. Fishy nudged Papwa to greet the caddie master too.

"Morning, Master," Papwa mumbled.

"Who are you, boy? Do I know you?"

"Kitchener asked him to caddie for him. Raj isn't here yet and we were one short," the one who'd offered to take him to the caddie master explained.

"Ever caddied before, boy?" the caddie master asked. He looked young, younger than Papwa had expected.

"No, sir."

"So why you think you can work here, boy? Why you waste my time? You know how many Coolies want to work here, want to be caddie boys? Look how puny you are, no muscles or anything, boy!"

"I know golf," Papwa replied. "I'm stronger than I look. Please sir, my mother is blind and my father is late. Not even a week he's gone ..."

"He's the brother of Mohan – Mohan who used to caddie here?" the third boy piped up.

The caddie master sighed. "Okay, boy, you can work today, but don't get any ideas. If you do well today, you can come back. You better get going, it's past nine already. Don't be late!"

The three boys shouldered their bags and set off for the tap. Papwa followed. In this way he learned that the first order of business was to clean his player's kit. Emulating the others, he wet the cloth on Mr Kitchener's bag and began wiping the clubs. He examined each closely, wishing for the day that he too would have clubs like these. He could see that they were of different sizes, but the letters on meant nothing to him.

"Have a sip of water before we go," Fishy advised. "All that walking can make you thirsty."

As the four of them walked towards the first tee, all dwarfed by the bags they carried, Papwa realised that he looked no different to the other boys. They were all thin, painfully thin Hindu boys. Nor were they dressed any better than he was. Though they were clearly older than Papwa, they did not appear much older. It had been wrong of him to feel so nervous when Mr Kitchener had selected him. He was sure that he was a better player than all three, but he tried to put such thoughts from his mind. Ma would not approve of his boastfulness.

The first man went up to the tee. Though he himself was not playing, Papwa felt that familiar mixture of excitement and tension he always felt when he took his first shot, but the man was calm, composed. The older boys had warned Papwa to remain silent as a player lined up his ball. Silent and unmoving – well out of the players' line of sight unless called upon for a specific reason. Smoothly, the ball drifted down the fairway. The three other players applauded and commented on how well the ball lay in relation to the flag.

For the first time, Papwa heard words like "par" and "birdie". This here was golf, real golf, he thought to himself, too pleased to even try to disguise his grin.

"You think that's funny, boy? Watch this!" The second player approached the tee. His ball whooshed across the green, but did not land as close as the first player's. The man muttered under his breath and this time Papwa stifled his grin.

The third player's ball stumbled, the worst so far, and Papwa watched as he took his frustration out on his caddie – thrusting his club at the boy as if it burned his hands. The fourth player was the one for whom Papwa was caddying. His opening shot was the best by far. Papwa was pleased.

"They usually tip better if they win," one of the caddies whispered to Papwa. Hefting their bags, the boys scurried to where the players' balls lay.

So it went, for the next five hours. Papwa followed the other boys' lead and cleaned Kitchener's clubs after each shot. Then he carefully replaced them in the brown bag he hefted to the next destination. The sun blazed. Papwa's thirst came and went, he was hungry and his muscles strained under the bag's weight, but he was exhilarated. He was on the greens, he had business here – was no longer an outsider looking in.

After Kitchener played an especially good shot, Papwa had been unable to contain a low whistle of admiration. Handing Papwa his club, he asked: "Ever played golf before, boy?"

"Yes," Papwa answered proudly. "I play on the beach."

Kitchener smiled at the boy. "That must mean you're good at bunker shots, then."

Papwa thrilled to be recognised by another golfer as such.

At the end of the eighteen holes, won by Kitchener and his partner, the man paid Papwa the highest compliment: "I like you, boy!"

Papwa beamed and beamed even brighter when Kitchener placed a shiny, new *tickey* in his hand. He couldn't wait to take the money home to Ma. She would be so surprised!

Trailing the three other caddies to report back to the caddie master, Papwa was reminded of Pa with the rod over his shoulder and pail in his hand as they walked home with their catch. The boys had yielded the bags to their owners, but they seemed weighed down still. After a morning's fishing Pa would be tired too, his shoulders hunched over in the same way. Papwa realised that until then, he'd forgotten to be sad.

NINE

"I heard you did well today, boy. Kitchener was happy. If members are happy I'm happy, remember that!"

"Yes, sir."

The caddie master stared at him, as if taking Papwa's measure. The man was friendlier than he'd been earlier, still it was unsettling, this penetrating gaze, making Papwa very aware of where he'd be found lacking. If he'd known he'd be offered this opportunity he'd have worn his best trousers and a clean shirt. His family might be poor, but Pa had always said: "Cleanliness is next to godliness." His sisters, Rani and Basmati, kept the few items of clothing he owned spotless and in good repair – washing the family's clothes in the river with the other women. Sometimes they'd guide Ma to the river too so she could enjoy the company of her friends who lived further away.

"How old are you, boy?"

Papwa panicked. He thought that perhaps the master would think that he was too young to work. The money *Bhai* brought in working for the Corporation was not enough to support their household. *Bhai* had quit caddying some time earlier, the shillings he earned too few and far between to contribute much to the family's expenses. Pa had been working then too. Thinking about the impossibility of their situation, Papwa felt the weight of his responsibilities – heavier than the heaviest golfing bag. Would caddying even make a difference if *Bhai's* caddying had not when Pa had been alive? But then he thought of something else Pa always used to say: "A bird in the hand is worth two in the bush."

He straightened his shoulders and stood as tall as he could. "I'm twelve years old, sir – thirteen next month," Papwa said, remembering advice Fishy had whispered to him earlier when he'd told him to say he was almost thirteen years old.

The caddie master stared at him more intently, then with a sigh, he said: "Good, come back tomorrow and be on time. You need to be here by six. We'll take it day-by-day until you're thirteen. At least Mr Kitchener seemed to like you. If the players approve of you, you won't have any problems with me. Members rule over here, you'll do well to remember that."

"Yes, sir."

"Before you go, I must ask the question: can you play golf? Mohan used to talk about a brother who played. Was that you?"

"Yes, sir." Papwa wondered why the caddie master's question made him feel so shy.

"And you're good?"

Papwa dropped his eyes, remembering his mother's words about being humble at all times.

"Raise your eyes, boy. If you're good, then say you're good. You have enough against you without adding modesty to the pot. How about you show me what you can do?"

Papwa was starving. He was eager to get back home for a meal, to hand over his earnings to his mother and tell her how the caddie master had said he could come back the next day, but here was the chance to prove his golfing abilities. When had he stopped believing, he wondered, that his father would summon up the courage to stroll through these very same gates and politely ask permission for his son to prove his prowess to someone who knew what to do with it?

When he and Pa had fed each other their dreams of how he would be someone some day, someone more than what he'd been born to be, he'd believed it – but only up to a point. Yet despite those doubts, it had always been, "Yes, Pa," accompanied by a grin that stretched the skin of his cheeks painfully. Perhaps he'd sensed that his father needed to believe these things. Perhaps he'd meant to follow through on his promise, but not even *Bhai's* working at the club had aided his father's plans to demonstrate his son's ability there.

Papwa followed the caddie master to a patch of green outside the office. The master handed him a club and positioned the ball on a tee.

"So, show me what you can do, boy."

Everything else shimmered away. The master; the other caddies who'd come out to watch, flicking bottle caps strung with wire; the members in the distance; and everyone at home. Only his father was a palpable presence in Papwa's head. He was doing this for his father as much as himself, he thought – finally seeing the dream through. And he would not disappoint.

He placed his hands in the familiar way, not hearing the titters about his "upside down" grip. Bending his knees, he hit the ball with the full force of his frustrations and hopes. When he came to, he heard the whistles and applause, a faint echo of the earlier foursome.

"Where did you learn to play like that?" the caddie master asked after a few tense moments of silence.

"We live in Riverside, sir. I used to come to the beach here to fish with my Pa. When my Pa let me, I used to watch the players."

The caddie master frowned. "I hope you haven't been making a nuisance of yourself, boy. No Coolies on the course. It's the rules." He said, as if that explained it.

"No sir," Papwa hastened to assure the caddie master. "I only watched from the beach. I never set foot on the course before today." It was a lie, but a small one, Papwa rationalised. Of course he'd set foot on the course. He skulked around the course in search of bounty whenever he had the chance: early in the morning before the caddies and other workers arrived and late in the evening once everyone had gone home. He'd half-expected the master to have recognised him from the way he'd haunted the grounds.

"You've got potential boy, no doubt about it," the caddie master said. "Definite potential. Come back tomorrow and on Monday morning you can play with the other caddies. As long as you're off the greens before nine on Monday, you should be fine, but not a minute later, you hear? Also, there's a competition every month. I think you'll do ..."

TEN

"Monday morning, Monday morning, Monday morning, Monday morning ..." Papwa repeated the words like a mantra as he walked home. He'd known about the Monday morning games even before *Bhai* had started working there. For years he'd kept his distance from the golf course, for years he'd obeyed the rules his father had set: don't go, not without him; don't get too close; don't go looking for trouble.

He had not been able to help himself when he'd seen that abandoned five-iron which became his first "real" golf club. Nor could he resist when he spotted balls trapped in sand or in bushes or left visibly on the green. What was a boy to do when there was no one around? He knew the corollary of the rules: don't get caught. He had never been caught, at least not by any of the members.

The caddies were another matter. Papwa had made the acquaintance of most of the caddies before *Bhai* had begun working there – knowing them by sight if not by name. He'd kept his distance at first, until the day one of the caddies had caught him trawling for lost balls. No one had better eyes for spotting lost balls than Papwa. Although he'd have preferred to keep his finds, he was smart enough to know that having potential allies at the course was more important than adding one more ball to his collection.

"They allow you to play, then?" Papwa remembered asking – the first of many questions.

"Ha! Don't be crazy, boy! Only time they allow us to play is Monday mornings. Have to be off the course by nine. Caddies only, so no ideas, boy! Maybe when you're a little older, right, lightie?"

Papwa ignored the slight. He didn't mind being called a child. In that moment he'd decided that he would become a caddie. That for him was the first step. Thus far he was not sure what the ensuing steps would be, but of the first step he had no doubt.

Now he was a caddie, well, almost a caddie, and come Monday morning, he'd play. Was step two about to manifest?

First, there was an entire week to get through before Monday. He'd have to be patient and practise so he'd give a good account of himself. Pa would be so proud, that much he knew.

On his second day, the caddie master instructed one of the older boys to teach Papwa the different kinds of golf clubs and their uses once the day's caddying was done. As with all things golf-related, the boy proved an astute learner. Papwa learned which club to use for what distance. For the first time, he learned to tell the difference between numbers because clubs with lower numbers could hit the ball for a longer range than clubs marked with higher numbers. Patiently, Gopaul wrote the numbers one to ten on the wet sea sand. Papwa traced each one awkwardly with a finger until he could write the numbers by himself.

Instinctively, he learned to distinguish between woods, irons, wedges and putters. He would tell anyone who cared to listen that woods, with their large, rounded heads and flat bottoms, were for the longest distance. His mother was his most rapt audience: "You know a driver is a type of wood, Ma? And it's not even made out of wood." Or, he'd say to Harilal: "You know irons and woods have numbers and wedges have letters, right?" Even his sisters were not spared his new golfing wisdom. "The club you use to knock the ball into the hole is called a putter, because you putt it in! Putt it in, get it?" He laughed at his own joke, but his sisters failed to appreciate the humour.

And so, within a short period, the new caddie came to be considered somewhat of a phenomenon at Beachwood. He hadn't been there three days when the player for whom he'd been caddying played his ball into the bunker. As the man attempted to play the ball out of the sand trap, he hit the lip and the ball rolled back in. Papwa looked at the ball and thought of the hours he'd spent hitting his golf ball on the sand with his wooden stick. Before his mouth had a chance to catch up with his brain, he blurted out: "I can do it sir, please can I try? Sir?"

"You want me to learn from a Coolie? Where did you learn to caddie, boy?"

Fishy, Gopaul and Jayendra were dumbfounded, but as always, the possibility for mirth loomed so they edged closer. At least Gopaul, the most level-headed of the three, had the decency to try to deter Papwa from his course by shaking his head vigorously and moving a finger under his throat in warning. Immediately, Papwa wished he could take his wild words back, but it was too late.

"He's new," Fishy answered on Papwa's behalf. "He's only started here this week."

"No caddying experience before," Jayendra confirmed. "He forgot the rules maybe, sir."

"I have to see this," one of the man's partners said. "Let the boy play!"

The other two players agreed and Papwa had no choice but to join the man in the bunker.

"Okay, boy, let's see what you can do."

Barefooted, Papwa curled his toes into the sand. He arranged his left hand below his right and placed the club on the sand.

"You know you're holding the club wrong, boy?" The man said.

"He holds the club like that, sir," Fishy said.

The four players laughed.

Papwa hesitated, but managed to drown them and his friends out. Imagining himself once more on the beach, his father watching approvingly, he shifted his weight onto his left foot, kept his head down and exerted the finest stroke the spectators had ever seen. All eyes followed the ball and rushed to where it fell. Papwa had sunk the ball.

For a moment he did not hear anything other than the sea in the distance. Everyone went quiet. Soon the players began debating amongst them whether it was a fluke or not.

"I owe you one, china," Gopaul said, pocketing the *tickey* Jayendra tossed to him. "I was the only one said you'd make it. Don't forget you owe me, Fishy!" he said, pointing at the other boy.

Papwa's play was not only above par, his instincts were impeccable. He proved this before the week was out.

"Damnit! Damnit! Damnit!"

Papwa tried to ignore the player's curses as he looked for his ball in the rough close to the eighth hole. Papwa followed him with his bag, his eyes eagerly scanning the ground. With the ball found, the player and Papwa both assessed the distance to the hole. Papwa was learning to measure distance in terms of club lengths and would later prove to be outstanding at estimation. He bent down to feel the playing surface and to envisage the ball's path to the hole before standing straight.

"Hand me a –" Before the man could complete his request, Papwa had passed a wedge to him, the perfect club to reach the height needed over the shorter distance. And he had learned to discern the correct club by shape and feel alone.

"Third time he's done that," the player exclaimed to his friend. "Gave me what I wanted before I asked." He addressed Papwa: "You're good, boy, uncanny, but good."

Fishy, caddying for the other player, grinned at Papwa conspiratorially once the players' backs were turned, his head bobbing to a tune only he could hear.

ELEVEN

Not everyone tolerated advice from a caddie and Papwa soon learned that it was the players who made the caddying experience. Some treated him with kindness, like Mr Kitchener had that first day. Others, like the team of four who were playing today, dealt with him and the other caddies like they were nothing more than the Coolies they called them.

The day had been long and tiring. Unusually for Durban and that time of the year, the heat was stifling, without a hint of moisture in the air. There was not even the most listless of winds to blow cool air off the sea. The players were hot and sweaty, turning florid under the sun. Papwa became aware of the smell of his skin and hoped it would go unnoticed. The bag he was carrying felt like it was filled with rocks.

Then the trouble started: with Jayendra and the man for whom he'd been caddying. The man had sliced his tee-off shot, curving the ball back instead of forward. The ball had not yet come to a standstill when the man made as if to smash the club into the turf. Then, as if realising where he was, he thrust the club at Jayendra, scowling. Before Jayendra could grip the club, the man dropped it, forcing his caddie to pick it up. Papwa's player had already taken his shot. Another had yet to play. Papwa watched as Jayendra cleaned the man's club. His face was placid, but a vein on his temple throbbed visibly and his face had turned ashen despite the heat that had flushed it earlier. Jayendra avoided Papwa's questioning gaze. The boys and the players made their way down the fairway once the fourth player had taken his shot.

"Don't say anything," Gopaul warned.

The game continued in that fashion. Jayendra's player was the weakest of the lot; the slice shot his particular failing. He missed another shot then tracked back towards where Jayendra stood with his bag. Pointing his finger in the boy's face, he shouted: "You need to get out of my line of sight; you're standing in the way! Who taught you to caddie you good-for-nothing Coolie?"

"Calm down, son," one of the other players, an older man, tried to placate the irate player. "Leave the boy alone and let's finish. There're only two holes left."

The player allowed himself to be pacified and the game concluded without further tension. In the caddie's changing room, Papwa watched as Jayendra flung a glove against one of the lockers.

"We're nothing to them; they treat their animals better than they do us!" Jayendra railed. "He didn't even tip me. Can you believe that bastard *gora*?"

Papwa's own tip had been better than normal that day. Perhaps his companions had been embarrassed by the man's behavior.

"That's nothing, remember the time that one *gora* bastard tried to beat me with his nine-iron? I had to run, I tell you brother," Fishy said, directing his comments at Papwa. "Chased me down the fairway, but I was too fast for that fatso." He imitated the man running.

Even Jayendra laughed at the picture of the skinny Fishy being chased by an irate player: a fat one too, huffing and puffing after Fishy with his spindly legs.

"What did the master do about it?" Papwa asked Fishy.

"Nothing, just reminded me that members rule, that's all."

"Members rule, all right," Jayendra jeered, as he made a crude sign with his hand, leaving no doubt about which member's rule he was referring to.

"Sticks and stones, my brother, sticks and stones," Fishy said. The boys looked at him expectantly. Fishy was not one to caution passivity, especially not when he was the one slighted. "I should have beaten him with a stick and hit him with a stone," Fishy grinned.

Papwa smiled nervously. He could not help but admire the bravado of his new friends.

It was Papwa's fifth day as a caddie. Every morning that week his trusty five-iron had accompanied him to work. He dribbled a ball the entire way there, dragging out the walk so that he was forced to wake earlier and earlier to be at work on time. Caddie Master was a stickler for the rules; the other caddies delighted in his nickname, bestowed by Fishy of course – Members Rule. While his fellow caddies inspired Papwa to be braver, the caddie master made sure to rein him in, lest he take on too much of the other boys' insolence. Like Pa had been, the master could be strict when the occasion called for it.

That evening, as the day's light was fading, Caddie Master surprised Papwa on an outlying fairway. Without any preamble, Papwa directed his ball into the hole. He wanted to make the most of the remaining light and enjoy the freedom of the greens for those moments. The fresh smell of the grass, mown that morning, lingered and the boy wished he could burrow into it like a blanket.

Slow clapping disturbed his thoughts, freezing his hands in place before he could strike the retrieved ball again. The caddies knew where he was and would not disturb him. They loved to tease him about his "Coolie golf stick," but they were not malevolent. They encouraged him to break the rules, as much as he could get away with, and they encouraged him to play, pointing out how unfair it was that the club restricted their playtime to a miserable couple of hours a week.

"What on earth do you think you're doing, boy?" Caddie Master hissed.

Papwa remained frozen in his stance, unable to find the words to defend himself.

"It's not Monday morning. Why are you playing? Do you know you're not only risking your job, but mine too?"

Papwa had no answer to the caddie master's questions He played because he had to, because it was more important than his job, more important than anything else, but he could not find the words to explain this. "I'm very sorry, sir. So sorry, sir," he answered.

"Don't be sorry, be careful! Next time, you're fired."

"Sorry sir."

Caddie Master softened. "I don't make the rules, boy. You're one of the best bloody players I've ever seen, but save your games for Monday. I know you need your job. Don't disappoint your Ma, right? She depends on you. How is your Ma, boy?"

TWELVE

Finally, Monday morning arrived. Amongst the players lined up were some caddies Papwa hadn't met before.

"Watch out for that one," Fishy nudged, pointing to a boy Papwa had heard being addressed as Raj.

"Who is he?"

"Name's Raj, you probably haven't seen him because he misses so many days. Wins so much on a Monday morning he doesn't need to come to work! Rich family too – Red Hill." Fishy hawked a wad of spit at the ground.

"Ah, he was the one who didn't show up that day?"

"What day you talking?"

"Day I started," Papwa clarified.

"Yes, right. Only way he keeps his job is 'cause he's the best player we got. Club wants to win competitions, so Caddie Master allows him to come and go as he pleases. Rich family and all, it helps, I tell you. Wait until you hear him talk."

"But even with his proper talk and all, Raj is welcome as long as he plays on Monday mornings only, and remembers: members rule!" Jayendra added, having heard the tail-end of the conversation.

Papwa frowned, but Fishy and Jayendra laughed, so he joined in too.

"Heard you're supposed to be good," Raj said as he approached, ignoring Jayendra and Fishy.

Papwa could see that the boy was different to them, his freshly pressed clothes were of a high-quality fabric and new, while it was clear that, like Papwa's, the clothing most of the other caddies possessed had had at least one prior owner.

Papwa nodded, not wanting to say more lest he appeared boastful.

"We'll see about that, *lightie*. Right?"

Papwa watched as the boy teed off. His club was a proper club, not a wooden stick and not a cut-to-size five-iron. His tee-off was impressive too.

Sensing his discomfort, Jayendra handed him a driver: "Use this – okay, right?"

Papwa tested the weight of the club, then arranging his hands, prepared to tee off.

"Look, he's holding it wrong!" Raj said to his handful of friends. Papwa wasn't certain whether they actually worked at the club: they were well dressed too. The boys laughed.

"It's the other way around, okay?" Raj tried to position Papwa's hands into the conventional grip.

"It's no use," Gopaul explained. "Leave the boy alone. Let him play the way he knows."

Raj raised his hands in resignation as he walked away. "Was just trying to help the *lightie*, *bru*."

Papwa hit the ball, but it was not his best shot.

"Ignore him, Papwa," Gopaul called. "You can't think about anyone else when you're on the course."

So the game continued, with Raj oscillating between being helpful and condescending. It soon became apparent that Raj's friends had no connection to the golf course and were just there to support him, keen to make a few pennies on the game. There was a patent rivalry between the two lots of boys, the rich against the poor, but it didn't go beyond teasing.

After a couple of hours, Raj, with a score of 79, was declared the winner. Papwa didn't have a bad showing either – he scored 84 points and was awarded second place.

"We told you this lightie could play, right?" Fishy said to Raj. "Can't believe you nearly got beat by a lightie, a tickey-line lightie and all!"

Papwa knew the others meant no harm. They were as poor as he was and seemed to enjoy taking the rich boy, who'd taken their money, down a peg or two.

He hastened to the changing room, enjoying the jangle of the coins he'd won in his pocket. During the past week he'd learned to love his job despite the occasional insults he suffered from the players. He earned one and six for every game he caddied. Some players thought this was enough and saw no reason to tip him further. For the freedom of the greens for those few hours on a Monday morning, he'd learn to swallow the insults. He'd learn to kowtow to the caddie master too, if necessary. For the sake of Monday mornings he would be a good boy, a boy who knew his place. He would speak when spoken to, offer advice only when bidden to do so. He knew what was expected from him in his job: to carry, to clean, to find the ball; to be pleasant, polite.

And on Monday mornings his smile would remain on his face at all times. It would be genuine – not a mask. Here was where he was happiest, with the yielding sensation of the soft grass beneath his bare feet, the sun on his face. In those moments, Papwa could forget that he was a poor boy from Riverside. No, when he was playing the game, against people who could play, when he was playing well, then he was the richest boy he knew.

THIRTEEN

Over the next few months, Papwa's reputation continued to grow. While he was not yet as good as Raj, it was only a matter of time. So Fishy, Gopaul and Jayendra hastened to assure him. He'd beaten Raj fair and square on more than one occasion even if the older boy had found excuses for this happening: he was tired; he wasn't feeling so well or more commonly, one of the other boys had distracted him.

Papwa could never tell whether Raj liked him or despised him. During Monday morning games he'd be downright derisive, but when the two of them were alone, Raj would be helpful, kind even. Like Jayendra, Raj had no problem circumventing the rules and encouraged Papwa to do the same. Instinctively, Papwa knew that the consequences would not be as grave if he was caught contravening the rules in Raj's company. Fishy said that the master treated Raj so well because his sister was married to his uncle or something. Gopaul said no, it was because Raj's father was rich, plain and simple.

The golf course had been deserted that day. Out at sea a storm waited on the horizon, the water dark and flat and still. On days like those, the caddies would huddle inside to keep warm, hoping they'd be able to pick up a game. That day, only two foolhardy players had come, and they'd abandoned their game before the ninth hole. The boys played cards to keep themselves busy, chatting loudly about the game, the players and of course, girls – some spoke from experience and others from wishful thinking. Papwa lost interest once the golf talk was exhausted and he was a better golfer than cardsharp.

"Hey, boy, want to help me with a club selection?" Raj stood up and motioned to Papwa. "Come on, I'll give you three to one on longest tee-off."

Papwa hesitated. He'd lost money on the cards and couldn't afford to lose more.

"Five to one, okay? Best odds I've ever given. What? You're scared or what?" Raj persisted. "You can owe me if you don't have the money."

Handing Papwa a driver, Raj motioned for him to follow him outside. Some of the other caddies tailed along too. The air was pregnant with the impending storm; not a soul was on the course and the clubhouse itself appeared deserted, bunkered down.

"You crazy or what?" Fishy demanded of Papwa. "What about Members Rules? You know it's your job, right?"

"The *larney's* probably catching a *dos* right now. It's fine, Papwa, come. Five to one, boy, right?"

"What's that mean, five to one?" Papwa asked Fishy under his breath.

"You put down ten. If he wins, he takes your money. If you win, you get fifty."

"Pence, right?" Papwa asked.

"Pence, shillings, whatever, Papwa – whatever you want to bet."

"Okay, but I pay you. Monday, okay, Raj?"

"Okay."

"Don't worry, you won't lose," Fishy winked. "Here, I've got a shilling. I'll pay so long. Actually, make that two, two for you and two for me."

"Hey, I also want to put money down," Jayendra called.

Gopaul began taking bets from the assembled spectators.

"Ball closest to the hole wins," Raj clarified.

"Closest to the hole, okay-right," Papwa agreed, hoping to make it a quick game.

Making sure that indeed no one of authority was around, the boys trooped to the tee-off area.

Grinning confidently, Raj tossed a golf ball at Papwa, who caught it on the club. Calmly, Papwa tapped the ball in the air as he walked to the tee-off position. Deferring to Raj, he let the ball drop. No one noticed the caddie master's approach as Raj lined up. He stopped to watch as Raj's drive flew down the fairway.

"Looks like the caddie record!" Raj boasted.

Papwa became aware of the master as he stepped up to the tee, but he refused to panic. Raj had reassured him that he would take all the blame if they were to be found and for some reason, he believed him. If he was going to do this, with an audience, he'd do so properly he decided. Switching to a conventional grip, he attempted some warm-up swings.

"Where's the voodoo grip, then?" Raj laughed.

No one else laughed, Papwa noticed. He considered the fairway then switched stance, reverting to his familiar grip.

Caddie Master moved closer.

Papwa closed his eyes and breathed in the acrid scent of the gathering storm. The sky had turned black: swollen rainclouds hid the sun, casting ominous shadows over the entire course. As his breathing slowed, Papwa drowned out everything else: the coming rains which could mean no work for days, Caddie Master and his threats, which could mean no work, period, and the fact that no work meant no pay and no pay meant no food ... and Ma?

The caddie master would remember the smile that wreathed the boy's face just before the ball shot into the air. He'd wonder whether the boy's eyes had been open – they seemed closed, he thought – and he'd replay in his mind the trajectory of the ball and how it splintered the lifeless air. The ball flew, soared high and far, landing past Raj's lie and rolling to a stop much further ahead.

No one spoke. Even the caddie master found himself awestruck, and he a man who prided himself on his decorum and calm – necessary traits of the job.

Eventually, Jayendra broke the tension, launching into a bout of clapping that was soon taken up by the other boys.

"Do it again!" Raj demanded, tossing another ball at Papwa.

Without hesitation, Papwa drove the ball with a power and speed that sent Raj jumping out of the way. The ball hit the fairway near his first shot, but rolled ahead. This time the applause was instantaneous with even the caddie master joining in dazedly.

"Now *that's* the caddie record!" Gopaul asserted. "And you owe him ten shillings."

The sum mentioned stunned the boy who'd stunned everyone else.

Ten shillings was more than a week's pay. They'd be able to eat well for days. Seeing the caddie master standing there, Papwa's confidence wavered and his earlier worries returned. "Sorry, sir," he began, not sure how to continue. He knew he'd transgressed the rules and knew he'd be punished. All he hoped was that he'd still have a job.

"Don't worry, boy, I didn't see anything. But just this one time, okay? No more chances. Right?"

Papwa stared at the caddie master silently. For a while now, as much as he loved his job, he had been feeling dissatisfied. As much as he loved the freedom to walk the fairways without fear, on the days when a heavy bag grew heavier with each hole played and his frustration ratcheted as the players for whom he caddied missed shots he could play with his eyes shut, on such days he almost resented his role of Coolie. One of the other boys had told him that "Coolie" meant a porter, which was just another word for someone who carried things.

He wanted to be more than a Coolie, a caddie or whatever they wanted to call it. No, he wanted to be the one driving the ball down those immaculate greens, he wanted to be the one sinking the ball in the hole; he wanted to be carrying his own clubs and balls. Contrary to his father's teachings, these feelings of dissatisfaction had awoken the first, uncomfortable stirrings of envy within him. He could barely articulate these feelings churning inside him. All he knew was that when he got to hit those balls on the fairway – on Monday mornings and in the forbidden moments he snatched for himself – he felt well and truly comfortable in this skin of his.

As if sensing these emotions within the boy, the caddie master moved closer. "I must talk to the club about letting you play in the championships as a caddie," he said, softly. "You've got something they need to see. You're someone everyone needs to see."

FOURTEEN

Papwa raced home, the master's words echoing in his head. How proud Pa would have been to hear them. *You're someone everyone needs to see.* His father had believed it, had believed in his son. Yes, Papwa was convinced after all, one day Pa would have found the strength to breach those gates with him. He just hadn't found an auspicious time to do so.

If Pa wasn't there to hear the master's words, there was still Ma. As Papwa hurried the ball along, he pictured Ma's face as he handed over his winnings. She'd be so pleased, he knew, thinking of all the things the money could buy. He wondered whether he should stop at the market, maybe buy her toffees or some ribbon for her hair, but the rain had turned the well-worn path between their home and the golf course to mud and Papwa knew Ma would be angry if he were to catch a chill.

In his haste, Papwa had not been concentrating on his putts until the ball caught in the mud. He pondered the different strokes needed to play it out. He tried once and lifted it a few yards out of the sodden ground. Over and over again he hit the ball into the mud, eager to perfect his game under boggy conditions. Sometimes the sea sand had been damp when he played, but this mud was soft and squelchy, messy. Such a challenge and so much fun.

Ma's eyes had failed her, but her hearing made up for it. "Where's the boy? Where's Papwa?" she asked Rani. "I hope he's not playing in the rain. First his father and now the boy; does he want to catch his death? My high blood, *arré*! That boy gives me so much to worry about. Where can he be?"

"It's okay, Ma. Papwa will be home soon," Rani reassured her mother.

"He better be," Ma said. "Why that boy makes me worry so?"

They were sitting with the other women in the sheltered courtyard of the big-house, grinding spices and chewing the betel nuts that stained their teeth yellow. One of her daughters was always close by these days. Her eldest girl was her mother's right hand, a good girl. Soon it would come time for Rani to marry and leave home. Yes, she been just a little older than the girl when she'd married and come here, Ma thought, but times were changing and who would make matches for her girls now that Pa was gone?

"Your middle boy's at Beachwood?" one of the other women asked.

"Yes –" Ma replied.

"Always that golf-golf business," another woman interrupted.

"He's a caddie," Rani answered, defending her younger brother. "He carries the players' bags and they pay him for it."

"His *bhai* should try to get him in at Corporation or one of the factories," Sushilla, the lady who lived in the big-house, suggested. "Enough with this golfing business. Caddying what? That boy must learn a trade. One day he will marry and how will he provide for a family?"

Ma shook her long hair loose, gathered it up again and fastened it in a knot behind her head. Slowly, she got to her feet. "Come, Rani," she said. "We need to start the meal. Soon your brothers will be home." And then she laughed. "Big boys with big appetites."

"Papwa likes golf, Ma."

"Yes, my daughter," Ma replied, "but the women are right. He should learn something else."

"Yes, Ma."

By the time Papwa arrived home, his teeth were chattering from the cold and he was covered in mud – from his caked feet to splattered shins, up to his thin shorts and yellow t-shirt, which was now more brown than yellow.

"Ma, Ma," Papwa called from outside.

"What happened to you?" Basmati asked, following him in.

"What happened to Papwa?" Ma asked. "Rani, what's wrong with the boy? And you?" she said, directing her attention to her youngest daughter. "Where you were?"

"Ma, Ma, I have a surprise for you!" Papwa shouted.

"*Arré*, Papwa, you want to give me heart attack, what? Calm down, boy. Tell me the surprise."

"Here, Ma, I won!" Papwa said, placing the folded note in her hands.

Ma unfurled the note, and smoothed it out in her lap to its limit. She raised it to her face and sniffed at it. "Ten shillings?" she asked, guessing the amount by its size. "Where you get this money, boy?"

"I won it, Ma. I just told you."

"You told me nothing, boy. Now where this money comes from?"

"There were no players today, Ma, so Raj challenged me to a competition to see who could hit the ball closest to the hole. Raj thought he had me, Ma, but you had to see how far I hit that ball. Then Raj made me do it again and this time I hit the ball even further, just like Pa always used to make me hit the ball from farther away. It was so far that Gopaul said it was a caddie record. When Caddie Master saw he wasn't angry that we were playing on the course and it wasn't Monday and all. He told me, Ma, that he would try to get me to play in the championships as a caddie and then he said that everyone should see me play. Can you believe it, Ma?"

"Slow down, boy. What about the money?"

"Oh, the money, Ma? I won the bet when Raj said who could hit the ball closest to the hole. He said five to one odds and Fishy gave me two shillings to play, and all the other boys bet money too and Raj had to pay out, Ma, because I won!"

"Oh, my son!" Ma cried. She raised a hand to his face and stroked his hair. "You're a good boy, but now go and dry yourself or you'll get sick, right?"

Ma sighed. She thought of the woman's words about Papwa getting a more respectable job and sighed again. She was pleased the boy had won. She remembered all those conversations she'd had with her husband about the boy playing that game. It would have been different if he was here. He'd have been so proud of the boy. Look how he'd always encouraged him, making him a stick and all. The family would survive on whatever money the boys brought in. If they were hungry, there was always fish. No, let the boy have his golf course and his friends. It was good he had friends; the boy had always been a loner, just him, that little white ball and that stick. Maybe when he was older Mohan could speak to him about getting another job.

At the caddie master's request, Papwa was granted permission to play in the club tournament as a caddie and had a respectable showing – reaching the quarterfinals. He was eleven years old. Thereafter he began entering caddie competitions and won his first place prize – a crate of cool drinks that he shared with his friends though he saved enough to take one home for Ma and each of his siblings.

Life in the home was good for a while. Papwa often went to the market with his friends and came home with gifts for his sisters and for Ma – metal bangles to add to the many that already jangled around their wrists; lengths of shiny ribbon in beautiful colours, for their long hair; coconut oil and fragrant whole spices.

Ma was too pleased and happily took the coins he dropped into her handkerchief – one of Pa's – that she knotted and kept hidden between her breasts. She might be blind, but no one could outwit her with money.

"I'll buy sovereigns one day," she mused with a satisfied smile.

She spent her days sitting cross-legged in a circle with the other women, under the lime trees, peeling potatoes and grinding spices, or slicing green mango for pickling. Her daughters were close by, learning the culinary arts from her and the other women, or they were washing the clothes in the river. The older women chewed their betel nuts and clucked away in Hindi, their saris draped over their legs. They laughed as the day wore on.

Her sons were growing up too. Mohan had his job at the Corporation and on his days off, he took Harilal with him to the North Shore where they spent their days with the men who went out to catch fish. Papwa, of course, spent his days on the golf course, perfecting his game when he wasn't caddying, or practising his numbers with his fingers in the sand.

There was much to celebrate. A bride had been arranged for Mohan. The men in the young girl's family had brought the news that the family had accepted Mohan's proposal. Everyone was pleased. She was a Northern girl like them, and came from a decent family. Ma was proud of her eldest son. After all, he had been educated and had a regular job with the Corporation.

No, life was good. Even with this white man's war that meant new things like shortages and the barbed wire on the beach. But with the white man's war, many of the Beachwood players had gone off to fight in Tobruk and Egypt and some on the island of Madagascar. Many days there'd be no games for Papwa to caddie and his tips were smaller too.

Mohan had his concerns.

"The boy must learn to do something other than golf. How will he support a family one day?"

"Not to worry, he does well on the golf course, my son," Ma said.

"But where will it take him, Ma? There's no future for him in golf! It's a white man's game."

There was silence in the home. All eyes were on Papwa, who held his breath, feeling a lump rising in his chest. The sea echoed in the distance; a mother chastised her young child somewhere close by. The oil lamp hissed on the little wooden table in the corner, next to the brass Ganesha. What would Ma say? Would she defend him or would she agree with *Bhai*?

Papwa hung his head as he waited. Ma remained silent, waiting too. In the years since their father's death, *Bhai* had taken to the role of head of the home like a duck to water, Papwa thought. Even if Ma defended him against his brother, he knew who would prevail.

Eventually *Bhai* spoke. "Beachwood is nice, the people are nice and all, but it's not enough money, Papwa. Ma needs your help. You're no longer a boy ... I was working when I was your age."

"But you were working at Beachwood," Papwa tried to reason with his brother.

Papwa knew that the seven, sometimes eight, shillings he earned per week was not much, not enough. However, privately, he knew he'd work for free if that's what it took: to be out on the course where he belonged, and for those few hours he got to stride the greens, not as a caddie boy, but as a player – a winner. But he was too practical and too respectful to mention any of this to his mother and eldest brother. Besides, *Bhai* was to marry soon. Everyone said a wedding was an expensive occasion – not only for the bride's family. He had two sisters, who would one day be brides too. Then there were the day-to-day concerns. Papwa knew he would agree to whatever *Bhai* suggested, but even as he prepared himself to concede, he could not help but wish that his father was still here. His father would have made a way. He'd always done so.

"You have to start looking for another job, Papwa. Quit Beachwood and find work in one of the factories. *Budhape ka sahara*," *Bhai* reminded Papwa: a son is his elderly parent's walking stick.

Papwa bowed his head, acknowledging the truth of his brother's words. "Okay, *Bhai*," he acquiesced, his voice small.

Bhai smiled and Ma smiled too. What did she know about sport anyway and how much golf meant to her son? Papwa squashed the disloyal thought. Soon the conversation moved to the pending wedding.

Papwa said goodnight, but that night sleep wouldn't come. His mother couldn't sleep either.

"One day you will have a family of your own, Papwa," Ma whispered in the darkness. "How will you feed them then with this caddie-caddie business? You need to think about these things, you're not a young boy anymore. I was married with one child already when I was your age!"

"It's different for girls, Ma."

"What nonsense you say, boy. It's getting time for you to think about such things, but not now. First your brother needs to get married and we need to save for the wedding. We want a nice wedding; he's been a good son, more specially since Pa left us. No, he must have a nice wedding, not too flashy. No one expects that. And what a lovely girl, I believe!"

FIFTEEN

Papwa worked the week out. Caddie Master assured him that he was welcome to try and pick up caddying jobs over the weekend and to play in the Monday morning matches but-of-course. With *Bhai's* ultimatum still smarting, Papwa began looking for better-paying work.

Papwa began his search at the height of the Second World War. While the war had amplified demand for manufactured products, the young boy faced increased competition in the market for unskilled jobs. As a consequence of the war effort, white females and black men and women were more readily absorbed into the labour market. At the same time, growing numbers of black people were abandoning the outlying reservations where they'd been shunted by the notorious Natives Land Act of 1913 – which restricted African land ownership – and were now relocating to large cities like Johannesburg, Cape Town and Durban to find work.

Papwa searched fruitlessly for several months. Each morning he'd depart the house early – while the air was yet a grey smudge and dew hung heavily on the leaves of the mangrove trees and even the monkeys and Myna birds were still asleep. Morning had always been his favourite time of the day. When Pa still lived, early mornings were for time spent at the beach, hoping to get ahead of other fishermen with the same idea: the early bird catches the worm, but the early worm catches the fish. "As long as I have these two hands and there are fish in the sea," Pa had always said, "our family will never go hungry. Remember this, boy."

Papwa had taken note of his father's words and looking at his own hands, had made the same promise. By mid-afternoon he'd be on the beach with his line in hand, after another day's search had come to naught. He'd look wistfully at the golf course and try to block out the calls of "Fore!" or "Get in the hole!", or sometimes his friends' laughter and shouts to join them if they caught him watching. His clubs remained at home. No, he had to put those things behind him now he was almost a man. Golf was for children with no responsibilities.

Eventually, Papwa found work at a garment factory in Prince Edward Street where he was employed as a thread cutter. The job paid fifteen shillings a week – five shillings less than a pound – but *Bhai* reminded him that this was "more than the peanuts" he'd received at Beachwood.

Ma was happy. "Nearly a pound my boy earns and he gives it all to his Ma, no complaints!" she'd tell whoever cared to listen.

Neighbours speculated that she'd always had a soft spot for that boy. *Bhai* married his nice Northern girl and the newlyweds moved out of the home, since the two rooms were already strained to bursting. *Bhai* and his wife remained in the same settlement, however, as part of the joint family system. Though Mohan was no longer living under their roof, he was still their *Bhai* and demanded the respect of his younger siblings. Every Friday evening after he was paid, before he returned to his wife, *Bhai* would stop at the family home, dropping a few coins in Ma's lap. In Hindu culture, caring for one's aged parents was and always will be regarded as a son's prime duty.

Papwa tried to be a dutiful son too. In addition to covering the household expenses, he took over the cost of Hari's education so the younger boy could aspire to one day undertaking more prestigious work than that done by his older brothers.

After three years of cutting loose threads from finished items of clothing Papwa returned to Beachwood – returned to carrying the heavy bags on his back, returned to his friends, the caddie master, the players and his beloved greens. He'd missed playing golf too much and the factory work had proven monotonous and stifling for a man who preferred to be outside in the fresh air. Plus, the war was over and many of the members had returned.

Older now, Papwa became a regular participant in caddies' competitions. These round-robin tournaments were held one Monday a month. Each club's caddies would play against the caddies of another

Durban club. For instance, one month the Beachwood caddies would play against those from Royal Durban, caddies from Kloof would travel to Mount Edgecombe, until each club had played the other – from Amanzimtoti along the South Coast right up to Umdloti Park along the North. These caddie matches would go a long way in helping Papwa cultivate his legendary match temperament. He learned to drown out the voices within the crowd: the taunts and cheers of those with money on the game, yelled instructions from others, like Gopaul and Fishy. Win or lose, the caddie master would insist on a lengthy post-mortem after each match. And woe betide him if he let Beachwood down! To escape censure after a loss, Papwa got into the habit of winning.

Soon, the young champion came to the attention of organisers beyond the caddie circuit. One morning Papwa arrived at work to find an envelope stuck between the slots of his battered metal locker. A letter was always bad news: disciplinary action of some sort, or a dismissal at worst. Although he was unaware of having committed any infractions recently, Papwa anticipated the worst. Never before had he hated his inability to read more than he did on that morning. It was for this reason that he paid for Hari's schooling, so his baby brother would not be hampered in the same way.

"Ooh, la! What have you done?" Fishy asked, coming over to take the envelope from Papwa's hand. "You're just going to look at it or what?"

"It's nothing," Papwa replied, refusing to yield the letter to Fishy's grasp.

"It's not nothing!" Fishy said. "You must be in some kind of trouble, look at this seal on top!"

"Stop teasing the boy," Gopaul shouted from across the room.

Papwa walked over to him. "Do you know what this is?"

"Open it, see for yourself," Raj suggested.

Papwa looked at Gopaul pleadingly. While his friends knew that he could not read, he hated to give Raj another reason to tease him. The older boy had found that one of the ways to snap Papwa's concentration during a game was to make fun of him, and although Papwa was good at tuning out insults along with everything else, this was Raj, and around the older boy he'd always felt inferior, except of course when it came to a round of golf.

"Here, let me open it if you're too nervous," Gopaul deflected.

All eyes focused on Gopaul as he slid a long fingernail beneath the flap of the envelope and retrieved the letter with no little amount of theatrics. Papwa watched his face as he read.

"Stop worrying, Papwa, this is good news! It's an entry form for the Natal Amateurs. All the best Non-European players, and they want you. Come on, let's fill it in!"

Raj gasped. "You can't be serious, brother! I'm always the one to play. I've represented Beachwood these five years now, sent in my entry last week and all. How come he got an entry?"

"Because he's good," Jayendra answered for the rest of them, "was good then and is better now. You know how his game's improved since he's back full-time and all ... Papwa's the best player I've ever seen: better than you, me, and all of us put together."

"Yes," Fishy agreed. Jiggling the coins in his pockets, he taunted Raj: "And I've got the winnings to prove it. This here boy's a racing certainty, every time, my brother, right?"

"But what he is going to play with?" Raj asked. "What he is going to wear? He'll embarrass us one and all."

"No Raj, come on now. Not everyone's like you."

No one noticed that the caddie master had walked into the room. "I see you've got it," he said, pointing to the entry form in Papwa's hand. "You must play. You deserve to play. Here," he said, handing Papwa a relatively new-looking driver. "I think you'll need this."

"Only *gora* can think to throw away still-good things," Jayendra said, placing a putter in Papwa's hand. "You know I have two of these, right? You show them what you can do with this, Papwa!"

One by one, the other boys handed Papwa a club. Like the three clubs Papwa owned then – the five-iron had been joined by a seven-iron and putting wedge – these clubs were castoffs from the members, old but precious to their owners. Papwa felt too overwhelmed to speak. By the time Raj came over to place his golf bag in Papwa's hand, he could only nod his thanks. These people believed in him, he realised, believed that he could be someone. It didn't matter that he was a poor boy from Riverside with a blind mother and a late father. It didn't matter that his clothes were worn and he had only one pair of shoes. They seemed to think that he could be a winner, maybe. He would not disappoint.

Established in January 1929, the Durban Indian Golf Club was the first in the Union to be founded by Non-European players. Its initial membership consisted mainly of caddies and numbered approximately one hundred in its first year. The nine-hole course was located at Curries Fountain, a Durban landmark.

Curries Fountain was the site of Durban's first reliable water source and drew its name from HW Currie, a Durban city councillor and mayor, who'd converted a spring on his property into the eponymous fountain. The waterworks had served the city for about seven years only. In 1925, after a period of disuse, the grounds became a sports facility serving Durban's Indian community. Over the years, the site had hosted a variety of sporting codes including motor racing, golf, cricket and boxing. In addition, Curries Fountain had long been a place of protest – dating back to 1913 when six thousand people gathered there to listen to political activist Thumbi Naidoo speak out against the land tax law.

In December 1946, Curries Fountain hosted the Natal Non-European Open championships. As with other Non-European golf courses in the Union, the standard of the course at Curries Fountain was very poor. The greens were hard and sloping, with a limited fairway close to each hole. The allocation of par had been done in a haphazard fashion and was very different to what Papwa had come to expect at Beachwood. Play was repeated from different tee-boxes in order to turn the nine holes into the requisite eighteen.

At the time of the tournament, Beachwood was regarded as being one of the toughest courses in the Union with the expectation that if one was able to play well there, one would be able to play well anywhere. However with its immaculate greens Beachwood would have done little to prepare Papwa for the sandy expanse that made up the Curries Fountain course for the most part. Luckily, Papwa had honed his game on the sand dune behind his home, on the undulating path between his home and the golf course, and on the sometimes hard, sometimes soft, tobacco-coloured sand at the beach where he and his father had fished.

Dressed in borrowed shoes and clothing, his hair slicked back with coconut oil, Papwa was beset with nerves as he warmed up. He knew he needed to relax, but he found his usual calm deserting him, thrilled as he was to be competing against the more seasoned players, players he'd only heard about in his small playing community – like this caddie from Kloof Country Club or that one from Eshowe Golf Club, or even one of the mythical members of the Durban Indian Golf Club itself – scratch golfers.

The first two holes were short holes of between 135 and 165 yards, the others ranged from 300 to 350 yards give or take. In an inauspicious start, Papwa bogeyed the first two holes, both of which had a par three rating. He was disappointed in his own performance and the crowd were disappointed too, expecting better play from the boy from Beachwood who was supposed to have such an exceptional short game. Papwa concentrated on drowning out the spectators' comments. Still, voices drifted through.

"You can do, it Papwa!" Fishy, Gopaul and Jayendra shouted.

Upon hearing the familiar voices, Papwa broke his focus and looked up. Theirs were not the only faces known to him. So many of his friends were there, he wondered who'd remained at the club to caddie. With his friends shouting encouragement, Papwa was able to transcend his fears.

The seventh, eighth and ninth holes were especially tricky: the course meandering across the main grounds, taking in a race track encircling a football field, surrounded by stands. To get from one hole to the next, players had to clear the distance from the football field to beyond the stands. Unsurprisingly, this was a feat difficult for most. Papwa thought of all the times he'd endeavoured to impress his father with his long shots. He cleared the distance easily, and after his rocky start, won the competition with an under-bogey score. He was sixteen years old, one of the youngest contenders and an unexpected champion since many had discounted the abilities of such an unassuming boy, especially after they first saw him play. Most importantly, this was his first win away from the familiar Beachwood course, and his first title.

Few spectators that day would forget the boy's shining eyes or his shy smile as he stood up to collect the oversized trophy in his white jacket and too-long trousers, a club perched awkwardly under his left arm. Though many people were sceptical, considering a win at his age a fluke, others were more confident. "Watch that boy," the men muttered to one another, "he plays like he's bewitched. With talent like that, he'll go far, mark my words, brother ..."

Dazed, Papwa could not recall much of the ceremony. Perhaps if his family had been there, he'd have felt differently, but there was such an unreal quality to the entire prize-giving, as if he was watching it happen to someone else. He worried that he'd say something to embarrass himself or the club. If only he had Raj's way with words ...

It was only later, as he and Fishy walked back home to Riverside, taking turns to carry Raj's old bag, that Papwa began to feel the euphoria of his win. Fishy began whistling the tune to Johnny Mercer's "Zip-A-Dee-Doo-Dah", one of the year's most popular songs and Papwa couldn't resist joining in, singing the chorus out loud. Fishy then switched to popular Hindi songs, gambolling and gyrating in the manner of a lumbering elephant or drunken wedding singer. Papwa laughed, but soon followed his friend's lead. He couldn't wait to tell everyone his news. He felt like a hero, he thought to himself privately, or a bridegroom off to claim his bride.

SIXTEEN

At the age of twenty-two, Papwa was very much a boy – a breadwinner for his family and the champion of several tournaments, but still a boy. Golf was his entire life. Women were of little interest to him.

"A man needs a wife," someone, one of the caddies, said. On slow days in the caddie hut, long after talks of swings and grips had been exhausted and games long lost and won had been revisited and replayed, talk would turn to the mysterious charms of the fairer sex. A few of the older caddies were married already and would hint smugly about the pleasures of married life. The rest of the caddies made do by comparing the looks of popular leading ladies: the ravishing Madhubala, ethereal Nargis and wide-eyed Meena Kumari, not to mention Kamini Kaushal or Suraiya!

"I need a daughter-in-law," his mother said, "a nice Northern girl to help in the house and take care of y'alls. It's hard for me now that your sisters are married and out of the house. A man should marry and have children," she added.

Papwa remembered his late father's stories of the first Indians in Durban. How there were never enough women, despite the stipulation that women were to make up a certain percentage of each shipment. Men comprised the majority of each ship that docked in Natal, often outnumbering the women by one to five in those days.

According to Pa, who'd heard it from his father and his father before him, it had been hard for the men to adjust to life without wives. Some men dreamed of returning home to find wives; they spoke of the women they would meet and those they had left behind: beautiful, respectable women from their home villages, villages to which they imagined returning either as heroes or strangers. Others spoke of the women who would come, marriages approved by the Brahmins and astrologers and arranged by families, because everyone knew that a marriage was not only between a man and a woman, but between families.

Those men who dreamed of finding wives had known that families could be broken up at the whim of an official's pen. They shared stories of mothers being separated from their children, husbands from their wives, fathers from their sons when they were allocated jobs. Still, they believed in family, in marriage as an act of *dharma*, a spiritual sacrament that joined together a man and a woman in this life and for up to seven or more lives, during which time the couple helped each other to evolve spiritually.

When he'd told those sad stories of the old days of the ships and the cane-fields, Pa always reminded his son that family was everything and that it was a man's duty to take a wife. Now Ma was talking the same talk. It was only he and Hari in the house now, the only two yet to marry. Hari was too young to take a wife. Papwa knew that Ma needed assistance in their home since Rani and Basmati had married and moved in with their husbands' families these past years as was customary. *Bhai* lived nearby and his wife came over to help some days, but Ma complained that she was a cheeky girl and would not learn to do things the way Ma expected her to. *Bhai* was too lenient, Ma said. Just like her late husband had been. If Pa was here, Papwa would have been married long ago, Ma reminded, because as much as Papwa needed a wife, she needed a daughter-in-law.

Papwa was nothing if not a dutiful son. He promised that he would marry whomever his family chose.

For three days in January 1949, African went to war against Indian in Durban, after an Indian shopkeeper in the Victoria Street area assaulted an African youth. The shopkeeper did not deny smacking the boy whom he said he'd caught stealing. Everyone in Riverside agreed that the crime warranted the punishment. Overnight, this incident lit the smouldering flame of resentment that everyone assumed Africans held for Indians. By noon the next day, large numbers of Africans, armed with whatever weapons they could lay their hands on, descended on the Indian business area around Grey, Victoria and Queen. Witnesses and even those who hadn't been there spoke of the orgiastic violence and looting that spread out to areas like Cato Manor with its large Indian community. "And this white man's government's not doing anything about it," was the continual refrain of frightened and angered Indians whenever they got together. "We need to defend ourselves," others said, forgetting all of Mr Gandhi's talk of nonviolence.

Papwa did not know many Africans. He'd passed them in the street. He'd even worked with several Africans in the garment factory where they were employed to do jobs even more menial than trimming threads off clothing, like sweeping the floor and making tea. In a country where separation of the races was encouraged, Papwa had stuck to his familiars: poor Indian boys like himself.

Though Jayendra and Raj seldom agreed, one of the things they agreed on was politics. "Those boys are too interested in politics and whatnot," Caddie Master had said after overhearing one of their conversations. "One of these days it's going to get them into trouble, ask me!" Then he'd turned around sharply and walked out of the room.

"Africans are upset because they believe that we Indians are treated better than they are," Raj tried to convince the others. "Violence is inevitable as long as government treats people differently – all because of the colour of their skin, or which gods they worship or where their families come from."

Gopaul's cousin had been injured during the first day of rioting. By the second day, Gopaul was talking about joining up with one of the protection groups that had sprung up in response to the violence. "So it's all right for these *umfaan* to rape our women and children, burn down the homes of honest, hardworking Hindu men and women, even with them in the house, *arré*! I've seen it with my own eyes, in Cato Manor ... people attacked with bush knives and daggers. What those people do to them?" He made as if to spit on the ground.

"They don't trust the shopkeepers," Raj tried to explain. "They don't trust the landlords, the bus owners. They think we think we're better than them."

"Of course we're better than them!" Gopaul scoffed. "Look how long is Hindu history. Our people built the Taj Mahal while their people were still living in huts!"

"Not everyone's the same," Papwa suggested, but was cut off.

Even Fishy, who never missed an opportunity to make light of serious business, had strong opinions on the matter: "No my brother, you cannot trust a Zulu. These people will slit your throat in your sleep. It's always been that way. From the cane-fields and all!"

Raj shook his head. "You can't stereotype like that, Fishy. Papwa's right in a way. Not everyone's the same, but in another way, we are all the same. Who are the people who are battling in Natal? In this Union of South Africa? Right, we chār-ous and pekkie-ous, that's who! When the first Indians came to Natal, the white man made sure to separate them from the blacks. Already Africans outnumbered the whites. Imagine if our two races stood together? So they made Africans overseers in the cane-fields, put Indians in charge of Africans in other places. Instead of calling each other names, we need to learn to stand together ..."

"Easy for you to say, eh Raj? With your talk of chār-ous and pekkie-ous. So fancy you are with your Harris Tweed jacket and your Crockett & Jones shoes. What do you know about battling, boy?"

The other caddies agreed with Fishy's assessment. The noise levels rose above the level expected of the club's caddies as the discussion became more heated. Alerted by the raucous sounds, the caddie master returned, glaring at each boy, his nostrils flared as if he was trying to sniff out the troublemakers. Then focusing his attention on Papwa: "Pay no heed to these boys Sewgolum, okay? They'll only lead you astray. Keep out of politics, play your golf. You'll be fine that way, you'll see."

Afterwards, although Raj called into question the validity of the commission of enquiry into the riots, labelling it a sham, he told the other caddies that more than 140 people had died during the hostilities. "African, Indian, even white, what-you-have." So many homes were destroyed, he said, that hundreds if not thousands of people had to be moved into refugee camps – mainly set up in Indian schools. "Black and Indian in the same camp, can you believe it?" Raj said. "Just like when the African National Congress supported us during the passive resistance campaign," he added, referring to the defiance campaign against the detested Ghetto Act, introduced in 1946, which was ostensibly aimed at improving living conditions. In effect, the Ghetto Act meant homes, clearing land destroying and moving Indians further to the periphery. Resisters had courted arrest by occupying land claimed by the Act, but no one could recall whether Raj had actually been part of the resistance movement as he now claimed.

"Sure Gandhiji, no problem!" Fishy replied, causing the others to laugh at Raj's expense.

"Actually Gandhi was not so much interested in pursuing rights for African people," Raj said, about to launch into another lecture, but it was too late.

Someone suggested a game of putt-putt on the small green recently constructed outside the caddie hut for this purpose and the conversation was forgotten.

It was during the 1949 riots, as part of a defensive patrol, that *Bhai* became acquainted with a family from the Seven Tanks area near Umlaas. When Mohan mentioned that his brother was an up-and-coming golfer, a respectable, observant boy in need of a wife, his new friend informed him that he had a daughter of marriageable age in need of a husband. Papwa and Suminthra had both been raised to obey their elders, even in the case of an elder brother as with Papwa. Once the Brahmin chose an appropriate day for the wedding to take place, the prospective pair agreed to marry, sight unseen.

SEVENTEEN

Suminthra had been born in Cato Manor, at a time when Indian property owners were leasing plots to African families who were not allowed to own land in Natal themselves. This resulted in a community where Africans and Indians lived side by side in a sprawling area a few kilometres from the centre of Durban. When she was very young, Suminthra's family moved to Thornwood in the west and later to Seven Tanks, so named for the seven water storage tanks that formed such a major part of the landscape. For many years after the 1949 riots, these tanks would feature in Suminthra's nightmares: persistent dreams of being chased by African hordes while she cowered in their shadow. Though her upbringing was sheltered, she'd heard the horror stories of what African men would do to young Hindu women if they found them alone. Yes, all things considered, Suminthra was relieved to hear that her groom-to-be lived in Riverside in the North of Durban – far away from Seven Tanks, in the South.

Truth be told, Suminthra could not wait to marry and move away from her father's homestead. As the oldest of four children – three girls and a boy – she was expected to pull her weight. This became even more so after her mother's death and her father's remarriage. Not only was she responsible for helping to care for the younger children born to her stepmother, she gathered firewood, picked cress and other herbs both wild and cultivated, and on occasion even ploughed the fields! Her father had not been one to spare the rod and as the oldest daughter, Suminthra had often found herself being punished for one of her younger sibling's misdeeds. Yes, her father was too-too strict and though she'd heard stories of mothers-in-law and their demands, she looked forward to marrying the boy who by all accounts was said to be gentle and soft-spoken.

She did not know much of her groom, other than that he played golf and worked as a caddie boy. The family did not have much money, she overheard her stepmother saying, but her father's money and property had not made her happy, nor had it made her stepmother happy either, it seemed. In any event, Suminthra acknowledged that her hopes were modest hopes. All she asked for was a husband who did his best. She looked forward to having children and for that, she needed a husband. Yes, a family of her own and a husband who did his best ... perhaps a kind mother-in-law. This would be her family.

Suminthra's father had always reminded her that as a daughter, she was *Paraya Dhan* – someone else's wealth since she would belong to the family into which she married. With two sisters from her father's first marriage alone, not to mention her two half-sisters, Suminthra knew what it was to feel like a burden. "A man has to feed and clothe his daughters, provide a dowry too, but it is her husband's family who benefits!" her father said often. He was not a bad man, her father, he was frustrated, that was all; she told herself. Still, she looked forward to her wedding day. It was a day she had dreamed about for so long.

Papwa was excited about the new suit he was having made for his wedding. An orange Viyella suit – not too flashy, it was the first item of clothing that had been tailor-made just for him. As the younger son, he was used to wearing *Bhai's* castoff clothing. Sometimes the members of the club who knew the boys well donated not only their used kit, but clothing too. Hopefully he'd get new shoes too, Crockett & Jones, just like Raj, and somehow Ma would find the money to buy his wife the set of jewellery every Hindu bride, no matter how humble, expected from her in-laws. For years she'd been putting money away. Only gold would do for the wife of her Papwa!

In her decadent pink sari threaded through with silver, Suminthra felt like a princess. Her gold and glass bangles tinkled as she moved, reminding her for some reason of a picture she'd once seen of a horse with bells on its bridle. For the first time in a long time, maybe since before her mother had died, she felt cherished and beautiful. Even her stepmother had treated her kindly. Her father too, but her stepmother reminded her that her wedding day was the most important day of a woman's life.

That morning, her bridal preparations or *solah shringar* had begun early. *Solah shringar* refers to the sixteen adornments that every Hindu bride wears on her wedding day in honour of the Goddess Lakshmi, the model of wifely devotion and symbol of feminine beauty, fecundity, fortuity and prosperity. As part of this beautification ceremony, Suminthra's female relatives began readying her from head to toe. They anointed her hair with oils and then applied a paste of milk, *gram* flour, turmeric and sandalwood powder to the skin of her face, hands and legs. Once the paste was rinsed off and her hair washed, Suminthra was made to relax in a long and luxurious bath fragranced with sweet-smelling oils. After her bath, the women helped her into her bridal sari: first she donned the petticoat and then the tight-fitting *choli* worn on top. Her stepmother helped her drape her sari, though Suminthra knew very well how to drape one herself.

"I married in a red sari with gold threading," her stepmother reminded her as if she was not able to remember the day her father had remarried. "It's the most auspicious colours for a bride, but never mind, *sona*," her stepmother addressed her with flowery endearments in front of the other relatives. "Pink and silver is still nice, maybe a more bright pink, but what you have? You're lucky such a nice boy wants to marry you. And you know he plays this golf business?" She addressed the room. "My husband believes the boy has great potential."

Once the not-so-auspicious pink sari was draped to the gathered women's approval, Suminthra's long hair was brushed and the shiny black tresses fashioned into a thick plait at the nape of her neck. One strand symbolised her father's home, another represented Papwa's family home and the third represented Suminthra herself: uniting the two families. It was a nice thought, Suminthra mused, feeling a sad tenderness towards her birth family now that she was leaving them.

Putting such thoughts aside, Suminthra concentrated on her adornment ceremony instead. Her plaited hair was decorated with flowers and jewellery. A veritable mat of delicate jasmine sprigs was placed at the back of her head – from the top down to the start of her braid. One of her aunties placed fanlike jewels along the length of her plait and then she was turned so they could concentrate on her front.

Carefully, lest the jasmine blossoms get crushed, a *maang tikka* with a filigreed pendant of red stones that came to rest on her forehead was placed down the middle parting of her hair. Just below the *maang tikka*, the same aunty stuck a gold *bindhi* – the sacred symbol of a married woman – at the centre of her forehead.

"Time for the makeup," one of her younger sisters suggested.

Suminthra stood as still as a doll as her eyes were rimmed with black *kajal* to make them stand out better. She felt feathery touches around the *bindhi* and above her brows and when she opened her eyes saw that someone had painted red and white dots there. She was transformed and bursting with pride as she imagined what her bridegroom would think.

"Ooh, what about the jewellery?" her youngest sister squealed. She'd seen enough brides to know that jewels formed a large part of the adornment.

In swift order the plain gold nose ring was placed in Suminthra's left nostril and strung to a chain that extended behind her corresponding ear. Heavy earrings were forced into her pierced ears, but they were not too heavy as to require being supported by a chain passing over the crown of her head as she'd seen some brides wear. Gold necklaces inset with chips of semi-precious stones were placed around her neck, while a gold armband with a red stone to match the *maang tikka* was placed over the hemmed sleeve of her *choli*.

"We need to do the *mehndi* before we can put the other jewellery on," her youngest aunty said. Jayshree had been her mother's youngest sister and Suminthra was soothed by her presence. In a way, it felt like her mother was there for her special day since the two had looked so much alike. Another lucky thing was that Jayshree was renowned for skills at applying *mehndi*. "Come sweetie, sit here," Jayshree motioned and Suminthra was relieved to get off her feet. The room was becoming stiflingly hot with so many bodies in it, chattering all at once. Suminthra felt faint from the heat and from lack of food since she'd been fasting since morning and would only be allowed to eat once the vows had been exchanged.

"Hands first, and then feet," Jayshree instructed as she checked the consistency of the khaki-coloured paste.

Suminthra frowned at the colour and smile.

Sensing her disgust, Jayshree kept up a constant patter. "*Mehndi* is for love," she said, "and how strong your marriage will be."

"It's not a love marriage, Aunty," Suminthra said softly.

"Maybe not now, but I know these things. Love will come."

"What's this girl talking about love?" her stepmother scoffed. "No one marries for love. There are more important things than love," she proclaimed. "You know that girl! Right?"

Most of the women in the room agreed, but Suminthra noted that it was not a universal agreement.

Undeterred, Jayshree continued. "It's a pity we couldn't do the *mehndi* ceremony yesterday. It's best done the day before the wedding, but never mind, sweetie. This will be a nice dark colour. You'll see when it dries. Lucky you're only getting married later on."

"The darker the colour, the better the love," one of the older aunties winked, causing clumsily stifled titters amongst the married women.

"And the more children you'll have," her stepmother added.

"Reaching for Suminthra's foot, Jayshree pursed her lips in concentration. "Honeymoon can't start until the groom finds both your names in the patterns," she said slyly. "And no helping!" She laughed, wiggling her fingers in her niece's face.

Suminthra blushed. She hated being the centre of attention and once more found herself squirming at the ribald comments and endless innuendo that had accompanied her dressing ceremony. She wondered whether Papwa was enduring the same treatment and whether he was as easily embarrassed as she was.

The *mehndi* dried to an attractive burnt orange colour, sufficiently deep-hued to the women's satisfaction. In no time at all, the remaining adornments were placed on Suminthra's body – so many of the gold and glass bangles that they nearly reached each elbow, rings were shoved on her fingers and a belt called a *kamarband*, fashioned from looped silver disks, was placed around her waist to match her sari and keep it in place. Then her feet were lifted from the ground and silver anklets were placed around each ankle as well as a ring on the second toe of each foot. Finally, Jayshree dabbed fragrant *itar* on the insides of Suminthra's wrists and the sides of her neck, so her niece could seduce her groom with her scent, she said with a wink.

"Stand still, girl," the women demanded. Suminthra blushed again as she felt the women's eyes upon her, looking for the tiniest flaw in her façade. She was nervous, she realised, not only about meeting her groom, the ceremony and the wedding night, no, she was nervous about disappointing her groom and in some small way, shaming her family. She held her breath, waiting for someone to speak.

"She looks very nice," her stepmother said eventually.

"Perfect," the women agreed. "Yes, so beautiful – with all that makeup and jewellery and whatnot, no one will even notice her dark skin," one of her stepmother's cousins offered. The other women looked at the speaker; she was known to be a bitter woman ever since her husband had passed away two weeks after her own wedding. Suminthra could not even recall the woman's name. "What?" the cousin shrugged. "This girl is as dark-skinned as a girl from the South, right?

No one replied, but the hopeful mood had been broken, like the fragile membrane of an egg. Suminthra asked to be left alone for a few minutes so she could make her final devotions and prayers before her groom arrived.

"Such a devout girl," the women clucked as they left her to her *puja*.

EIGHTEEN

Mohan had arranged for a friend with a car to drive them from Riverside to Seven Tanks – the motley group of friends and relatives that made up Papwa'st groom's procession. In addition to his relatives and neighbours, Papwa was accompanied by several of his Beachwood colleagues. Caddie Master was there and it was good he was there, because Papwa found his authority calming. Fishy lightened the mood while Gopaul and Jayendra went further by placing bets on whether Papwa's bride would actually go ahead with the marriage once she laid eyes on her groom and of course whether she was a beauty or not. Even Raj attended and since he had a car, he'd also ferried some of the guests there. When Papwa offered to pay for his petrol, he'd waved away the gesture saying that Papwa should consider it a wedding gift. Papwa was overwhelmed by his friends' generosity. On the morning before his wedding, he'd found a pair of black patent leather Crockett & Jones shoes trimmed with white and still in the box, on the bench in front of his locker.

The cars stopped a few streets away from the bride's parents' home where the wedding was to be held. Papwa, dressed in his bright orange suit, a saffron turban and those gleaming shoes was made to ride a bicycle to the smallholding where Suminthra's family lived. Someone suspended streamers of tiny marigold flowers strung together from the edge of his turban while Fishy joked that Papwa was lucky they had not made him ride a mule as men did in the past. As he rode, the men danced and sang popular songs like "Shola Jo Badke" from the movie

Albela and "Khayalon Mein Kisi Ke" from *Baware Nain*, which were both popular that year.

On arrival at the wedding venue, the procession was heralded by the melodic sound of *shehnais* – the traditional Northern Indian double-reed oboes made of wood with a metal bell at the bottom of the instrument. When the music piped down, Papwa and his party were welcomed – first by Suminthra's father and then the rest of her family. Her stepmother placed a *tilak*, a vermillion dot on Papwa's forehead and someone else placed garlands of marigolds around his neck. With the welcome concluded, Papwa entered the tent hired for the occasion to the sound of *tabla* music. He took his place on the podium and awaited his bride. Already he felt nervous, this house and the plot on which it sat was bigger than he'd anticipated, his wife's family more splendidly dressed. How could he, a poor caddie boy from Riverside, compare? How would he be able to provide his bride with the lavish lifestyle to which she was no doubt accustomed? Papwa resolved to put these thoughts aside as he waited for her, but Jayendra and Gopaul's stupid bet played on his mind. Was she beautiful? Would she be happy to have him?

Suminthra had remained in her bedroom while the welcoming was taking place outside. She'd heard the music as the groom's procession neared, differentiating between the exuberant songs of the men as they neared her home and the more subdued sound of the *shehnai* – louder, but somehow more solemn.

"Come, it's time," Suminthra's eldest male cousin, Sanesh, urged. He would be taking the place of her brother in the ensuing rituals, since her half-brother was too young.

Suminthra followed him to where her father and stepmother were waiting to lead her in – at the head of her own procession. It was a short walk, but Suminthra knew that she would not be the same person leaving the tent as the one who walked in – to the sound of a love song, the name of which she could never remember though she knew all the words. Taking a deep breath, Suminthra entered the tent. Immediately inside, her gaze slipped to the podium where her groom sat waiting in a lurid orange suit almost the exact colour of the flowers around his neck. She tried to make out his features through the gauzy screen of the *pallu* that obscured her face. She'd heard stories of brides wearing mirrored rings so that they could spy on their grooms during the ceremony, but she'd thought it superstitious nonsense. Mind you, a mirrored ring would not have helped, since the marigold curtain dangling from his turban hid as much of Papwa's face as her *pallu* did hers.

A man, whom she assumed to be Papwa's older brother, she'd been told that he had an older brother, came forward and gave her the usual assurances that he would take care of her if anything were to happen to her groom. She sat stock-still as Papwa was officially invited into her family and given a libation consisting of curd, honey and *ghee* to drink. Once Papwa had drunk his fill, Suminthra's father stepped up to the podium and placed her hand in Papwa's to show that her family were entrusting her to him. Papwa and Suminthra chanted mantras for a harmonious union and the Brahmin motioned for them to exchange with each other the garlands they wore around their necks. This was the start of the actual marriage ceremony.

During the exchange, Suminthra had seen her groom's eyes and thought they appeared kind. Physically, he was not much taller than she was, perhaps a head or thereabouts and she was of dainty stature herself. He was slim too, but muscular which she assumed was due to all the golf she'd heard about. From his voice when they'd chanted the mantras, she suspected that he was as soft-spoken as he'd been said to be, or perhaps he was as nervous she was.

Again Papwa and Suminthra's hands were joined, this time signifying that the two families were bound together. Her female relatives came to the podium to bestow gifts upon the groom and his family. Then it was Devashnee, Suminthra's younger sister's turn to participate in the ceremony; she tied a corner of Suminthra's sari to the tangerine-coloured scarf Papwa wore with his suit. From weddings she'd attended previously, Suminthra knew that this gesture was to demonstrate the eternal bond that now existed between her and her groom. The Brahmin led them in prayers of which she remembered only snatches: that they'd accepted each other and agreed to abide by the Vedic scriptures.

Fire, one of the five elements, formed a big part of Hindu weddings and the rituals around fire had always thrilled Suminthra the most. During the first fire ritual, she and Papwa prayed to Agni, the God of Fire for longevity, health and prosperity and then jointly offered *ghee* and puffed rice to the fire. This joint offering symbolised how the couple would sacrifice and work together. Before the second fire ritual, Papwa helped Suminthra place her right foot on a millstone to show that she would remain firm in the face of adversity, and that together the couple would solve any problems that arose. They then held hands and circled the fire four times while the Brahmin chanted mantras. During each revolution, they again offered grains to the fire while vowing to carry out the moral duties required of all Hindus.

The *Saptapadi* or seven steps is often considered the most important part of a Hindu wedding ceremony. During these seven steps that the couple take together, Papwa and Suminthra said their vows, invoking the blessings of Lord Vishnu. They promised to provide for their household; to develop physically, mentally and spiritually; to grow their wealth by righteous means; to gain knowledge, peace and bliss through mutual love, respect and trust; to practise self-restraint and to strive for a long life in which they would remain friends and partners both.

"With these seven steps we become husband and wife ... with an everlasting bond."

Suminthra held her breath as her new husband traced the red powder of the *sindhur* on her forehead that marked her as a married woman. What an act of faith marriage must be, Suminthra thought, especially one such as this. She had just united herself with a man who for all intents and purposes was as much stranger to her as she was to him. Yet she was not worried. She and Papwa had made their pledge in front of God, the Brahmin and their community. Hindu marriages did not fail. As soon as she'd accepted the betrothal, she'd resolved to be the kind of wife a good man would deserve. It was how she'd been raised; she knew no other way. Whatever happened, she would accept.

Papwa wondered about his wife. She'd seemed shy, but that was not unusual for someone of her background. He looked forward to the singing and dancing that followed the marriage ceremony. Did his new wife like to dance? He hoped so. Perhaps he should have asked *Bhai* about that when he'd brokered the wedding, but it hadn't seemed important at the time. Suminthra – he had to get used to saying her name – knew that he loved golf. *Bhai* had told her father about Papwa's first golf club and how he loved golf so much that he continued to work at Beachwood just for the chance to play. Papwa sobered, at once thinking about his father and how he'd missed all his children's weddings. It was on such occasions that one really missed one's father, Papwa realized, still feeling the pain of his loss after all these years and on this most auspicious day.

NINETEEN

Papwa and Suminthra departed for Riverside the morning after their wedding. Traditionally, a bride would be sent off to live at her new home a week after her wedding, but there was neither the time nor the money for a huge leave-taking ceremony. Papwa had to return to work and Ma could not be left to fend for herself for so long. Her other children lived nearby, yes, and Hari was still in the house, but Papwa never forgot what Pa and *Bhai* had both told him: that he was his mother's walking stick.

So within the space of one day, Suminthra found herself newly married and moved into the two-roomed tin house a world away from her father's home in Seven Tanks. When she cast her eyes upon her new home for the first time – a shack really, though she would never insult her husband by referring to his home as a shack – she laughed at herself. "You wanted to move as far away from Seven Tanks as possible!" Still, she reminded herself, her father's house had never been her home, not really – not when she would forever be regarded as *Paraya Dhan* in the family into which she had been born. Her marriage to Papwa was her *karma*.

As a concession to their privacy, Parvathy vacated her bedroom and the newlyweds had the room to themselves. It was not much, but it was theirs. Suminthra strung new hangings on the walls, scenes from the *Ramayana*, the romantic story of Rama and his wife Sita, particularly those dealing with the trials and tribulations Rama had to endure in order to retrieve Sita after she was abducted by the demon king Ravana. Papwa was only too obliging. He carefully set new nails into the corrugated iron walls, anything to please his wife, he said. He saw how she was making a new home for the two of them; she'd replaced the bedding on the double bed with an embroidered spread. "Imported from India," she told him casually, as if the beautiful light-blue cotton spread with its spirals and swirls of silken embroidery done in reds and yellows and blues was nothing of consequence.

The walls were thin and the house much smaller than any in which Suminthra had lived before, but despite the close quarters, and a mother-in-law whose hearing had heightened to compensate for her lack of sight, Suminthra was happiest in those early days than she had memory of ever being. Papwa was a kind and gentle man. Yes, he deferred to his mother, but that was a sign of his respect for his elders and had not her stepmother told her that the way a man treated his mother boded well for how he would treat his wife?

Hindu tradition dictates that a bride is not expected to perform housework until her *mehndi* has faded. For a few days, Suminthra revelled in the feeling of being spoiled – by her husband, by her mother-in-law and by her sisters-in-law who came to assist with the household tasks. Suminthra expected to work. She was happy to take over the cooking as it had always been a task she'd enjoyed in her father's home. She expected to put the house to rights, getting into all the nooks and crannies that Parvathy had been unable to reach. But once Suminthra's *mehndi* faded, she discovered a new side to her placid mother-in-law.

Parvathy clearly adored Papwa. She cossetted all three of her sons, but held firm beliefs regarding a woman's responsibility to maintain the home to her exacting standards of hygiene. Suminthra soon discovered that though her mother-in-law was blind, she always knew where Suminthra was and how well she'd executed her tasks. "There's too much oil in your curry," or "your *roti's* flat and dry," she'd complain, before launching into the virtues of a good *roti*: light and puffy and both surfaces perfectly flecked through with golden brown specks, "but be careful not to burn it because no one likes too dark *roti*!" Suminthra wondered how her mother-in-law could possibly know the colour of the specks on the *roti* just by tasting it, but she bit her tongue. Parvathy would always end her tirades by wondering where Suminthra had learnt to cook, as if asking the gods why they had saddled her with such a useless daughter-in-law.

As for Suminthra, she wished she could have explained to the older woman that her stepmother had had little interest in teaching her stepdaughters the domestic arts, but even in the early days of her marriage, she knew no explanation would placate her mother-in-law. There was no question about it, Parvathy was a real authoritarian and Suminthra was forced to assume the role of the subservient wife and daughter-in-law. It was the role to which her father and later her stepmother had trained her, so Suminthra felt few qualms about her circumstances. No matter how many times her mother-in-law made her grind already finely-ground spices, or made her dust pristine surfaces or complained about the colour of the specks on a *roti* she could not see, it was better than pushing a heavy plough, Suminthra reminded herself, and Papwa was not the type of man to raise his voice, let alone his hands, to a woman. Suminthra had to be thankful to his mother for teaching him that much, she decided.

Suminthra came from a religious Hindu family and she had always found solace in her religion. Her devotion was the one thing she had in common with her mother-in-law. Though the house was tiny, the family's altar took pride of place. It became Suminthra's job to light the oil-soaked wick in the little recess of the brass *Aarti* plate as a daily offering to Lakshmi, the goddess of the home. By lighting the lamp each evening, just as dusk began to blanket Riverside in a cloak of smoke and fog, Suminthra was not only bringing light into the home, she was welcoming in prosperity.

These rituals and Papwa's quiet support, though he worked six days out of seven and departed early in the morning and returned late in the afternoon, helped Suminthra adapt to her new life. A few weeks after her wedding, Suminthra arranged the beautiful cups she'd received as a wedding present on hooks against the wall in the common room. Like the bedspread imported from India, it gave her great pleasure to look at them.

Over time she made friends with the other women living on the property and was pleased to discover an ally in Mohan's wife, Saras. When they walked to the river to wash clothes, far away from Parvathy's uncanny hearing, the two friends would mimic the shrill tones of their strict mother-in-law. Suminthra was surprised to learn that though her husband's brother took his duty as his mother's walking stick as seriously as Papwa did, Mohan often took his wife's part in arguments with his mother, which was the real reason they'd moved out of the family home. After only a few months of marriage, Suminthra saw that Papwa was blindly loyal to his mother. She knew that even if she were to have the courage to complain about the way Parvathy treated her, Papwa would hear no ill about his mother. Sometimes Suminthra longed to return to her childhood home – just for a visit and to be around familiar people and places, but Parvathy would not allow it.

Still, those early years of her marriage were happy ones, Suminthra considered. She and Papwa shared a love for Hindu films and on his days off, the couple would go to the Avalon Theatre in Victoria Street to see the latest films from India featuring stars like Guru Dutt, Raj Kapoor and Dilip Kumar. Like her, Papwa loved music and dancing and the two attended enough weddings and festivals to get plenty of practice. She did not know much about Papwa's work, but knew that he loved his job and loved golf. He was a good man, her husband. On Fridays he brought all his money home. He didn't drink and he didn't smoke, nor was he one to raise his voice in anger if in fact he did become angry. No, Papwa was a calm man and other than her mother-in-law's moods from time to time, she had few complaints.

Papwa and Suminthra's daughter, Romilla, was born a little over a year after their wedding and the couple adjusted to parenthood. Life was good and could only get better. There was this new government of course, in power for more than five years, but everyone said that the new government was just like the old government and that apartheid was just a new word for the way the whites had always treated the Indians and the Coloureds and the Africans in the country.

TWENTY

The early years of his marriage were indeed happy ones. Ma had help in the home and Papwa had the companionship of a spouse. Suminthra was quiet and caring, a modest woman in all ways. Since Papwa was quiet too and mostly modest; they were a perfectly matched pair. Like his wife, Papwa had entered into his marriage knowing it was not a love union as some of his friends enjoyed, but had been told that affection would grow and indeed it had. Suminthra encouraged him to enter as many competitions for which he was eligible, but drew the line at watching him play.

"Golf is your job," she explained. "A wife does not watch her husband do his work."

Ma would not have approved of Suminthra standing around a golf course either. Both Suminthra and Papwa knew that.

When he returned home after each tournament, Suminthra would soothe his muscles with liniments and oils while Papwa recounted the day's play. With a trace of pride, Papwa told her often how no one could beat him during the Monday morning matches, no one at Beachwood and none of the other clubs' caddies either.

"A, man should always endeavour to be his wife's hero," Raj had told him as part of the premarital advice doled out by the other caddies.

Papwa remembered thinking how easy it was for his friend to appear heroic to his own wife. Raj had turned his back on caddying and had finally begun working as a salesman for his father's cool-drink factory. But when he saw how his wife's eyes sparkled at the tales of his success, Papwa thought how right Raj was. A man really should be a hero in his wife's eyes and golf was the only way Papwa knew how to be a hero.

After his initial win of the amateur title in 1946, Papwa went on to win the Natal Non-European Open Championship in 1954, 1955 and 1958. He was beaten in the 1956 playoffs. Spectators at these and other events still spoke of him as an unassuming, friendly golfer, quick with a smile and a friendly word or two. The only difference between those first events and now was the expectation that he would win, and by large margins too – often by up to ten strokes fewer than the next best contender!

Outside of competitions, Papwa continued to excel on his familiar turf. As word of his golfing abilities spread, his pay was raised with the caddie master averring that Papwa had what it took to become a caddie master himself if only he'd learn to read and write! There was a tacit support for the promising caddie, with several members, who now vied for his services, encouraging his talent. The club turned a blind eye to his practising on the empty greens as long as the members did not complain.

Beachwood is a par 73 course. At the time, the official club record round was held by Sandy Guthrie with a score of 66. Papwa's personal best at this time was 64, two strokes less than Guthrie's and an astounding nine under par. Furthermore, Papwa regularly finished in the 60s.

With an abundance of stories relating his various achievements at Beachwood, it often proved difficult to discern between what was truth and what was legend. Witnesses told of the time he hit a hole-in-one at the 720-yard fourth hole with a par rating of four. Others said no; it was the 271-yard fifteenth hole, also with a par rating of four where he'd holed his tee shot. "Or was it the sixteenth hole?"

Still others – Fishy, Gopaul or Jayendra – said, "No my brother, it was on all three that our boy hit those holes in one!"

"And I've got the winnings to prove it!" another would add.

"He's not done yet!" someone else would point out.

The boys, men now, would grin, their faith in their friend and his abilities absolute. Papwa would grin too, but even the most confident player would not expect to hit a hole-in-one on each of the course's eighteen holes.

Papwa had always been better known for his short game – chipping and putting – anywhere around fifty to one hundred yards, but as his holes-in-one showed, and whatever they numbered, he was no slouch over longer distances either. He hit long off the tee, more often than not landing in the middle of the fairway, while his long irons hit firmly and accurately. Papwa soon gained a reputation for being deadly on the greens, but he knew the importance of the long shot: "If your ball is not up there, it will never go in," he'd tell whoever cared to listen.

People were beginning to listen, and more importantly watch, eager to emulate the unconventional golfer's style of play. Yet as much as his reputation grew, Papwa remained down-to-earth. As quick as he was to dispense golfing advice and tips to his friends and those who wanted them, with age and the maturity of marriage and fatherhood, Papwa had learnt to temper his wisdom to those willing to receive it. Some members spoke of the shy, but engaging caddie who, when drawn out of his reserve, would speak about life in Riverside, a life punctuated by a kind of poverty they could not comprehend. Others spoke of his timidity and reticence, while yet others spoke about his confidence and uncanny ability to "read" the golf course.

Whichever version of himself Papwa presented to the world, beyond the club, the caddie and the Natal Non-European circuit, others were taking notice of the quiet Indian golfer with the awkward grip. Reg Sweet, sports editor of the *Sunday Tribune* and *Daily News* was one of the first mainstream journalists to champion Papwa. In his 1957 article, "Back-to-front Indian Golfer (Plus 1) is a Champion," Sweet wrote: "Papwa plays to (and he really does) a handicap of plus 1. In fact he is the only 'plus' Indian golfer in Natal." Stating that "in the matter of golf at the top level, he compares with the best of them," Sweet urged: "There are good reasons why golfers as good as this should be given every encouragement."

In 1950s South Africa, as it had been since his birth, there were very many reasons why a man such as Papwa with a golfing talent such as his, would not receive "every encouragement." Though Papwa struggled to get his head around politics, through his interactions with Raj and Jayendra and a few of the other, older caddies, he knew that white interests had always formed the heart of South African politics. "They keep all the power for themselves and make sure they don't share it," Raj had explained when the new government had first come into power in 1948.

"New government's much the same as the old," Jayendra had said.

"Yes, my brother, it's the same old people in parliament, this Malan and all the other Afrikaners," Raj had agreed. "All of them – from the very first days of the Dutch East India Company to the formation of the bloody damn Union, and don't forget how the British treated us Indians! All they wanted was to ensure that the white man ruled."

"Yes, apartheid's just a new word for something that's been around forever and it's us who get screwed," Gopaul had added, making an obscene gesture.

Even if he'd tried, Papwa would not have been able to avoid the word "apartheid." Raj had explained the difference between the so-called grand apartheid and petty apartheid to him.

"You see here, my brother. Grand apartheid is where this government wants to divide South Africa into one country for whites and one country for blacks. You see why they make the Africans carry this *dompas* thing."

"Won't be long before we have to carry a pass as well," Jayendra had warned.

"And petty apartheid is all these laws they make up so they can justify this damn system," Raj had continued.

Papwa had heard the term "apartheid laws" before – too many times, in his opinion. In 1950, the Population Registration Act, which sought to place people into various narrowly defined race groups was introduced and served to underpin apartheid legislation. A person's racial category became paramount and would affect where one lived and what rights one would be entitled to. Other laws introduced included those banning interracial sex, marriages between white people and those classified as not white, segregating residential areas, as well as the segregation of public transport and amenities such as schools, beaches, toilets, parks, stadiums, cemeteries and hospitals. While the Indian Representation Act which had allowed for those white representatives of Indian interests in parliament was scrapped in 1950, at least Indians were not required to carry passes to move around in the cities as African people were, Raj had said.

None of the caddies had known what to make of the new government at first. When it had first come to power, they'd expected it to function much as the old government had. It seemed that even Raj and Jayendra had been taken unawares by the extent of apartheid's tentacles. In 1956, the apartheid government succeeded in getting Coloured people in the Cape taken off the common voters' roll and Raj started talking about black people, whom he'd described as anyone who was not white ("don't give me this non-anything, my brother") having no future in the country. That was the year he'd left Beachwood, hoping to make as much money in his father's business as he could because a rich man had options, he'd said, and a man would not become rich working as a caddie.

"You need to do something about your game or leave," Raj had warned Papwa on his final day of work.

Papwa did not know what to do. His job was safe and he needed to earn a living. He was happy to play on a Monday morning, happy with his wins. He did not know what more he could do to take his play to another level. It would take a chance meeting on the Beachwood links to give Papwa's golfing career the boost it needed.

TWENTY-ONE

"My caddie can play better than you, I'm sure!" the tall man joked as one of their four fouled his shot.

The four caddies looked at one another warily. They were used to players ribbing each other with that line of a caddie being a better player. Frankly, it was insulting, if true, particularly in the case of one of the caddies. No, they'd been caddying here long enough to know that such comments were not complimentary, not for the caddies at least.

The insulted player frowned as they expected he would. An unhappy golfer was one who'd have arthritis when it came to putting his hand in his pocket at the end of the day's play. Papwa held his breath. Today it was his misfortune to be this man's caddie. Jayendra was the one who routinely drew the most disgruntled players. Papwa supposed that today was Jayendra's lucky day.

Three of the four were members of the club. He'd caddied for those three before – polite, energetic men who made up in enthusiasm what they lacked in skill. Usually, they were good tippers; usually they did not play with men like the fourth. Sometimes two of the men played together, sometimes all three with a fourth joining. Because they were relatively new members, Papwa had not felt comfortable talking to them about himself or making too many recommendations unless requested. Yes, it was frustrating caddying for players poorer than he, but that was the only way in which they were less fortunate than he. What could he do? Caddying was his job and for his pay and the promise of a tip, he'd happily put up with the man's biting comments and growing frustration.

"Caddies are like dogs, we make good targets for the white man's ire," Raj used to say.

"Except you can't kick a caddie!" Jayendra would warn in a mocking falsetto, wagging a finger for emphasis.

"That's what you think," Fishy would add, aiming a kick at his friend's shins.

Fishy too had found new work. These days he sold buttons and zips and what-you-have at a haberdashery in Victoria Street. Papwa missed working with him, but with three children to support in addition to his wife and parents, Fishy could no longer survive on a caddie's wages. Now it was just him and Jayendra of the old caddie crew. Gopaul had moved inside the club and now worked behind the bar, but at least he was able to play in the Monday morning matches. Now there were new boys, just a little older than Papwa had been when he'd started. Caddie Master hadn't needed to ask him to show them the ropes. But-of-course not! Only, sometimes he felt uncomfortable about what he had to teach.

"Stop day-dreaming, boy! I asked you a question!"

"Yes, master," Papwa replied, unaware of what he'd missed.

"I asked what club you'd suggest, boy. Since my friends seem to think you can do better than me, perhaps it's only right I bow down to your superior knowledge," the man said, bending at the waist as if to bow, but only fractionally.

The three other caddies looked at Papwa, waiting to see his reaction. They knew that Papwa was not a volatile man, but that was the crux of the matter, he was a man. He might have begun here at Beachwood a boy, but he was a man now in truth and in temperament. And as a man, he no longer needed Mohan to remind him of how much he needed his job.

After a quick surveillance of the player's lie in relation to the green, Papwa answered. "Six- or seven-iron, sir," he said, quietly but firmly, modulating his voice to the man's mood.

The man frowned. The green was approximately 160 yards away. In his experience, six-irons were more suited to shorter distances, but he felt as if he had a point to prove. The other players had been getting on his nerves all morning. The day was hot and humid. To add to his irritation, when not making sport of his shots – very unsporting if you asked him – Graham and Jack had been talking between themselves;

wondering if one of these boys was the famous Coolie caddie from Beachwood who'd won all the non-white tournaments. He could not imagine why they'd be interested in knowing such a thing.

The man lined up behind the ball, took a few practice swings and struck, his hips flexing with the shot as if directing the ball with his body. The ball whizzed in the air and all eyes followed to see where it would land. Once it came to a stop, it was clear that while not exactly a bad shot, it was far short of where he'd wanted it to go.

"I thought you're supposed to be a first-class caddie," the man said, his face reddening with rage. He tossed the iron at Papwa, who luckily had good reflexes or he'd have been whacked in the chest.

Heat rushed to Papwa's face too. He wasn't sure if it was the tossed club or the way Jayendra and those young boys he was trying to train looked at him when the man spoke to him like that, that compelled him to put the man's bag down gingerly on the grass and walk away.

"Where do you think you're going, boy?" The man strode towards him threateningly, but Papwa no longer cared whether the man hit him or complained to the caddie master or even to the club's manager for that matter, about his insolence. He was tired and yes, sometimes a man needed to be a man.

"Leave the boy alone," the man they'd called Jack intervened.

Papwa turned around, straightening his posture so his spine was elongated though the man still towered above him and outweighed him by about fifty pounds. He did not need the man's friend to fight his battles. "I'm done here, sir," Papwa said. "I'll get you another caddie to carry your bag. First-class caddie, right? That's what you want?"

"But I didn't say you could go," the man replied, baffled by the boy's insolence.

"Let him go," said the man called Jack.

The man they called Graham walked towards Papwa. He was the one who had started all of this with his teasing, Papwa thought uncharitably.

"Wait. Why did you think a six-iron would work?" Graham asked.

Though surprised at the change in direction, this was a question Papwa could answer. He'd had no doubts about his suggestion. "I play sir. I said a six or seven because that's what I would use."

"And you'd make the green?" asked the player who missed the shot. "This I have to see!"

Papwa nodded – a defiant movement of his head, not his practised, subservient barely-a-nod, the one he'd tried to instil in the new boys.

"Here." The one called Graham handed him his own six-iron. He motioned to Papwa to place the ball where the man's ball had lain.

This was something caddies were strictly forbidden to do, but the men's determination and his own desire to prove a point impelled him forward.

"Don't worry, I'll say we forced you if anyone asks," Graham added, no doubt aware of the club's rules.

As Papwa addressed the ball, he did not think about the placement of his hands or whether the players would have anything to say about it. He'd already taken note of the wind, of the grass and the sun when selecting the choice of clubs for the man, but he checked again. Taking one final look at where he wanted the ball to land, he swiftly and surely made contact with the ball.

All eyes watched as the ball soared – "majestically" the third and largely silent member of the four would describe it later. The ball came to a rest within a foot of the pin.

It happened so fast that the four players and the three other caddies were silenced, as if they'd collectively held their breath waiting for the ball to land. Papwa realised that he'd been keeping his breath too. He'd been confident that the ball would land where he'd wanted, he'd played that shot time and time before in heat or rain, with the grass cut or not, playing the ball and the conditions of the day whatever way he found it, just happy to be allowed the chance to play. "But still, it's never good to be over-confident," Caddie Master used to say. "And if you mess up a shot, just play the next one."

Papwa always remembered the caddie master's words, which is why he was never disappointed in a shot. There was no time for recrimination if there was another shot to play. Still, this shot was different. It was not a tournament, or championship game, yet in some inexplicable way, the stakes felt higher.

All eight of them made their way to the pin. As they approached, the one called Graham stopped midstride and turned to Papwa: "You're really good, boy, do you play in the Monday morning competitions here?"

"Yes, master," Papwa replied.

"No one can beat him, sir," Jayendra elaborated. He knew Papwa was not someone to sing his own praises, and this man seemed interested, genuinely interested, in his friend's abilities.

"Is that right, boy?"

"Yes, master," Papwa said.

"And you work here as a caddie, fulltime? When else do you get to play?"

"He plays in the caddie competitions, sir." Jayendra had appointed himself Papwa's spokesmen. "No one can beat him there too. And he's won the Natal Open Championship and all!"

Graham frowned. "Ah, so you're the one they all talk about! What did you say your name was, boy? Why don't I know your name? With talent like that, why haven't you played in the Natal Open proper and the other competitions?"

"He can't, sir." Jayendra shrugged. "It's the law."

The other players looked at Graham quizzically. Surely he knew this?

"Hmm," Graham said, fingering his moustache. He knew the realities of racism in South Africa. He'd grown up in South Africa; had seen it in the Transvaal and seen it in Natal too. No, apartheid had never sat well with him, but he was not an impetuous man. He'd take the measure of this Papwa boy and see what he could do for him. He seemed like a decent sort and talent like that should not go to waste. He'd see if the boy had the chops to do anything about it.

TWENTY-TWO

Tall and bluffly built with a distinctive handlebar moustache he'd cultivated for many years, Graham Wulff was somewhat of an unusual man. Like Papwa, Graham had experienced the loss of a father at a young age. His father had died when Graham was four years old, and he and his two siblings had been raised by their mother on a Johannesburg farm. Unlike Papwa, however, Graham's education had been prioritised and upon matriculating, he was employed as a laboratory assistant by a dynamite factory in Modderdam. Working there ignited an interest in chemistry and led to his completing a Bachelor of Science degree via correspondence.

After qualifying as an industrial chemist, Graham worked for a number of organisations, including a stint at the Industrial Development Corporation of South Africa, setting up wool-washing plants. While based in Durban, Graham began studying the cosmetic benefits of lanolin, a fatty substance derived from sheep's wool during the scouring or washing process. Legend had it that Graham's research was a labour of love – to find an alternative to the thick, waxy beauty creams packaged in shoe-polish tins used by his wife, which left a greasy residue on her skin. After much trial and error, Wulff, with his wife's input, perfected the formula for the preparation he called Oil of Olay, the name a play on the word lanolin.

At the time, he described the delicately scented, pink-hued preparation as being as near as possible to skin sebum, the oily secretion from the sebaceous glands that lubricates skin. Product testing proved the fluid to be easily absorbable – it dried to a matt finish within ten minutes of application and left skin feeling soft, moisturised and restored. From his wife's experiences, Graham knew that it was not only how a beauty preparation affected one's skin that was important to a woman, but the positive, more imperceptible attributes she associated with the product – hence the pink colour, subtle fragrance and attractive packaging.

In order to reach as many potential consumers as possible, Graham contacted an advertising agency and it was here that he met his future business partner and friend, Jack Lowe. In 1952, the two, along with chemist Edmund Anderson, the third golfer on the day Papwa proved his prowess with the six-iron, set up a company, Adams National Industries (ANI) to produce and market Oil of Olay. Within the space of a few short years, Oil of Olay became very popular amongst South African women – both due to the efficacy of the product and an innovative promotional campaign. The partners soon began talking about expanding internationally.

All three: Graham, Jack and Edmund were ardent golfers and all three were members of the Beachwood Golf Course. Graham played there at least once a week and over time was able to evaluate Papwa better. He learned more about Papwa's home life: Ma's blindness and Papwa's pride in his children. Graham was a father too, and the two men often spoke about their children. Graham was approximately twelve years older than Papwa, but a friendship of sorts developed between the two of them. Their mutual love of golf bridged the divides of race, background, education and status. On the course, they were just two men talking about the game, discussing shots and talking about their dreams and limitations.

When no other members were around, Graham and Papwa surreptitiously played together. Despite all his skills as a businessman, Graham knew that he could never hope to play even half as well as the timorous Indian man. He felt it such a waste that Papwa was restricted to playing in the Non-European competitions, believing Papwa's talent to be equal to the best golfers in South Africa, if not the world.

"You can't be your best if you can't play the best, old chap," he said to Papwa. "You're wasted as a caddie; you should be entering all the competitions, making a living from golf. Look at Gary Player!"

It had never crossed Papwa's mind to even aspire to pitting himself against the best players in the country. He knew about the country's laws and the restrictions he faced. They were after all, the restrictions he faced every day and had faced all his life. He had always been a modest man; encouraged to do his best, but not to get ideas above his station. As an adult he'd learned not to make waves and if anyone were to ask him, he'd say he was happy with his lot. His friendship with Graham made him realise that perhaps he was setting his own limits to his play.

"I'd like that," Papwa agreed. "But how? How does one make a living from golf?"

"Come work for us," Graham offered. "In the mornings you can fill bottles in our factory, and in the afternoons you can practise your game."

"I don't know anything about filling bottles in a factory," Papwa demurred.

"Don't worry about that, old chap. It's not so difficult. I know you need to support your family, but this way you can do both. Work and play golf. You'll need to practise every day; you have to if you want to play golf at the level I think you're capable of – the professional level. We'll find the competitions for you to enter, even if we have to look overseas."

Graham noticed that Papwa had not mentioned the laws that curtailed the competitions in which he could play. He knew that the club turned an occasional blind eye when Papwa practised on the greens or during lulls or even when he caddied for Graham, but they could only do so much. In South Africa, the National Party's hold on the country had been strengthened by several key moves. The party had won the general election of 1953 by a larger margin than that which had seen it come to power in 1948.

In 1956, the year Papwa accepted Graham's job offer, government finally succeeded in removing Coloured people from the voter's roll after enlarging the Senate and thus earning the requisite two-thirds majority vote to do so. Coloured people had been the last of the non-white race groups to retain any form of voting power till then, and had traditionally voted for the United Party, the National Party's opposition in parliament. At the same time, widespread protests against the pass laws that now compelled African women too to carry reference books, the dreaded *dompas*, began. These protests included the burning of these books and impeding their delivery, sometimes by stoning official vehicles. Many women were arrested as a result. On 9 August, an estimated twenty thousand women of all races and from all over South Africa marched to the Union Buildings in Pretoria to present a petition against the pass system to Prime Minister JG Strijdom, who had succeeded DF Malan two years earlier.

In December 1956, the anti-apartheid movement experienced a further setback when 156 leaders of the Congress Alliance: members from the ANC, South African Indian Congress (SAIC), the Coloured People's Organisation and the Congress of Democrats (white sympathisers of the ANC) were arrested and charged with high treason. They had the previous year approved a draft version of the Freedom Charter, a list of basic democratic rights, at a meeting known as the Congress of the People. The stage was being set for apartheid to become even more firmly entrenched into South African life. Graham knew this and worried about the future of the country.

Papwa, however, remained disinterested in politics, especially without Raj and Jayendra to goad him into being more politically aware. He'd always lived life one day at a time and would continue to do so. With regular practise at the non-white course close to the Umgeni Road factory, and a properly outfitted golf bag, a gift from his employers, Papwa's game improved markedly.

Ma and Suminthra both were proud that their Papwa was employed in the white man's factory and pleased with his regular pay cheque – almost double what he'd earned at Beachwood. Papwa was grateful that he no longer needed to rely on the ups and downs of players' tips to augment his salary, no longer had to worry about whether his demeanour was pleasing or whether he'd say the wrong thing and offend the wrong person. Caddie Master had been unhappy to see him go, but since Papwa had a standing invitation to continue his participation in the Monday morning matches, he knew that he'd continue to see the employee whom he'd come to regard as a younger brother.

Graham soon came to realise that the promised entry for Papwa into the historically white competitions as well as requisite membership into the golfing unions might be harder to procure than he'd previously thought. He'd known some of the difficulties faced by people the government classified as non-white, but he had no idea how deeply these ran or how difficult they would be to counter. Though he'd had no truck with the concept of apartheid, he felt almost guilty when he realised how much his white skin and privileges as a highly-educated, successful businessman had insulated him from the habitual indignities Papwa and several other of his factory workers had to endure and somehow overcome. To this end he would later set up scholarships to pay for the tertiary education of his factory workers' children, but for now, helping Papwa become the world-class golfer he was meant to be, and expanding his business internationally were his primary concerns, though not necessarily in that order. With luck, those goals would intersect, and Graham was a lucky man. After all, a person made his own luck, he believed.

TWENTY-THREE

"Look Pops, I don't think the South African PGA or the Golf Union's going to grant you membership. We can try, but in my opinion, we'd be butting our heads against a brick wall and all that. You know them. They'll hide behind the rules of this damned country and at the end of the day the outcome will be the same. We need to be clever here, Pops. Find a way to force them to allow you to play. They mustn't think they are doing you a favour."

Papwa knew that the South African Professional Golfers' Association and the South African Golfer's Union had rules. A golfer who was not an accredited member of the PGA would be not be allowed any share of the purse put up at a championship meeting under the control of the Golfer's Union.

"In other words, you can't win in any of the white competitions," Caddie Master had explained when the caddies had first spoken about putting Papwa's name forward into those tournaments. "Of course you can appeal the ruling, but the chances of succeeding, or even being granted professional status is slim to none, my friend."

And that had been that. Papwa had stuck to the Non-European tournaments. Indeed, it was frustrating, knowing that he was better than most of the white players he'd encountered on the Beachwood links, but Papwa had not been one to bash his head against a brick wall.

"Know your limits; you'll be happier that way," Caddie Master had cautioned. Papwa had definitely been someone who'd known his limits. His world had been circumscribed and safe ... until Master Graham began talking about wonderful things like "potential" and saying: "We need to challenge the status quo."

In a way it was strange for a white man to believe in him so strongly. Papwa had often been afraid of anyone with any authority over him, but with Master Graham and the others on his side, he was learning to be the daring boy he'd once been. A boy who'd found a golf ball and had learned what to do with it.

"The problem is that the PGA here is under the Golfer's Union. Why a professional body should fall under the control of the amateur organisation makes no sense to me. Then again, I suppose, so much about this country makes no sense to any rational person," Master Graham continued, interrupting Papwa's thoughts.

Papwa nodded. He was at a loss to discuss the rules, associations and the government, particularly as Master Graham knew so much about these things. Talking with him about these issues was unlike his discussions with Jayendra and Raj, both of whom had felt it necessary to educate Papwa about his lack of political awareness. Master Graham assumed Papwa had some knowledge of what was happening in the country. Papwa struggled to keep up with the man's rapid reasoning and thoughts, but was able to follow the gist of his conversation. Often Master Graham would veer from one discussion to another. When that happened, all Papwa could do was nod.

This was not to say that Papwa was ignorant of what was going on in the country. As an Indian man living in a land geared towards the satisfaction of its white citizens, Papwa did not have the luxury of ignorance. He knew all about the new laws, the separate entrances at certain buildings, the signs on park benches and train stations – on the golf course too. Whether one could read or not, these signs had become important to recognise, for the penalties and humiliations attached to being on the wrong side of the signs that marked out "European Only" and "Non-European" areas were severe.

He didn't need to be around Raj and Jayendra every day to hear what was going on. Most Indians in Durban were following the Treason Trial, especially after the arrest of people like Farid Adams, Ismail Meer, Dr Chota Motala, Dr Monty Naicker and Billy Nair; not to mention Yusuf Dadoo and Ahmed Kathrada from the Transvaal. Now, so many months after the first arrests, the trial continued. Certainly, some of those arrested had been released, but people said it wasn't right that the government had acquired evidence against those charged by seizing documents from the offices of the Natal Indian Congress and the *New Age* newspaper.

"Indians have always been against government," someone, Papwa was not sure who, said. All Papwa knew was what people told him and even then he wasn't certain what to think. Master Graham had explained the laws they would use to disallow him from playing in the white tournaments.

"It's the government's policy that white and, as they say, 'non-white' sports should be separate, just like everything else. They make no bones about that. The Minister of the Interior has said so on record. They won't allow mixed teams to go abroad, and if foreign teams want to play here, all the members have to be white if they want to play against white South Africans. Otherwise, 'non-white' teams can play against other 'non-white' teams."

"Is that all, sir?"

"No, Pops, there's more. They've amended the Group Areas Act so that anyone who is not white will not be allowed on the premises of one of our clubs as a member or guest. There're other amendments too, but I suppose this is the one that will affect you most."

"Group Areas Act," Papwa rolled the words in his mouth like a wad of sour-tasting tamarind. He'd heard them before – from Jayendra and Raj – and could in fact recall the first time he'd heard the term.

"They're controlling where we can live," Raj had said.

"Nothing new, brother, they've always controlled where we live."

They'd been away from the golf course on that occasion, at the wedding of one of the club's waiters. Papwa remembered the conversation almost word for word, though he could not for the life of him recall whether the groom had been Dinesh or Rajesh – brothers who both worked at the club.

"This is Ghetto Act all over again," Jayendra had said.

"No it's different this time," Raj had countered. "Before it was just Indians here in Natal that they were aiming to remove from their so-called white areas; now it's everyone, everywhere. They'll keep the best part of this country for themselves and we can battle it out for the rest. Mark my words brothers; it won't be long before we're all living in reservations like the African people do. Riverside –" he'd said, circling widely with an outstretched arm, since the wedding was taking place there, "Riverside's going to look like a happy dream, a memory, by the time they're finished with us."

"You don't even live in Riverside," Papwa had pointed out, uncharacteristically sharp.

"It doesn't matter. That's not the point at all. My wife's family is from here. And come on, I've worked at the club for so long and with you lot all this time, you might as well say that I myself am from Riverside," Raj had said, a tight smile softening the countenance he assumed when he spoke about government and politics.

The others agreed and they'd spoken of other things before the dancing began, putting paid to all political talk.

Papwa asked Master Graham the question he had not wanted to ask Raj then: "Do you think it will ever change, sir?"

"Things are changing, Pops, but this government is a powerful government. Others are trying to challenge the rulings too, you know that. There's the Committee for International Recognition calling for non-racial sport. There'll be new committees and organisations to come. You can be sure of it. I don't know where we golfers will stand in all of it. Only time will tell. All I know is that we can't merely accept that the government's way is the only way. You have so much golfing talent, an embarrassment of talent. And the main embarrassment is that you have to let all that talent go to waste on those penny ante competitions when you could be playing with the big boys. You need to do something with that talent, Pops. You shouldn't have to be a caddie. You deserve more out of life than filling bottles in a factory."

"Yes, Master Graham, sir."

"Don't worry, Pops, we'll find a way for you to play. Here or abroad. Jack's going to go to Australia for a year to get us started there. Perhaps we can arrange an Australian tour for you, like they did for that Gary Player chap. Jack, Edmund and I will put our heads together and we'll see what we can come up with."

Graham knew, but did not say that the government could refuse to allow passports or exit visas to those sportsmen and women whom they suspected would damage the country's reputation abroad. In any case, he couldn't imagine mild-mannered Papwa doing such a thing!

Given the spectacular local success of Oil of Olay and within a few short years at that, the partners had long been talking about setting up in places like Australia, the United Kingdom, selected European countries and the USA. Now the talk was about to become a reality. The first phase of the plan was for Jack to set up a manufacturing source and distribution system in Australia – another English speaking country in the Southern hemisphere. While he was there, the three partners agreed that he should lobby the relevant authorities to grant Papwa permission to play in the local tournaments.

In order to convince the Australian golfing authorities of Papwa's abilities, peculiar grip and all, Graham arranged for a film to be made of Papwa playing with Phil Ritson, a renowned golfing coach and former South African Open champion. However, despite the promotional film and the partners vouching for him, Papwa was denied a visa by the Australian government.

"The Australians can criticise our country all they want, but they don't encourage dark skins in theirs either," Graham had told Papwa at the time.

Papwa hadn't known what to think when Master Graham had first spoken about his playing in Australia. On the one hand, listening to Master Graham and Master Jack talk about the opportunities he'd find in Australia, so far away from the tentacles of apartheid, he'd been keen to go. On the other hand, the fact that Australia was far away made him uncertain. He wondered what it would have been like to be away from Ma and Suminthra and the children for so long.

Then, when he heard about the Australian government's decision, he thought that perhaps South Africa was not the only country that treated its non-white people so badly. Pa had always said: "Better the devil you know than the devil you don't." This was why he'd encouraged *Bhai* to work for the Corporation and probably would have encouraged Papwa to follow in his footsteps too, had he lived that long.

After the Australian fiasco, Graham decided to call the South African PGA's bluff and applied for membership on Papwa's behalf. As expected, his application was denied. No reason was given. None was required. On the application form, he'd had to fill in Papwa's race – Indian.

Much had changed in South Africa during the past year. Prime Minister JG Strijdom had died in office and was replaced by HF Verwoerd, one of the most intransigent cabinet ministers elected to the Senate in 1950. In his first year as Minister of Native Affairs, Verwoerd had ushered in the Population Registration Act and the Group Areas Act. These had been followed shortly by the Pass Laws Act in 1952 and the Reservation of Separate Amenities Act of 1953. Those in the know had begun to refer to Verwoerd as the architect of apartheid, his views so strident they'd have put his predecessors in the shade. As it was, the policies introduced by Verwoerd and his cohorts alienated many more moderately-minded white citizens and dissuaded them from supporting an already distasteful system. More and more, Graham became convinced that if Papwa was to have a chance at realising his potential, it would be best if he pursued a career outside of South Africa.

When Jack returned home, after having successfully introduced Oil of Ulan (as it was known there) to the Australian market, it would be Graham's turn to travel to Great Britain and begin operations there. Never one to miss an opportunity, he decided to submit an entry into the British Open on Papwa's behalf.

"They accept entries from all over the world," Graham explained to Papwa. "This is why it's called an open, because entry is open to all who apply. If only it was as easy in South Africa, eh Pops? Here they may call them opens, but we know how so very closed they are!

"If your entry is accepted, it will allow you to play in the qualifying rounds. Of course you'll have to prove yourself to get into the next rounds of the championship proper, but that will be up to you. The British Open is one of the oldest in the world. Golfers play for a trophy called the Claret Jug. It's a big honour, even though the purse is not so big ..."

"I've heard about the British Open, sir. My father used to tell me stories of the great Bambata from Durban who went to play in it."

"That's right," Graham laughed, surprised that Papwa's father had known the story since, by all accounts, the man had not known much about golf.

TWENTY-FOUR

On 27 May 1959, three people set off from Stamford Hill Aerodrome in a four-seater Piper Twin Comanche 250 ZS-DRT: Graham Wulff, his wife and Papwa. A small crowd of family and well-wishers had come to see the three off. In addition to the British Open which had approved Papwa's entry, Wulff had entered Papwa into the French, Dutch and German Opens and was waiting for confirmation of Papwa's acceptance into these events. In many ways, the trip was an act of faith for all three. Wulff was hoping to set up United Kingdom operations for Oil of Olay, or Oil of Ulay as it would be called there. Papwa's task was no less daunting. He was about to test his mettle against some of the best golfers in the world.

That's why I'm nervous, Papwa thought that morning, after a sleepless night. He knew that it was not the competition and the field that had him worried. He would handle the golf one round at a time, one hole, one shot. It was his first time flying, and each time they landed in a new country, Master Graham had said he would have to sign his name on a card. For weeks they had practised together, the master showing him how to grip a pen and helping him to trace the letters to spell out the name: S-E-W-S-U-N-K-E-R--S-E-W-G-O-L-U-M. It reminded him of when Gopaul had taught him his numbers by writing in the wet sand outside Beachwood.

"Why not Papwa?" he'd asked, preferring the shorter name he'd mastered signing for the scorecards, but Master Graham had explained that Papwa was a nickname and the authorities would want his official name, the one written on his passport. Master Graham had taken him to get the passport and had filled out all the forms then. Ma couldn't remember if Pa had registered Papwa's birth at Indian Affairs when he'd been born. There were no papers to show, so Master Graham had filled in the dates himself. Peering at Papwa, he'd said: "You look about twenty-eight, twenty-nine, so we'll say you were born in 1930, okay?"

Papwa could not understand the white man's need for such precision of detail, but he had accepted Master Graham's reasoning that it was "government business."

Ever since receiving word of his acceptance into the British Open, Papwa had upped his training. Master Graham and Master Edmund had insisted that he adopt a strict diet. They'd bought him vitamin tablets and warm clothing so that he could withstand the Scottish weather, wet and chilly, even in July!

"It was the rain and cold that did Bambata in," Master Graham warned Papwa when he wondered why he had to take the vitamin pills. "These will ensure you won't get sick."

"So you *have* heard about the Great Bambata?" Papwa had asked him, surprised that a white man would have heard about the Indian golfer. Master Graham hadn't said much when he'd mentioned Bambata before.

"Every golfer in Durban knows the story of Bambata, Papwa. Did you hear about the time that he won a bet against JT Barry, one of the best golfers in South Africa then? Barry offered him two cents for every hole he won. Bambata played each shot with a putter only, but at the end of the round Barry had to pay up seventeen half-crowns."

Papwa laughed at Master Graham's story of the irascible golfer taking each shot with a putter. Not so long ago, he'd played entire rounds with his trusted five-iron alone. He laughed until he wanted to cry, the lump in his throat threatening to undam in a burst of emotion. He felt such an intense longing for his father then, his father whose life had been cut so short. Pa had set him on this path, he knew. Pa had supported him even if he'd known little of the game. He would have been so proud, Papwa thought, thinking back to his own big talk of one day surpassing Bambata's achievements and returning home a hero.

Yes, it was not only that he was nervous of flying, nervous of embarrassing himself – on the plane, in the hotels Master Graham said he would be staying in, in the foreign countries, not to mention in front of the other golfers. It went much deeper than that. He would miss his family, Papwa realised. Their happy chatter seemed a world away. And what of the smells of Riverside? The faint, but familiar stink of the river, the appetising aroma of curries cooking in the houses he passed. Would there be curry where they'd be going and who would prepare it? He'd been so caught up in the momentum of going, of achieving this impossible dream, not only for his family and himself, but for Master Graham and all of them at the factory too, that he hadn't stopped to consider what it would be like to be away from his home and his family for so long. Romilla would soon start school, Beepraj was younger than her and Dennis was still a baby. This would be the first time he'd be away from his children. And Suminthra? Would she be able to manage on her own and help Ma too? What if Ma took ill? What if something happened to one of the children?

At least they'd have money to last while he was away. Not only were his employers covering the cost of his trip, they'd paid his salary in advance and ensured that his family would be taken care of in his absence. But that morning, when Master Graham and Master Jack had arrived to take him and his family to the Aerodrome in Argyle Road, he'd almost told them that he'd made a mistake and had changed his mind. As soon as they'd heard the cars' hooters, Romilla and Beepraj had raced outside as children do; excited by the novelty of not one but two motor cars outside their home. They'd so been looking forward to driving in the car that they too had battled to sleep. This was a good thing Suminthra had said, as it had distracted them from the fact that their father would be leaving. But what do children know of distance? Even he struggled to get his head around it. To his children, he could have been going just a bit farther down the road instead of across the sky. How would it be when they realised that he was not returning home that night?

When the children raced out with an anxious Suminthra in pursuit, Papwa had remained inside the house. With tears in his eyes, he wished his mother farewell and dropped to his knees to receive her blessing.

"*Maar ke agana mar keh ne ana* – come back victorious, think of me when you are playing," Ma said.

Papwa dried his eyes so the men and his children would not see that he'd been crying.

Fishy, Gopaul and Jayendra had come to see him off too. His friends carried his bags to the car, all three joking that they wished he'd consider taking one of them with him as his caddie. It would have been a help, Papwa thought wistfully, but knew he could not be ungrateful for all the kindness the white men had shown him.

"I'd like to think of you as a friend," Master Graham had told him, more than once. "Call me Graham," but Papwa could not bring himself to do so.

Yes, if someone like Gopaul could go with him, it would help, Papwa thought. Gopaul could read and write, where all Papwa could do was scratch out his name and clumsily write numbers on a card. He hated writing so much that he kept a tally of scores in his head – his own and those of his fellows, agreeing to the totals at the end of each round.

Papwa was about to hoist his red leatherette golf bag into the boot of the car when Ma called him back. "Bring it here," she called out. Ma stood in the doorway. She stared at him so intently, as if she could see him and perhaps she did, in her mind's eye at least, for when he asked what he needed to bring her, she'd answered with: "Your golf bag but-of-course."

When he approached, Ma felt until her hands reached the synthetic material of the bag. "May you have the strength to hit the ball as strongly as Lord Hanuman; may the blessing of Lord Shiva keep all evil thoughts and negativity away from you, and may the blessings of the Mother grant you health, wealth and prosperity, my *beta*. Travel safely. I am always with you."

"Are you ready, Pops?" Master Jack motioned that they were ready to leave. Papwa, Suminthra and the children trooped into the car. Hari would stay behind with Ma while the rest of the family went to the aerodrome to see him off.

Ma heard the soft ticking over of the motors as the men started their cars. Her son was leaving – the first of her children to travel in an airplane. Overseas seemed so far away, like the word said, her Papwa would be going across the endless sea to a land on the other side. She remembered going to the beach with her late husband, Sewgolum, when they'd been newly married. They'd stared at the horizon in the distance as if it housed the future and spoke of the hopes they had for their children not yet born. She and the late Sewgolum had never imagined that one day one of their children would be leaving on an airplane to go so far away. And with a white man and a white woman too, come to think about it.

She thought of how she'd tried to encourage her husband to get the boy involved in other interests, but her husband had known best. Papwa was a grown man now, but still she worried. How would he cope in that cold, cold place? What would he eat? Was her son lost to their community or would he be a source of pride for them all? One of the neighbouring women had read the newspaper article to her that spoke of her son's plans: "Papwa is going to play with the *goras*!" That's what everyone was saying, that Papwa was going to fly in a plane, and play golf against white men overseas.

Papwa gazed out of the window as they drove. They passed the beach where he'd fished with his father. Even now, fishermen were lined up on the shore, men and boys, fathers and their sons. When Beepraj and Dennis were older, he would teach them to fish, he vowed. He waved at the fishermen, but they must not have seen him, for they did not return his greeting. Who was he anyway – just a man in a car, about to go overseas. Yes, he was afraid. But surely this was what he dreamed of when he'd imagined himself playing golf on the beach.

"Look, Pa, look!" he said beneath his breath.

It was nice to think of one of those men as his father – fishing placidly while his son played with a ball and a stick.

On the beach, one of the little boys waved at the car as it passed and Romilla waved back. Children wave at passing cars, Papwa remembered, and at strangers. He thought of a boy on the beach with his dog, and a man who'd thought he was nothing more than a Coolie boy with ideas above his station. Was he?

"How are you feeling Pops?" Master Jack asked, turning briefly to look at Papwa sitting on the seat next to him. "You have a wonderful family. Everything's going be alright, you know. Graham is very fond of you and will take care of you".

Papwa smiled wanly, but did not answer him. Romilla was chatting to her mother at the back, while Dennis had fallen asleep, his little head nuzzled into his mother's shoulder. Beepraj wouldn't sit still and Papwa could sense that his wife was struggling to keep the two older children in check. He wanted to tell them to be quiet and sit still, but he could not bear the look of disappointment that would cross their bright, sweet faces at the slightest rebuke. He would not spoil this leave-taking for them, so instead he concentrated on the sea outside, the glinting grey waves with the sun hitting the water, the soft brown sand and the bleached-white carcasses of dead trees uprooted by long ago storms. The wind whistled through the open windows while Myna birds squawked overhead. It was such an ordinary day.

All too soon they arrived at the aerodrome. Master Graham had arrived beforehand and was already tinkering around: checking the undercarriage of the small plane and other things that Papwa did not understand. It seemed impossible to imagine that such a large machine would be able to stay aloft, but Master Graham had explained that the plane was actually quite small. Peeking inside Papwa saw that it was smaller than he'd imagined and then he wondered what it would be like to travel so closely with Master Graham and his wife. He knew that they'd fly during the mornings only as Master Graham had explained that he was the only one who could fly and the plane did not have an automatic pilot, which meant that he could not leave the controls untended and they'd also need to refuel.

Papwa looked around him. So many people had come to say goodbye – faces he knew: Caddie Master in his sharply pressed work clothes; Raj with his wife and children; a handful of the club's members. Amongst the familiar faces were strangers too: a man taking photographs; Indians who'd read about his trip in the newspapers; and others whom he assumed were just golf fans or Master Graham's friends. All applauded as Papwa and Master Graham posed for photographs. Papwa drew his children closer. He bent down and hugged Romilla and Beepraj. Then straightening, he chucked Dennis on his chin. The little boy, who was propped on his mother's hip, laughed, but Beepraj, sensing the ominousness of his father's departure, clung to his father's trouser leg.

"I'll go with you, Pa?" the boy asked winsomely.

"No, my boy, you need to stay and look after your Ma and *Aji*," Papwa replied, his heart contracting at the disappointment painted on his son's face. "You too," he said to Romilla who hung on to her mother's sari. "Do not make mischief; listen to your Ma and *Aji* while I'm away."

Suminthra was a shy woman, especially in crowds, but Papwa drew her closer. "I'll miss you, *Kanna*," he said, taking one of her hands in his.

"I'll miss you too, Papwa. Think of me and remember that Lord Hanuman is always by your side," she said. The two stared at each other wordlessly, as if saying all the things they hadn't been able to say to each other these past few days, and couldn't, in the throng.

"I'm really going," Papwa said, looking around him in disbelief.

"Yes, *Kanna*, you're really going. Papwa, please come back to me." She said it like a question.

"I'll always come back to you and my family," Papwa said. Then Master Graham came to tell him that it was time to go.

"Are you okay, old chap?" Master Graham asked once Papwa was strapped in.

"Yes, sir, I am fine. I am just thinking about what it would be like to be a champion."

TWENTY-FIVE

Graham piloted the airplane during the morning hours, devoting afternoons to sightseeing and business along the way. Beira was the first overnight stop. Within scant hours of landing, Papwa was on the links playing with a five-handicap golfer there – the manager of the hotel into which they'd been booked. The luxurious Grand Hotel in Beira was Papwa's first experience of indoor plumbing and having a room all to himself. Graham was surprised to find Papwa chipping balls across the king-sized bed when he went to check on him before retiring for the night. Further overnight stops were Dar es Salaam, Nairobi, Entebbe, Khartoum, Cairo, Tripoli, Rome and Nice – up Africa and over the Mediterranean to London's Gatwick Airport.

Save for a near miss when a sudden storm blew the small plane off course while Graham napped and his wife watched the controls, the pilot had become less vigilant about such things the longer they flew, the actual time in the air was largely pleasant and uneventful. They flew at a relatively low altitude and the travellers were able to see many features along the way, including Papwa's first glimpse of snow – the frozen peaks of Mount Kilimanjaro. The trio spent an extra night in Cairo and visited the pyramids and the Egyptian Museum to see Tutankhamen's treasures. Papwa also had the thrilling experience of riding a camel and could not wait to regale his children and his friends with the story when he returned home.

There were days when it was easy to believe that this was all one long dream, Papwa thought, marvelling at his changing fortunes. All he'd wanted to do was play golf. He'd never guessed how much golf would open up the world to him, a simple man from Riverside. Once the trip had been confirmed, Ma said that it had always been his destiny, set out before him by the gods and that he should do her and his late father proud.

Sometimes Papwa felt that it was not only Ma and Pa, Suminthra and their little ones, his brothers and sisters and friends who were relying on him to do them proud: he carried the hopes and dreams of all of Riverside on his shoulders – of all Indians for that matter, poor or not, who'd been told they were nothing more than Coolies; worthy of their second-class status in a country that only grudgingly accepted them and showed in so many ways, how it did not.

There were days when Papwa missed home so much. He missed Suminthra's cooking and faced with all the foreign food, including beef and pork which he would not eat, Papwa stuck to what he knew: bananas and biscuits, to the Wulffs' great amusement. In such close quarters, Papwa discovered that the couple's generosity did not falter. Papwa was grateful for all that Master Graham had done for him, but Master Graham was a trickster too.

"Papwa, don't you think it's wonderful that we don't get lost?" he'd ask, at least once a day.

And always, Papwa would answer: "Oh, I think the master's been this way before."

Graham had not in fact flown that way before and had relied heavily on a friend, who'd flown from Durban to Europe in a light aircraft the previous year, to help plan his journey.

There was another ritual they observed. Before setting off Papwa would ask whether the Comanche contained enough petrol to get them to their next destination. Graham had found the question hilarious the first time Papwa had asked. To humour him, Papwa continued to ask the question and the joke never grew stale. Other times Graham would pretend that he'd lost the way or that the plane was indeed about to run out of fuel just to see Papwa's reaction.

After nearly a fortnight's worth of travelling, they arrived at Gatwick – a landing that was not entirely free of drama. A mix-up with the Gatwick frequency and the Comanche's automatic direction finder caused the plane to be diverted to Biggin Hill, a Royal Air Force base, for refuelling before it could go on to Gatwick. "We nearly ran out of petrol there, Pops," Master Graham bellowed.

Papwa spent a few days with the Wulffs in London before Graham flew him over to Edinburgh so that he could acclimatise and practise at Gullane, North Berwick and Muirfield, the three courses where the British Open was to be contested.

Since most of his business was based in London, Graham was unable to remain in Edinburgh long. Moreover, with his company's international expansion drive, money was tight. He booked Papwa into a hotel some distance away from the courses and arranged for him to take a train back and forth from his practice sessions. However, the hotel's distance from the golf course and Papwa's inability to read and write hampered his mobility. Always a problem-solver, Graham devised flash cards with pictures of the train stations, the golf courses and the hotel for Papwa to carry with him. Graham made sure to include the address of each so Papwa could consult passers-by if he got lost. This worked for a while until a misunderstanding resulted in a ruinous taxi bill when Papwa neglected to discharge his driver after being dropped at one of the courses for a day's practise. After that Graham hired a university student to take Papwa around and moved him to a hotel closer to the New Berwick course.

Given the bewilderment he faced in the foreign country where people spoke with thick Scottish brogues as indecipherable as his Durban *chārou* accent, it was with great relief that Papwa encountered a fellow South African contender during one of his first visits to Gullane. That man was Gary Player and the meeting was the beginning of a friendship between a poor player from Riverside and a poor player from Lyndhurst, Johannesburg. One had lost a father at a tender age, the other his mother. Likewise, both had discovered a passion for golf whilst young, haunting golf courses during their teens. Their careers, however, would take two very different trajectories and years later would earn Papwa the media-bestowed title of the "Ugly Sibling" to Gary's title of the "Pretty Twin."

Seven years younger than Papwa, aged twenty-three at their time of meeting, Gary was by far the more experienced and worldly player. He had already started to make a name for himself in the international golf standings. Since winning the Egyptian Match Play event in 1955, he'd gone on to win several tournaments – in South Africa, Australia, the USA and Great Britain. That year in South Africa alone, Gary had won the South African Masters, Western Province Open, Natal Open, South African PGA and Transvaal Open. He'd won both the Australian PGA (1957) and the Australian Open in 1958. The USA was where the big money was to be found in golfing, and in 1958, Gary claimed his first US victory: the prestigious Kentucky Derby Open and was the runner up in the US Open played at Southern Hills Country Club in Tulsa, Oklahoma. With successes such as these, it was not surprising that Gary was highly tipped to win the British Open, and a man closely watched by the press.

Papwa also received his share of attention. The British press wrote not only about the burgeoning friendship between the two young South African golfers, but about the irony of Papwa being able to play in tournaments in a foreign country, while his own country denied him the right to play in anything but the non-white competitions. In a *Sports Illustrated* article written by Henry Longhurst, titled "South Africans at Muirfield," in a somewhat backhanded manner, Longhurst wrote of Papwa: "Like so many South African caddies he can beat the best amateurs in his club, and like Sam Snead [an American professional golfer famed for his folksy image], he reckons he plays his best in bare feet. He holds the club with his left hand below his right and in the first qualifying round went round in 71 in a downpour. So much for those of us who write books on how to play golf!"

It seemed there would always be this question around Papwa. Was he a talented amateur or did he have the ability to turn professional and vie with the world's best? Denied professional status by the South African PGA, there was little way of knowing into which category he belonged unless he travelled outside of South Africa. "To be a champion, you need to compete with champions," Master Graham had always said. At this stage of Papwa's career, the competition offered by the contenders in the non-European championships wasn't up to providing much of a challenge to Papwa – not when he regularly beat his closest competitor by ten strokes at least!

Papwa found a worthy opponent in Gary. During their first practice round, Papwa set off to a spectacular start, scoring three birdies within the first few holes. He reached the turn in thirty shots, but only managed thirty-nine strokes over the next nine holes to finish on 69. Gary had a good second half to finish on 70, losing to Papwa by a single stroke. The next round went to Gary with a score of 70 to Papwa's 74. Then the third round went to Papwa, who scored 70 against Gary's 78.

During the qualifying rounds, Papwa scored 147 to make it into the first round of the championship, but failed to make the cut for the final two rounds. When he dropped out of the competition, Papwa was just six shots behind Gary, who then went on to clinch the famed Claret Jug and a cheque of one thousand pounds. This was Gary's first Major Championship win – one of the four most prestigious tournaments (Masters, PGA, American Open and British Open), and the first of his three British Open victories.

Papwa was happy for Gary. He would never forget how Gary had helped him navigate the Edinburgh transport system, often arriving at his hotel so the two could travel to their practice sessions together. Years later Gary would recall the mistiness of the Scottish golf courses, the rain and a damp wind that chilled Papwa to the bone, even though he was dressed in waterproofs, which Gary conceded, restricted his friend's play.

Certain of his supporters would later claim that Papwa had fallen ill in Scotland and that was why he hadn't made the cut. Others believed that he'd been sabotaged by agents of the apartheid government. When asked, Papwa would only smile, and with a grace that had come to define him, would reply: "The best player won. I regard Gary as a friend and am proud of him. Still, I look forward to challenging him on various courses in the future. Who knows, possibly even in South Africa ... Who knows what the future holds?"

TWENTY-SIX

Graham had planned a mini-European tour for Papwa. Luckily, several of the larger tournaments were scheduled within a few weeks of each other. The French Open, the oldest national open in Europe, was next – due to be held within less than a week after the British. Papwa had been looking forward to playing in the French Open since he'd heard that South African golfer Harold Henning had been the runner up to the Belgian Flory van Donck the year before. Graham and Papwa arrived in Paris on the ninth of July. It was only upon arrival that they discovered that the start of the Open had been brought forward by one day, with the result that Papwa was ineligible to play. He and Graham watched the tournament, held at the La Boulie Golf Course in Versailles, from the side-lines. Ultimately, Welshman Dave Thomas with a score of 276 won the 1959 French Open, beating Englishman Peter Alliss into second place.

"He lost out on the British Open last year," Master Graham said of Dave Thomas. "Lost a 36-hole playoff to Peter Thomson from Australia, but never mind, I hear he won the Dutch Open after that!"

Papwa smiled, thinking that despite the failed trip, he was learning something valuable too. A man might lose one tournament, but there were always others to be won.

Starting on 16 July, the Dutch Open, played at The Hague Golf and Country Club, was next on the European golfing calendar. Founded in 1893, The Hague Golf Club was the oldest in the Netherlands. Tracing back to 1912, when it was won by Englishman George Pannell, the Dutch Open was another national tournament with a long and interesting history. English-born Sid Brews, who'd moved to South Africa in his teens and was regarded as South Africa's first world-class golfer, won the Dutch Open in 1934 and 1935. Bobby Locke, the first South African to win a Major and a highly respected golfer on the international circuit, claimed victory in 1939.

During his first round, Papwa scored 35 in the first half and then 32 in the second with three birdies to score a record round of 67 – the best of the tournament. He scored an admirable 69 in the second round of the day, which gave him a scoreboard-leading total of 136. Three-time runner up, Dutch professional, Gerard de Wit lay second with a score of 139.

Leading the field, Papwa entered the final day of play with an attitude of calm. He decided to play "non-attacking golf," by which means he hoped to maintain his lead and win the championship. For a while, this approach worked and by the fourth hole in the final round, he led by five strokes.

Papwa felt light-headed, ecstatic. Here, finally, was his chance to prove to South Africa and the world that he too, was a champion. Then the day turned. From the fifth to the ninth holes, De Wit shot four birdies and one eagle. By the start of the final half, Papwa found himself a stroke behind. Even his caddie seemed to have lost the fight, Papwa thought, wondering why the man thought it necessary to remind him constantly of his diminished position.

For a moment, Papwa felt himself giving in to the panic that suffused his veins. Had he come this far to let himself down with only nine holes remaining? He knew that he could hardly blame his opponent, despite the Dutchman's superb rallying and the support of the crowd. After all, the first lesson he'd learnt when he'd begun to take the game seriously, was that a golfer plays only himself and the course. "Play the ball as it lies; one ball at a time," everyone, from Gopaul, Fishy, Jayendra and Raj to Caddie Master and Master Graham had told him. Pa too, with his limited knowledge of the game, had said something similar.

Apart from himself, what about the other people he would be letting down? He thought of Ma blessing his golf bag and her parting words: "I am always with you." Ma had wanted him to return victorious. She'd encouraged him to think of her when he played. Now, it was as if she were standing next to him: her blind eyes seeing her son's need; seeing everything.

"My son, my son, are you all right?" Papwa heard her saying above the roar of the wind gusting across the course.

Papwa decided to attack.

By the eleventh hole, Papwa lagged one stroke behind. He hit a birdie, but so did De Wit. Papwa remained a stroke behind. He birdied the twelfth hole and repeated the feat on the thirteenth and fourteenth holes to claim a two stroke lead.

With only four holes remaining, both golfers had much to play for. De Wit had been denied the top spot three times in a row – from 1954 to 1956. Papwa too had much to prove, especially to himself. From the fifteenth hole to the start of the eighteenth, a long par five hole, they matched each other shot for shot with Papwa maintaining his two stroke advantage. He took stock of the wind, as he always did, blowing strongly across the fairway from the left. With a quick prayer to Lord Hanuman, Papwa asked that his nerves not fail him this close to victory.

From the tee, Papwa's drive rebounded off the fairway and landed a foot off the ground on wind-blown grass. Contrarily, De Wit's drive had gone straight – 240 yards down the middle of the fairway. Given the position of his opponent's ball, knowing that now more than ever he needed to play offensively, Papwa selected his four-wood and whacked. In so doing, he overcompensated for the wind and the ball landed behind a stand of tall trees to the left of the green. If he could not clear the trees to land onto the green, it would cost him the tournament. De Wit's second shot landed the ball firmly on the green. Using a nine-iron, Papwa's third strike overshot the green to land in the rough beneath a tree with low-hanging branches. Sensing victory in sight for their local player, the crowd cheered when De Wit's ball landed close to the hole.

Papwa knew that given the poor lie, he'd count himself lucky to reach the green. Again, just as he was about to succumb to his nerves, two American friends with whom he'd played a round previously, stepped up to offer him advice: "Take your time, Papwa, you can win this competition, it's still yours."

With this in mind, Papwa took a deep breath then hit the ball out of the rough to land within seven feet of the hole. So far so good, but he knew he had to sink the putt for the win, since barring a disaster, De Wit would achieve his desired four strokes with a ball lying six feet past the cup. Recalling with clarity those early mornings when he'd hit the ball swiftly and neatly into a tin can buried in the ground of their backyard while his father watched, Papwa tapped the ball ... and watched in a daze as it found the centre of the cup. Never was Papwa more grateful for Pa's advice to hit the ball ever farther and farther away from the cup. This was what all those years of practice had been for.

The din of the fickle crowd was such that De Wit had to wait for the applause to subside before sinking his putt. He did so in one shot, but it was too late for him. For the fourth time, Gerard De Wit found himself in that unenviable position: runner up to the Dutch Open. And by a single stroke, Sewsunker "Papwa" Sewgolum was the new Dutch Open champion.

His final score of 283 was the sixth lowest in the history of the Dutch Open. Coming twenty years after Bobby Locke's win in 1939, Papwa's victory was the first by a South African in as many years. Papwa's win made history in another way: he was the first non-white player to win such an important tournament in Europe.

Clutching his replica of the Dutch Open trophy and his prize-winning cheque for 200 pounds, Papwa told the gathered crowd: "I am happy to have won, but sorry that I did not have better scores on the final day. My putting went off."

News of Papwa's historic win was transmitted around the world and in the days that followed, well wishes poured in. Beachwood and the Durban Indian Golf Club cabled their congratulations. Back home in South Africa, when asked for comment, Gary Player replied: "Papwa has done very well. He is not only a fine man, but also a fine golfer."

TWENTY-SEVEN

Fresh from victory in the Netherlands, Papwa travelled to Hamburg to participate in the German Open. Master Graham had told him that Bobby Locke had clinched the title in 1954. Five years later, Papwa hoped to emulate his victory. It was not to be.

His first round score of 76 put him nine strokes behind the leaders and Papwa was unable to regain the lost ground. England's Ken Bousfield won the 1959 German Open in which Papwa scored 285, including a respectable 68 in the last round. Papwa and the Wulffs returned to London before departing for home. "I'm so happy to have won a championship here that I can hardly think straight," Papwa told an interviewer before his departure.

While travelling to Britain from South Africa, Papwa's talisman had been a Beachwood scorecard showing his record score of 64. This he'd stared at when he was not looking at the scenery below. On his return, he cradled his replica of the Dutch Open trophy – too precious to be stowed away as cargo. This time the question of how Graham knew where to go was obsolete. They returned the way they had come.

Despite disappointments like the French Open starting earlier than they'd expected, all in all, it had been a good trip. Graham had successfully arranged for his products to be manufactured and had outsourced a distributor; Papwa had his trophy. Papwa would be returning a hero, since the world's sporting press had written about him, from his time in Scotland until now. Papwa wondered what awaited him, but he didn't dwell on the thought. He'd missed his family and could not wait to be reunited with them. He couldn't wait to dangle his children on his knees, eat his wife's cooking and receive his mother's blessings.

On their return to South Africa, Papwa and the Wulffs were met by jubilant crowds, both in Johannesburg, where they cleared customs, and at Louis Botha Airport in Durban. In Durban Papwa's homecoming was particularly poignant. He arrived home to a hero's welcome as an estimated two thousand supporters gathered, all determined to shake his hand. Best of all, Master Jack and Master Edmund had brought his family along to greet him and though subdued by the attention and the fact that he'd been away so long, his children were thrilled to see him, peppering him with questions about his trip in the small airplane wanting to know what gifts their father had brought them from overseas. As a Hindu woman of her time, Suminthra was shy and preferred privacy for displays of affection and overt emotion, yet the pride she felt at her husband's achievement was reflected in her sparkling eyes and quiet smile.

The cheering crowds draped garlands of flowers around his and his sponsors' necks in traditional Indian fashion. Papwa himself was raised aloft by his hordes of fans and borne to a Cadillac convertible that would chauffeur him and his family home. The Cadillac headed the convoy of cars driving along the main South Coast Road to Riverside. All came to a halt in Clairwood, where frenzied supporters with outstretched arms converged upon the car to touch their own home-grown hero.

From the very beginning, Papwa's fans crossed racial lines – fellow South Africans delighted by his success. At a victory party held at the Lotus Club later than night, Papwa was congratulated by a host of dignitaries, including Durban City Councillor Ted Kerdachi and former City Councillor Jimmy Bolton, as well as D Kalideen, the president of the Durban Indian Golf Club, whose blazer and badge Papwa had worn throughout his official European appearances. At the same function, Graham was asked why he and his business partners had supported Papwa as they did. What was in it for them?

"People are constantly asking us what we are getting out of this. The answer is: nothing. We simply feel that anyone with great skill, regardless of colour, deserves his chance."

Papwa's prize money would not have been enough to share. There were, however, a few benefits to his win. Advertising money began trickling in. One such ad, for Five Roses Tea showed Papwa enjoying "a refreshing cup at the ninth hole". Natal Furniture Products, an Indian-owned store, presented Papwa and Suminthra with a new bedroom suite in recognition of his win. Other than the fame and glory, within a few weeks, life returned to normal. Or as normal as could be expected with strangers pitching up at his home in the evenings to meet their hero and talk golf! In the Indian community for a while, interest in playing the gentleman's game increased exponentially. Recognising his popularity and in a show of support, the Durban Indian Golf Club appointed Papwa as the professional of its yet-to-be-built golf course in Springfield. This was a hollow gesture as the nine-hole course would take two more years to be completed.

The new Dutch champion had little choice but to remain at his station on the production line of the Oil of Olay factory in Umgeni Road. Afternoons, as always, were devoted to honing his game. Oil of Olay's international forays had been so successful that the company expanded into new markets, including the USA, Germany and the Netherlands. With a hectic travel schedule and added responsibilities, Graham was unable to provide Papwa's career with the necessary nurturing. He'd set him on his way, now it was time for someone else to take over.

Louis Nelson, a former caddie and union leader, was one of the people who'd come to greet Papwa on his return from Europe. An avid golfer and able organiser, Louis had been instrumental in setting up the inter-club caddie matches in which Papwa had first begun to distinguish himself and as such, the two had a longstanding acquaintance. Shortly after Papwa's return, Louis took him to Curries Fountain where an interprovincial soccer match was being contested. Before kick-off, Papwa was invited to the centre of the field. Four golf balls were placed on the turf. Deftly and in swift succession, Papwa hit a ball into each corner. Excited at seeing the champion in action, spectators clamoured for a souvenir. Papwa found it hard to believe that here, on the now razed golf course, was where he'd won his first title in 1946.

"You've come a long way, Papwa," Louis said, looking out at the crowds. "You're a role model now. They're more interested in you than the soccer stars."

Papwa smiled, but still found it hard to believe how far he'd come.

In those days, all he'd been interested in was playing the game. He'd never imagined that he'd travel overseas in an airplane, sleep in hotel rooms and be treated like a white man. His smile broadened as he thought of the boy he'd been at sixteen, wearing borrowed shoes and clothing and playing with a cobbled together bag of clubs, most of which he'd had to return to their owners.

Louis patted him on the shoulder indicating they should vacate the pitch. "One day your name will be on clubs and balls. You're showing our people a new way, Pops. Your win has made people proud to be Indian again."

"They were not proud, before?" Papwa asked, but if Louis replied, Papwa did not hear his answer.

Aware of South Africa's race laws, the British PGA granted Papwa membership. This paved the way for him to play in all future UK and European tournaments. In November, the Papwa Trust Fund, aimed at raising enough money for him to travel to Holland to defend his Dutch Open title and participate in the British, French and German Opens, amongst other, smaller events, was announced. Louis was chairman of the trust with EI Hafferjee, G Pumpy Naidoo and T Lutchman making up the rest of the committee.

The fund's target was one thousand pounds. Papwa's employers and the sponsors of his first European tour contributed a cheque for twenty-five pounds, but the hope was that the public, particularly the Indian public, would contribute generously. A booklet, highlighting Papwa's achievements was written by Joe Francis for this purpose. Pages were sponsored by individuals and companies and contained short pieces by Rajendra Chetty, sports editor of *Graphic*, IA Khan, a reporter for the *POST* newspaper, Ronnie Govender, sports editor of the *Leader*, Reg Sweet, sports editor of the *Natal Daily News* and *Sunday Tribune*, who'd written about him several times before, and Obed Kunene, sports reporter of the *Ilanga Lase Natal* newspaper. Included in the booklet was a feature that demonstrated, with photographs, "How to Play Golf the Papwa Way." In his opening message, Louis anticipated "the generosity and charity of all in a worthy and deserving cause for a humble, poverty-stricken golfer of sterling capabilities."

Papwa capped off his watershed year, and the decade, by winning the

Natal Midlands Non-European Championship held at the Maritzburg Country Club. Although Howick caddie master, Lawrence Buthelezi, had been leading right up to the eighteenth hole, Papwa holed a twenty metre shot to a draw and in the playoffs held a few days later, thrashed his opponent with a score of 142 to 156. The *Golden City Post* named Papwa their Sportsman of the Year, succeeding cricketer Basil D'Oliviera, who'd been honoured the previous year. Papwa was being recognised at home and abroad and was well on the way to achieving the success that Graham and his other supporters had envisaged for him.

However, what none of Papwa's advisors had anticipated was how the South African government would react to Papwa's success, and the international attention it brought with it.

TWENTY-EIGHT

In 1936, American athlete Jesse Owens, the son of black sharecropping farmers and grandson of slaves, embarrassed Adolf Hitler and the Nazi regime when he won the first of four gold medals in the 100 meters at the Berlin Olympics. Hitler, disgusted at the fact that the supposed racially superior Aryan athletes were beaten by a "sub-human", left the stadium after the race – reportedly to avoid congratulating Owens.

So it was in South Africa when a little-known Indian golfer went to Europe, beating not only Gary Player in two out of three practice rounds of the British Open, but becoming the first black golfer to win a tournament the calibre of the Dutch Open against a predominantly white field of players. Like Owens's, Papwa's success exposed the fallacy regarding the superiority of the white race.

The non-white golfing community was eager to embrace Papwa. In January 1960, he travelled to Cape Town to participate in the South African Non-European Championships for the first time. Papwa had heard about the competition before. It had been started in 1949 – three years after his first tournament win. Some of the other caddies had spoken about getting Papwa to enter then. "We'll clean up if this boy plays, heh?" Gopaul or one of the others had said; referring to the lucrative side industry they had going at the time – making money by betting on their "boy". But after considering it, Papwa had decided that traveling so far away from home would not be worth his while. When questioned, Papwa would say that perhaps he'd enter if the tournament came to Natal, but it hadn't, not yet. Now things were different. Now he'd already travelled overseas. Now the organisers of the event had sent him a personal invitation, eager to claim the Dutch Open champion as their own.

That year the Milnerton Golf Club offered their course and the convenors gladly accepted. This was the first time that a traditionally white club hosted the tournament, and the first time the championship was being contested on a decent course. Papwa's appearance had been highly anticipated and during both days of play, spectators of all races jostled good-naturedly to see the player with the upside down grip and deadly short game. Papwa did not disappoint, tipping his hat at the crowd's frequent applause and winning his tournament debut comfortably. All in all, it was a strange and warm reception, Louis said. It was at odds with what government was trying to do with their laws and regulations to keep the races apart. "Golf is a gentleman's game," someone else said, "and fair play is bonny play."

Apartheid had been a way of life for more than a decade in South Africa. It was more than ten years since the first discriminatory legislation had been introduced, while the National Party had been in power for twelve years. The change of government had occurred three years after the end of World War Two in which South Africa had been an ally of Britain and the USA. The two superpowers turned a blind eye to the system. At the time, South Africa was one of the top producers of metals such as gold, platinum, chromium, manganese, copper and vanadium and minerals like diamonds and fluorspar. The strong mining industry, coupled with a sound infrastructure and a significant manufacturing sector, provided the basis for the strongest economy on the continent. Additionally, during the 1950s, South Africa was seen as a bulwark against the threat of communism in Africa.

On 3 February, 1960, visiting British Prime Minister, Harold McMillan, delivered a speech in the South African Parliament building in Cape Town. This speech, famously known as the "wind of change speech," signalled a shift in world reaction to the system of apartheid and the Nationalist government and it was the first time that a senior world politician had spoken against South Africa. In his speech, McMillan acknowledged that (presumably white) South Africans seemed concerned about the independence movements taking place on the African continent – almost every colony in Africa had a nationalist movement clamouring for independence during the 1950s.

According to McMillan, this drive towards independence echoed the independence movement that had spread across Asia fifteen years ago in the aftermath of World War Two. For example, in 1946 the Philippines gained its independence from the United States; India gained its independence from Britain and was partitioned into the independent states of India and Pakistan in 1947; and in 1949 Indonesia finally gained its independence from the Netherlands after a protracted revolutionary war.

"The wind of change is blowing through this continent, and whether we like it or not, this growth of national consciousness is a political fact. We must all accept it as a fact, and our national policies must take account of it," McMillan urged.

McMillan's speech was met with stony silence and several members of Parliament refused to applaud when he concluded. While he thanked Mr Macmillan for his speech, Prime Minister Verwoerd said that he disagreed with its substance, arguing: "We are the people who brought civilisation to Africa. To do justice in Africa means not only being just to the black man of Africa, but also to the white man of Africa."

A mere month after McMillan's ground-breaking speech, members of the South African police force killed 69 protestors and injured approximately 200 others who'd heeded a call by the Pan Africanist Congress (PAC) to leave their passes at home and hand themselves over at the nearest police station in protest against the pass laws. The police reacted by firing at the five thousand-strong crowd in Sharpeville, a black township in the Transvaal. On the same day in Langa, Cape Town, police charged a crowd of twenty thousand who'd assembled at police stations to offer themselves up for arrest since they too were contravening the pass laws. Individuals within the crowd attempted to defend themselves by throwing stones. Police opened fire on the protestors, injuring more than fifty people.

Inflamed by the heavy-handed police action, protests spread to other parts of the country. Government declared a state of emergency, detaining close to twenty thousand people in the weeks that followed. On 8 April 1960, the PAC and ANC political organisations were banned.

Images of bodies strewn on the ground – the casualties of the Sharpeville massacre, as it came to be known – were met with international condemnation. Share prices on the Johannesburg Stock Exchange went into freefall, forcing government to borrow heavily from US banks. Locally, the divide between white and non-white had never been more pronounced. Gun shops in the Transvaal and the Cape sold out as nervous whites sought to arm themselves, while foreign embassies were inundated by those seeking to emigrate.

While Papwa was not looking to emigrate, he was able to return to Europe for three months thanks to the money raised by the Papwa Trust Fund. During his trip, he successfully defended his Dutch Open title and participated in various tournaments. This time there'd been no Graham Wulff to either fly him or accompany him there, but despite being homesick, Papwa adjusted, enjoying the freedoms of a life lived without the spectre of apartheid over him. His movements, however, were carefully traced, both through the media and by a pair of Special Branch operatives who trailed him wherever he went – ever concerned that he would bring South Africa into disrepute. Papwa was not a political man and had never been one for pronouncements, but the mere fact of his competing on the international stage, and winning tournaments at that, did not sit well with apartheid's leaders. As in the previous year, Papwa made the cut for the British Open, held at St Andrews this time, but was knocked out after the first round. He had better success in the Yorkshire Evening News Tournament, placing fifth with a score of 281 – thirteen strokes behind winner Peter Thomson's 268. In Eindhoven he successfully defended his Dutch Open with a score of 280. Runner up, with a score of 283, was compatriot Denis Hutchinson.

Once back home, Papwa returned to the factory in Umgeni Road and continued to compete in the non-white tournaments. In June that year, the Natal Golf Association had been formed to serve black golfing interests in Natal with Louis Nelson appointed to the interim committee. Black golfers continued to face the restrictions they'd always faced: inadequate golf courses where they existed, and limited access to white courses save for caddie competitions and clubs like the Circle Country Club in Pinetown that allowed blacks to play on its greens on Thursday afternoons. The nine-hole Springfield golf course was no closer to completion and with it, Papwa's appointment as the club professional.

In December Papwa won the Natal Non-European Open for the fourth year running with a score of 294. Seasoned golfer RT Singh was runner up with a score of 313 – nineteen strokes more than Papwa's. The tournament attracted a field of 110 players, vying for prizes to the value of 150 pounds in the form of cash and gift vouchers sponsored by wine and spirits company W&A Gilbey Limited and shared amongst the top twelve finishers. Newly established Natal Golfer's Association administered the competition. W In addition to the title, Papwa and his partner in the team event, PL Paul, were awarded the Juggernath Trophy for the best score over the first thirty-six holes. In many ways, even with the Non-European Championship win in Cape Town, the year had shaped up to be pretty much a repeat of the last. Papwa needed new challenges. Everyone knew that; Papwa knew that too.

TWENTY-NINE

Both the Sharpeville massacre and McMillan's speech had served to foment the fears of white South Africans – both Afrikaners and those who identified themselves culturally as English. Verwoerd managed to parlay white fears that Britain no longer had the interests of white South Africans at heart. He urged for a referendum to be held, to vote on whether or not South Africa should become a republic – unbeholden to Britain or any other country. In October 1960, South Africa's white electorate voted narrowly in favour of a republic, paving the way for South Africa's independence from Britain.

In contrast to the moves to further entrench the separation of the races, in Durban, often called the last outpost of the British Empire, two ramparts of this outpost, Royal Durban and Kloof Country Club, opened their doors to the players, organisers and fans of the South African Non-European Open in early January 1961. Set within the grounds of the Greyville Racecourse, Royal Durban, or the Durban Golf Club as it was first known, had been established in 1892. Forty years later, in 1932, King George V granted permission for the prefix "Royal" to be attached to the club's name. It was around this time that the club acquired its motto: *Ludus Palma Potior*, which, loosely translated, means the game is more important than the man. Kloof Country Club can be traced back to 1927 when it was established on fifty acres of a farm belonging to the family of Thomas Samuel Field, a strong golfing proponent. The course at Kloof had been redesigned some ten years before the tournament in order to make way for a road linking Durban and Pietermaritzburg.

As reigning champion of the South African Non-European Open, Papwa looked forward to defending his title – in an enlarged field of 156 contenders, since many more centres were being represented than previously. The logistics of dual venues meant that the field was divided into two, with half the competitors playing at Kloof and half at Royal Durban. After the first round, they were transported by car and bus to play the second round of the day at the other course. According to reports in the golfing and mainstream media, players were made to feel welcome at both venues with tents and marquees set up, furnished with tables and chairs and catered meals.

On the second day, the fifty qualifiers finished the tournament at Kloof. Papwa fulfilled all expectations by retaking the title. Runner up and previous winner, Simon "Cox" Hlapo, a Transvaal player, scored 305 to Papwa's 297. Tied for third place were Papwa's friend, PL Paul and Western Province's Ismail Chowglay with scores of 307 each. Interestingly, Chowglay, who was left-handed, was also known for his unorthodox grip: he gripped the club with his left hand above the right. In addition, Papwa claimed the Harry Oppenheimer trophy awarded to the top scorer over the first 36 holes (75 and 73) and led Natal to win the Commonwealth Shield. Papwa and Paul also won the inter-club team event for which they were awarded the Cannon Trophy, named after the first white sponsor of the South African Non-European Golf Association.

Everyone had been most supportive, including leading white players, professionals and golf administrators. The New Zealand Golf Union cabled a message of support, while not to be outdone, the Australian Golf Union sent a shield. Media coverage of the event was quite high, with one cinema group sending out a cameraman to take photographs and stills.

When interviewed after the event, an unnamed member of the club said: "It was tremendously thrilling to see first-hand what Papwa can do with his unorthodox grip. He seemed a thorough gentleman, did Papwa. They were all gentlemen. Divots were replaced carefully – by the players themselves, not the caddies! Imagine that. I can't imagine why government finds it necessary to separate play the way it does. It is not good for them, and it is not good for us, but who am I to question the wisdom of government?"

After the championship, Papwa returned home to his family. Along the way, he'd asked the driver to stop so he could buy sweets and chocolates for the children. Ma, Suminthra and the older children would be so excited to see the new trophies, he knew. Slowly, but surely, the shelves he'd put up in the front room of their house were filling with trophies, joining the first one he'd won all those years ago and the replica of the Dutch Open trophy he'd clutched all the way home after his first trip. Suminthra kept the trophies sparkling with silver polish and an old rag. It was the least she could do for her Papwa, she said.

Romilla now seven years, enjoyed taking the trophies apart and reassembling them when her mother cleaned them. When her mother wanted to admonish her, Papwa reassured his daughter: "You're proud of Daddy, girl? One day you're also going to bring trophies home, but for your school work, right?" he winked.

"I want to bring trophies home from golf," the little girl pouted. Papwa smiled. He was not yet sure how he felt about his children playing golf. Despite the support of the white clubs and organisations, government continued to do all they could to make it difficult for Papwa to play in the whites-only tournaments and that's all he wanted, to play with the best regardless of the colour of his or their skin.

"You think they'll all let me play this time?" Papwa asked.

"I don't know, Pops, but there's no harm trying. My father always used to say: 'nothing ventured, nothing gained,'" Louis replied.

Papwa nodded. His manager came from a family of teachers and was often known to spout off English sayings when explaining something. Though Louis and Master Graham were very different men, in many ways they were much alike, Papwa found himself thinking, not for the first time. Come to think of it, his own father had used many sayings too.

"It will be hard for them to turn you down. You're the two-time Dutch Open champ. You've won all these other tournaments. How can they not allow you to play?"

Papwa shrugged. Earlier that year, the Natal Golfers' Union had rejected his application to play in the Natal Open Championship and that was only on the provincial level – in his home province. They'd tried to justify his exclusion by saying that Papwa's application had raised so many questions – questions they'd been unable to answer themselves and would therefore have to defer to the will and ruling of the South African Golfer's Union. But since that organisation was only due to meet once the tournament had already taken place, in the meantime and to their great regret, they'd have to turn Papwa's entry down as a matter of course. Since the provincial organisation had hidden behind the national body, what hope did they have that the South African Golfers' Union would agree to let him play?

"You're not thinking of backing down are you, Pops?" Louis asked, sensing Papwa's discomfiture.

"No, I don't think ...," Papwa began, but Louis interrupted him.

"We have to keep on challenging them or accept that we can't change a thing. What do you want to do?"

"I want to play."

"Okay, fixed up. I should warn you, though: I'm not going to beg them to allow you to play. I'll demand that they let you play. You're the current Non-European Champion and the reigning Dutch Open Champion; I defy the Golfers' Union to refuse you. Of course they'll kick it up to government, but can you imagine the stink it will cause overseas if they refuse you?"

Louis continued. "If they let you in, you'll be the first person of colour to play in the white-only South African Championship. And I have a feeling they will. We were meant to make history, my boy!"

As Louis predicted, the South African Golfer's Union accepted Papwa's entry on condition that the Minister of the Interior, Jan de Klerk, granted him a permit to play on the whites-only golf course. By the time they left Durban, the permit had not yet been issued, but Louis insisted they travel to East London anyway. After all, the permit to travel there had already been issued!

The official record says that Papwa was afforded "every support" by the East London Golf Club and associated bodies. After the tournament, however, one of Papwa's friends who'd accompanied him and Louis to East London, denied this, stating that when Papwa asked to be allowed a practice session on the course in the days leading to the event, his request was denied. "We haven't received the permit yet," the club's secretaries said. On the day before the event and still with no permit in sight, Papwa's request to walk around to see the lay of the course for himself, was refused on the same basis. At midnight, Louis Nelson received a call from the event's organisers with the news that Papwa's permit to play on the course had been granted. The reality of what this meant was brought to Papwa's attention the morning of the match:

"They'll let you play," Louis said. "They'll allow us to watch you play, but there'll be no fraternisation, no getting ahead of ourselves, no sir!"

"What do you mean?" Papwa asked.

"It means, my friend, no eating inside, no drinks at the bar or otherwise, no changing rooms, no lockers and definitely no usage of the ablution facilities! Heaven forbid you sit yourself down in the place reserved for the member's lily-white arses! I think that is what this government fears the most, the black man's naked arse!" Louis guffawed.

To be polite, Papwa laughed too, but he did not see the humour. All he wanted to do was play. Why was it so difficult? In order to come here, they'd needed permission from the Department of Indian Affairs to leave the province. They'd been forced to stay in the Milner Hotel, which was admittedly not a bad hotel, but the only one open to guests of a darker skin tone. There'd been no choice in the matter and that was what had hurt. It was not like this overseas. Why should it be so in the land of his birth? "No use dwelling on such things," he heard Master Graham's voice in his head, but the thoughts were his own. Such thinking would only give him a headache and he already had a throbbing hand to contend with.

The day before, his hand had been slammed in a door and that morning the wound was still bleeding through the pale, pink bandage. He hoped his injury would not affect his grip or the power of his swing. He'd come to East London feeling confident and strong. Louis and the others had reminded him time and time again that he was the Dutch Open champion; there was no reason for him to feel nervous. But was he nervous? Papwa thought not. Just ... it was a bitter pill to know he was only here on sufferance as Louis had said. Once more he felt the weight of the dreams of all black golfers on his shoulders, the hopes of the people back home in Riverside, his old friends from the club, and, to a lesser degree, all people who'd been told they were non-white – not good enough to be themselves, they were defined by what they were not. It was hard to be a symbol when all he wanted to do was play golf. Was it these distractions that had caused his accident, Papwa wondered. It had not been his fault, but the fact remained, if he had not been distracted, he'd have removed his hand in time before Jimmy had a chance to slam the hotel's door on it.

It was time to tee off, time to put such thoughts behind and concentrate on the game. "One hole at a time, old chap." Again Master Graham's voice came to him, but the man was not there. He was in America or some other place, trying to follow his own dream of building an international business, the dream he had shared with Papwa as they'd walked Beachwood's links all those years ago.

Papwa scored 76 in the first round, followed by scores of 77, 75 and 79 in the subsequent rounds for a total of 307. His hand continued to throb throughout the first day and by the time the pain abated, it made no difference. He tied for eighteenth place – out of the earnings, which meant that coming to East London had eaten his money and not added to it. The tournament was won by Retief Waltman, a rising star in his early twenties, with a score of 289. Barry Franklin, a seventeen-year-old amateur was the runner up.

Despite his own disappointment at his performance in the Open and his failure to pick up any of the prizes, Papwa's reputation was untarnished. The day following the tournament, he stopped off at the nearby town of Port Elizabeth en route to home. Here, at the Alabama Hotel, a banquet and dance was held in his honour. Garlanded and grinning Papwa proved especially popular with the ladies who clamoured for his autograph or a dance with their champion.

THIRTY

After the excitement and disappointment of his trip to the Eastern Cape, Papwa returned to his family in Riverside and his job at the factory in Umgeni Road. He might have made history as the first non-white player in the South African Open, but for the time being, Papwa's day-to-day duties were his main concern. Ma took ill – she'd always had weak lungs – and for a while Papwa thought she would not survive. Money had to be found for medicines and such, but Papwa did not bear the burden alone. His sisters and brothers helped too. By now, Hari had found his way to the Beachwood Golf Course, where he too served as a caddie. "This seems to be a rite of passage for the Sewgolum boys," Caddie Master said.

Though theirs had always been a fraught relationship, Suminthra nursed her mother-in-law diligently. When the day came that the older woman roused sufficiently to berate her daughter-in-law for the supposed untidiness of the home, Suminthra knew that she would recover.

Other than her mother-in-law's bossiness, Suminthra had little cause for complaint. Her children were healthy and joyful. In many ways, they helped unite the two women who loved them so. And in the neighbourhood people were saying that if Papwa kept on winning all those competitions, it wouldn't be long before they'd be wealthy people and all. Suminthra and Papwa were patient people, their family's needs small. Suminthra thought it would be wonderful if they no longer had to worry about having enough. Papwa said that as long as he was able, there would always be enough. Yes, her husband was a good man and life was fine.

Then it was the end of May and the republic for which white South Africans had voted came into being. The British queen was no longer the head of state; replaced by CR Swart, the former governor general, who was now the country's first state president. As he explained the changes, Louis told Papwa that though it might not appear so at first, the republic was for the better. "Things will have to change in this country now, Papwa," Louis said. "Hopefully, they'll change for you and me too. This is a good thing."

"Why is it a good thing?" Papwa asked, not even daring to wonder how things would change in his life.

"Ever since Sharpeville, the world has become more aware of what's happening in this damn country. Other countries can no longer ignore South Africa's racist policies. Not when people are being killed. Even those who have no problem with a little discrimination here and there found the sight of all those dead bodies lying in the street uncomfortable, evil."

Papwa felt the heady feeling coming on, the dizzying sensation that always overtook him when he thought about what had happened in Sharpeville. He'd seen those images too.

"This is an evil country we live in," Louis continued. "Apartheid is an evil system. There are no two ways about it. It took those bodies in the street for the rest of the world to realise what we already know. Do you know that after the massacre, other governments began speaking out against apartheid? In Norway for example, all their flags were flown at half-mast the day the victims were buried here. In New Zealand the Prime Minister called for a moment of silence to commemorate our dead. Canada's Prime Minister too; he openly said that his government has no sympathy for racist policies. I tell you Pops, politicians in England and America even spoke out against what happened. And it embarrassed this government no end when the Dutch parliament called them to task, saying a country needs to look after the welfare of all of its citizens. That means you and me, Pops. We Indians are officially citizens of this country, whether they like it or not! Talking of – in India, Mr Nehru said that the Nats were just like the Nazis. Mind you, India has always spoken out against the system in South Africa. Why, in 1946, India called for the treatment of Indians in South Africa to be investigated by the United Nations, but I'm sure you know that!"

Louis looked at Papwa as if waiting for a reply, but when none came, he continued. "When they first went after their independence, Verwoerd and his cronies thought South Africa would be able to remain in the Commonwealth as India did when she gained her independence. See, there're many benefits to being part of the grouping, economic development and trade amongst members, for instance. Verwoerd may be an evil man, but he's no fool. Anyway, some of the other members threatened to walk out if South Africa stayed in. People like Mr Nehru and Mr Nkrumah of Ghana began saying how apartheid went against the organisation's democratic principles and demanded that it be discussed at the Prime Minsters' conference. To save face, Verwoerd allowed the country's membership to lapse, rather than face further humiliation. The UN will be next, Pops. Mark my words!"

Papwa sighed. There was no stopping Louis when he got so excited.

"Even sportspeople have begun to take note." Louis's eyes glinted. "In Brazil, the government stopped a football match from taking place against a South African team; they recalled their ambassador from Pretoria too.

"I have no interest in politics," Papwa said slowly, without looking at him. When Louis finally halted his tirade, Papwa continued. "I want to play golf, good golf. That's all."

"You need to understand these things, Pops. One day you'll be called upon to come out against this damn government, mark my words. A man can never be too educated about these things."

"You Louis, always you and education," Papwa laughed. He thought of a subject to sway Louis from such conversation. It was nearly as bad as listening to Raj and Jayendra debate. No, Pa knew what he was talking about when he'd said a man shouldn't get involved in things he didn't understand. Try as he might, Papwa would never understand such intellectual matters as the others did. And even if he had understood the intricacies, he'd never have their facility with words to express himself.

"I'm a simple man, Louis," Papwa said sternly. "Your father was an educated man; my Pa was a simple man and so I am a simple man too. That is the way it is, right?"

"No it's not right, Pops. A man is not destined to become his father.

You can change your own destiny. Look, your father wasn't a golfing man, but you yourself are one of the world's best golfers."

"Just like I'm not an educated man, but my children will be," Papwa acknowledged, thinking of little Romilla who every night read to her parents out of her children's picture books from school. These featured children with pale hair and rosy cheeks, Janet and John. Romilla pronounced their names with such reverence for one so young.

Despite Louis's optimism, nothing much changed for him, for Papwa or in the country. If anything, things became much worse. Towards the end of June, Louis informed Papwa that they had not been able to collect enough money to send him overseas this time. The local media picked up the story, reporting that Papwa would not be able to defend his Dutch Open title due to a lack of funds.

Earlier that year, Louis had proudly stated that Papwa would undertake a European tour. When no tour was forthcoming, speculation abounded regarding the finances and record-keeping of the Papwa Trust Fund. Further rumbles centred on the nature of the fund and whether it benefited anyone other than Papwa. In his column in the *POST*, sportswriter Theo Mtembu, wondered why the committee of the fund consisted of Indian members only and whether it would "think about co-opting accredited non-Indian members."

Aware of the controversy, but feeling unable to do anything about it, Papwa deferred to Louis. He did not have the words to defend himself, nor the skills to oversee Louis's accounting or management of his career. Certainly, he trusted the other man implicitly. Even if Louis was inclined to talk too much about politics and how, together, they were going to change the nature of sport in South Africa. Papwa was not looking to make history, he reckoned. All he wanted was to be given a fair chance to play golf – good golf.

THIRTY-ONE

After few weeks after learning that the European trip would not take place after all, Louis came to visit Papwa at home. The conversation veered towards the latest developments in the fight against apartheid in sport as Louis found his stride.

"Brutus is claiming he's got a new plan that will end racism in sport by 1964," Louis announced, referring to Dennis Brutus. The previous year he had been one of the founders of the non-racial South African Sports Association, a counterpoint to the bodies representing white sporting interests only.

"What's the plan?" Papwa asked the question demanded by the conversation and the circumstances. He knew too well and all too personally that the apartheid government was in no hurry to open up sporting events to all of the country's designated race groups.

"He wants supporters to demonstrate against the segregated tours. This will put a stop to countries like Australia and New Zealand and even England from sending all-white teams over here to play our all-white teams. Also, there's to be a pamphlet campaign encouraging sports lovers to boycott all such racist matches and tournaments. Oh, and this might interest you," Louis said, training his gaze on Papwa: "They intend to ask all players to refuse to participate in those matches too."

"I don't understand," Papwa said.

"Matches like the all-white South African Open. Just because they allowed you entry once, doesn't mean they're not racist, or that they'll allow you to play again. We both know that!"

"But I thought their allowing me to play in January changed all that," Papwa protested.

"You and I both know that's not true," Louis said carefully. "Remember what they said when they granted you the permission. The provinces will kick the matter up to the national body; the national body will allow you to play if the Minister allows you to play. You know how the story goes. One day the Minister will grant you a permit, but you can't be sure that he'll do so the next time and the time after that. It all depends on what the papers are saying and which other country's government is nosing in *this* damned government's business."

"I think you're right, Louis," Papwa allowed. "But I hope you're not. I used to think that once the organisers and the other players met me, they would realise that we're not that different after all. Just like Master Graham did."

"Still calling that man 'master'?" Louis shook his head. "Don't fool yourself my friend. Those other players don't understand what it's like to grow up in a country that doesn't want you. And you know this doesn't stop once you're grown either for that matter! Some of the players, professional or not, might talk about 'growing up poor'. But you don't need me to tell you that there's a big difference between our version of being poor and the white man's poverty! As for the Brutus matter, some of us have already been approached by the papers. We've given our support –"

"No one asked me anything," Papwa said. "I didn't speak to anyone at the papers ..."

"Where *do* you stand, Pops?" Louis asked. He stared deeply at Papwa as if trying to determine the answer from the other man's face. "One day you're going to have to decide this for yourself – playing in the white man's competitions if and when they allow you to, or being happy with our people's games. There's no money in the one and no guarantee in the other. I suppose you could always go overseas, play for India or maybe even England, like Dolly."

In April the previous year, the Coloured master batsman Basil D'Oliviera had left his pregnant wife behind in Cape Town to play for Middleton Cricket Club in the Central Lancashire League. The news had made all the newspapers and for a while, Dolly playing for an English club was all that the cricket-mad people of Riverside spoke about. Dolly might have been from the Cape, but they claimed him as one of their own.

"It's hard, Louis, I can't imagine moving to another country. My family is here; my home is here."

The two men sat in silence as night swallowed day and flickers of candles and paraffin lamps glowed through curtains shut against prying eyes. Old ways still held strong in Riverside. Street lamps sputtered on then, illuminating moths and other flying insects beneath the dull, yellow light. The two men looked out at the street as those lucky enough to have work returned home.

"Sometimes I think you'd have been better off if you never picked up a golf ball all those years ago," Louis said softly, still concentrating on the street.

Papwa pondered Louis's words in a silence punctuated only by the noises of the dusk. Eventually he answered: "But what would I be, Louis, without golf?"

Over the following months, Papwa concentrated on his job, his family and the small, local tournaments or friendly rounds with a few bob going to the winner. There were times that his conversation with Louis crossed his mind, but Papwa refused to contemplate a future without golf. He was playing at his best and believed that there were many championship wins in his future – if only he were given a chance to play.

Towards the end of August 1961, newspapers confirmed that Papwa would be defending his Griqualand West Open Championship title. The non-white tournament was slated to be staged later in the year on the new course of the white Kimberley Golf Club. At the same time, the papers reported on the challenges facing the hosting of the national non-white tournament in Bloemfontein, the major city of the Orange Free State province. The issue was especially pertinent to Papwa and his fellow Indian golfers since people of Indian origin were prohibited by law from staying in the Orange Free State for more than twenty-four hours. In order to smooth the way for their defending champion – Papwa – and the other Indian players, the organisers applied for special permits to allow debarred entrants to stay in the province for at least seven days since permits were usually only granted to Indians "in transit" to the Cape.

With a purse of more than one thousand rand, Papwa needed little inducement to defend his title. In an interview with the *POST*, Papwa said: "If they allow me, I will definitely enter. I like to play in the Orange Free State. Many Europeans from the area have seen me in action – and I am sure we will be happy to meet each other."

Representing the non-racial Natal Golf Association, Louis added that the organisation would not allow any of its members to participate if Indians were not allowed to play.

Rather than swaying the apartheid government, several setbacks had made it take an even harder approach against non-racial sport. In September the South African Sports Association wrote to the organisers of the Commonwealth Games protesting South Africa's plans to field an all-white team in the Games to be held in Perth, Australia the following year. Then, on 26 September 196, the white Football Association of South Africa was formally suspended from FIFA at the football federation's annual conference after failing to comply with a one-year ultimatum to adhere to FIFA's regulations on non-discrimination.

As for Papwa, during his early October trip to Kimberley, he not only retained the non-white Griqualand West Open Championship title, beating his nearest rival, Jacob Gumbi of Transvaal by twenty-three strokes, he also finished seven strokes under par, setting a new course record for the Kimberley Golf Club. Scoring 68 on the 73-par course, he smashed the 72 previously set by Gary Player.

For Papwa, this win was the turning point in what had in many ways been a disappointing year. He knew Ma would say: "After something spicy, something sweet," but no one knew quite how despondent he'd felt after the trip to Europe had failed to happen. Sometimes there was nothing sweet to soothe the sharp bites, but the win, and the large share of the purse he collected, allowed him to forestall once more the nagging questions he had about whether or not he had a future in golf.

THIRTY-TWO

"So you beat Player again?" Fishy asked, though Papwa was sure that his friend knew this was not the case.

"No, I beat his record on the course is all," Papwa replied.

"Why you think Gary would be playing in the *darkie* championship when he can earn the big bucks in America and all these white tournaments and all," Jayendra added.

"Right, why play for small-small stakes when he earns the money he does? You'd have beaten him for sure if he played, the man's lucky is all," Raj joined in.

"No, he's not lucky, he practises very hard," Papwa defended the man he still regarded as his friend.

"And our Pops never practises," Gopaul laughed.

"Hey what do you think this is?" Fishy exclaimed.

"I don't practise, I play," Papwa said, sucking his teeth.

"All those years he dribbled that ball from his *possie* to the Club. What do you think that was?" Jayendra punched his friend's arm. "Got all his practice in from a young age already!"

"There's nothing this man doesn't know about the game!" Fishy grinned, exposing a tan-toothed smile from his constant tobacco chewing.

The friends had met for a round of golf at the newly opened Springfield Golf Course, completed by the Durban Municipality after all these years. Despite being far superior to the one it had replaced at Curries Fountain, Springfield was a far cry from the white golf course on which all four had honed their game as caddies.

"It's playing on those uneven slopes with the monkeys and the potholes, the sand and the rain that's made him such a good player," Gopaul mused.

"And don't forget the putt-putt course at Beachwood; we built that ourselves," Raj said. "Helps with his short game."

"Short game, long game," Jayendra sniffed. "Look around you brothers, at our great new course. What do you see? Nine holes instead of eighteen. It's better than the old Curries Fountain, yes, but can you imagine the Gary Players and the Henning brothers being satisfied to play on such a course? That's why our Pops here is so good. Because of the shitty courses he's had to practise on!"

"There's also Beachwood. Caddie Master –" Papwa began.

"Yes, Beachwood's a good course, but it's a white man's course. Doesn't count anyway, it's not like you can just pitch up and play, no problems!"

"I tell you brothers, things are going to get worse before they get better," Raj said. "This government is not going to change its policies any time soon, especially not with sport – not now. If they'd wanted to make changes, they'd have done so long before. Look what they've done with Brutus. They've banned him now, you know? Five years under the Suppression of Communism Act."

"It's because he's responsible for getting South Africa banned from the Commonwealth Games," Gopaul added.

"So one banning for another, right? But seriously *bru*, how is it going with the *gora* tournaments? Louis doing a good job of getting you in and all?" Fishy asked.

"Louis tries," Papwa said diplomatically. "We're still waiting to hear from the organisers about the Natal Open again."

"I don't know about that, Pops. Don't get your hopes up. Look what happened last time. And look how our South African Open has to be moved to Kimberley because Bloemfontein wouldn't allow it. You'd be better off somewhere else my friend. We *chār-ous* count for nothing here. Things are going to get worse, I tell you!" Jayendra said.

"Yes, we all thought the UN would agree to expel this damned country from the organisation; force them to make changes, but we all know how that ended!"

"How?" Fishy asked. With the exception of Papwa, he amongst the friends was the least politically minded.

"Voted 7-2 against sanctions and expulsion," Raj said. "The UN 'condemns' South Africa's policies, but will do nothing about it."

"Said that all nations should take 'separate and collective action' against South Africa to force the government to abandon its policies. What does that even mean?" Jayendra added.

"It means, nothing will change, for you, for me and all of us," Raj said. "Like I've always said, things will only change once all the people this government calls 'non-whites' stand together. Take this course for instance. Government says it is for Indians only, what about the other players? Zulu, Coloured, so on?"

"Oh Raj," Fishy started, but then stopped.

A weighted silence settled as the four men made their way to the next tee-box. With only nine holes, players on the Springfield course had to double back to make up the requisite eighteen holes of a standard round.

"Anyway, there's the Natal Open next week. All this talk of politics makes me tired. Gopaul said. "Defending champion hey, Pops?"

"Non-European Natal Open Championship," Jayendra clarified.

"Yes," Papwa said.

"To be held at Umbogintwini, right?"

Fishy spoke before Papwa could reply. "Did you catch our boy here in the four-ball at 'Twini beginning of the month?"

"Ah, I heard about it," Raj grinned.

"I was there, brother I can tell you! Pops and two others with a white player making up the fourth, mind you. What was that white gentleman's name, Pops?" Without bothering to hear the answer, Fishy continued. "Pops and his partner didn't win, but you had to see the crowds that gathered to watch."

"Because of who Pops is?" Raj asked. "His name drew the crowd or what you say?"

Fishy guffawed. "No my brother, it's because between the four of them, they scored seventeen birdies in the last fourteen holes alone. Oh it was a spectacle, I tell you."

Papwa shrugged. "It was nothing, Raj, just a game."

"It was not nothing," Fishy scoffed. "A white club in Amanzimtoti and the crowds loved you. People wanted to see you play, fourteen birdies or not. It was your name: Papwa Sewgolum, on everyone's lips."

On the very day before the championship was to start, Umbogintwini received word that it had been barred from hosting the Non-European event. The club had been the first to offer its venue when it heard that the organisers of the Non-European Championships were looking for a Natal course to host the national tournament the previous year. Though hosting of that event had ultimately been shared by Kloof Country Club and Royal Durban, Umbogintwini's renewed offer to stage the provincial tournament was gladly accepted. Mischievous mouths said that it was because of that four-ball in which Papwa had played and the attention it received afterwards. Others agreed, but said it was not because of the attention, but that government was not impressed by the way the white crowds had supported Papwa, elevating his status even further.

"It's the fraternisation, they don't approve of," Louis said. "Apartheid is all about keeping the races separate, so it doesn't help when your supporters cross racial lines. And it definitely doesn't help to support the myth of the superiority of white players."

"But we never even won," Papwa said.

"Doesn't matter, win, lose, they don't want to see you play. Not on their courses at least and not against their players either. After all, you could have just as easily have won!"

Thanks to intervention by members of the white golfing fraternity, as well as efforts by Louis, who was now president of the non-racial Natal Golf Association, the chairman of the Umbogintwini Golf Club received a midnight telephone call, informing him that the championship could go ahead after all. Once notified, many contenders had to drive through the night in order to make the early morning tee-off time.

Papwa did not have to travel as far. The club in Amanzimtoti was about forty kilometres from his Riverside home. As expected, Papwa won the competition comfortably, taking and maintaining the lead from the first round. PL Paul, who'd partnered him in the team event of the same tournament the previous year to win the Juggernath trophy, was runner up – scoring 303 to Papwa's 290.

"It's a good end to a year of mixed fortunes," Suminthra said to her husband when Papwa returned home with the winner's cheque and one more trophy to add to the bulging shelves that lined the living room walls.

THIRTY-THREE

The year 1962 was not off to a good start. In January, Papwa travelled to Kimberley to defend his South African Non-European title. This was the event that had been planned for Bloemfontein, the city in a province so inhospitable to Indians. It had been moved when permissions were denied. In a surprise upset, Papwa relinquished the title to Cape Town's Ismail Chowglay – the left-handed golfer with a 'wrong way' grip. Chowglay scored 297 to secure the trophy and the winner's cheque. With a score of 308, Papwa tied for sixth place with G. Diamond from the Transvaal – behind runner up JF Mazibuko and third-placed JL Semenya, both from the Transvaal, fellow Natal and Durban Indian Golf Club player, PL Paul, and Transvaal players Simon "Cox" Nhlapo and R Ditsebe.

A certain lassitude had overtaken Papwa that month and he found himself losing another, smaller competition, the first championship of the Durban Indian Golf Club. Though an insignificant club competition, and though Papwa was the runner up, the defeat still warranted mention in all the local newspapers. In February Papwa redeemed himself by setting a new course record at Springfield Golf Course when he won the Naidoo Brothers Trophy with a score of one-under-par in the 18-hole competition. In reporting his win, the press again referred to the fact that Papwa had previously lost not one, but two club competitions.

Around this time, Louis informed Papwa that though the Natal Golfer's Union had sanctioned his entry into the 1962 Natal Open, the government had refused – claiming that his application to play on the white Royal Durban Golf Course, had been received too late to put the necessary permissions in place. Papwa once more tasted bitter disappointment, but he chose to focus on the sweet: fundraising efforts to send him to play in lucrative tournaments overseas.

When Ismail Chowglay won the South African Non-European Open, a resolution had been taken at a meeting of the South African Golf Association to send him on an overseas campaign that included an appearance in the British Open. A levy was placed on each of the nine affiliates to the association to assist Ismail's trip, which a Kroonstad businessman had committed to sponsor. Papwa hoped to raise enough money to join Ismail in his campaign.

That year, for the first time, the Non-European Transvaal Open was due to be contested on a white-owned course – the Irene Golf Course in Pretoria. This venue was chosen since non-whites in the province had no golf course of their own, playing on the open veld instead. Papwa was still in two minds about travelling to Pretoria, but Ismail agreed to participate and was the big draw-card for the event – one of his final appearances before his upcoming trip.

Ismail and several out of town golfers travelled to Pretoria at great expense in anticipation of the tournament. Yet, on the eve of the tournament, the government banned the event from taking place. Justifying this action, Minister of Bantu Administration, Michel Daniel Christiaan de Wet Nel, said in a statement to the press that non-white golfers would be "insulted by being disallowed clubhouse facilities." Furthermore, allowing the Open to take place would pave the way for mixed sport (since sixty-eight black, Coloured and Indian golfers had registered to play).

"He's trying to save face, the bastard," Louis said as he read the rest of the statement to Papwa. "He says that if they allowed the championship to take place on a white golf course, they would be 'shirking' their responsibility to provide sporting facilities to non-whites. Since when do they worry about shirking their responsibilities? I wonder!"

Without a venue, and with no available alternatives, the tournament was cancelled. Days after the banning, representatives of the 600-strong Transvaal Non-European Golf Union voted in favour of suing the government for their losses and humiliation.

"It's a good thing you didn't go," Suminthra said. She'd walked into the kitchen area were Louis and Papwa sat. "It would have been a waste of money."

Papwa agreed and that was that. That year, as with the previous year, the monies raised by the Papwa Trust Fund were insufficient to send Papwa on an overseas tour. Papwa had already resigned himself to staying home; Suminthra was heavily pregnant with their fourth child and needed all the help she could get. A man needed to be there for his family, Pa had always said.

Out of the blue, as if to make up for all the missed opportunities and rejections of the past years, Papwa received an incredible offer. The letter arrived through the South African PGA of all places. An American oil company wanted to pay him, and generously too, to travel to India to take part in a television series – "Wonderful World of Golf" – along with twenty-one other top international golfers.

About to enter its second season, the show was based on the concept of challenge matches between two professional golfers and was shot on location in various parts of the world. The winner would receive $3,000 – more than R2,000 – and even if he didn't win, Papwa was guaranteed a sum of $1,800 in addition to his travel costs and generous living expenses.

The letter had been signed by J. Edwin Carter, a larger-than-life character who'd served five years as the tournament director of the American PGA and now represented several of the world's best professional golfers for their film, television and other media appearances. Carter had been tasked to engage talented players from around the world to compete in the show. Not only would Papwa be exposed to millions of viewers, in terms of the contract, attempts would be made to introduce Papwa to the American golfing circuit – the most lucrative in the world.

The news could not have come at a better time. Suminthra had given birth to another girl in the meantime and Papwa had been worrying how he'd be able to support his growing family with what he earned at the factory and from the small tournaments in which he played. Suminthra was happy too, telling a journalist: "This is, perhaps, the big break he's always been looking for."

It was not.

A month after sending off the signed contract to New York, Louis informed Papwa that India had been eliminated from the competition and his selection and everything that came with it, cancelled as a result. To assuage his disappointment, the organisers hoped that Papwa would win a major tournament and thus qualify for the US Masters, one of the four major championships in professional golf. Were he to win the white South African Open next year, he was almost guaranteed an invitation to the Masters, Louis confirmed.

"Then that's exactly what I'll do, Louis!" Papwa replied, waggling his eyebrows in a show of confidence that belied the tension in his gut.

"I'll write to them, okay, Pops? I'll explain how few opportunities you have to play golf in this country. Perhaps Mr Carter can still help. You never know."

Gary Player, already regarded as one of the world's best players having become the first international player to win the US Masters the year before, was featured in the 1962 season of the "Wonderful World of Golf" – competing against Australia's Peter Thomson at the Royal Melbourne Golf Club.

THIRTY-FOUR

"This is going to be your year, *beta*," Ma said, smiling at her son. "I feel it in my bones. I know things didn't work out as we'd hoped, but I believe your luck is going to change."

"I pray it is so, Ma. We can all do with some bit of good luck," Papwa said to her.

Suminthra did not add to the conversation, but gently placed her hand over her husband's, covertly darting a glance at her mother-in-law.

The family were celebrating *Diwali*, the festival of lights. "*Diwali* is not only to celebrate the power of light over dark, good over evil; it reminds us that hope is stronger than despair," Ma said.

"Yes, Ma," Papwa answered. He could not explain his despondency adequately, nor the feeling in *his* bones, that things were only going to get worse.

Suminthra smiled and cooed at the baby. Dennis, still feeling a little miffed since being usurped from his position as the youngest in the family, demanded his father's attention by tugging on his trousers. Though Baby was only a few months old, Suminthra was expecting again. By the time the new baby came, this one would be crawling and would no longer be called Baby. Dennis had been the baby for almost three whole years before his younger brother had been born. Though Papwa continued to worry about getting the ends to meet, children were a blessing. He'd been one of five too and even after Pa's passing, the family had been okay – no better nor worse than most others in Riverside. Something else, some other opportunity, would surely come up.

Now it was *Diwali* and *Diwali* was for children. Papwa smiled, remembering his own childhood celebrations. Ma would begin making the sweetmeats and other treats days before the time. During tougher years, especially right after Pa's death, wealthier members of the community and benevolent associations had helped out by delivering parcels of food and gifts to the family. All the children would help Ma with the cleaning and decorating of the house. The clay lamps they used now were the same ones they'd used when he was a child.

That morning Ma had rubbed purifying oil on the children's bodies to ward off evil and attract all that was good. She'd done the same when he was a child. Papwa closed his eyes to the memory as he inhaled the invigorating smell of the oil that still lingered on his young son's skin. Dennis had taken over his father's lap while Romilla and Beepraj demanded that their father tell them the story of *Diwali*. That was something Pa had done.

"Pa and his stories! I'm turning into my father," Papwa thought to himself.

Grinning, he addressed the older children, all three jostling to find a place on his lap.

"You know the story of how Lord Rama was sent away to live in a forest for many years by his father?" he asked the children.

"I know the story!" Romilla said, her body twisting into a wriggly dance of excitement.

Beepraj was silent for a while. "Did his father not love him, Pa?"

"A bad lady told him to do it, son," Papwa reassured the boy. "A wicked king wanted Sitaji for himself and tried to make her his wife, but Lord Rama rescued Sitaji and killed the wicked king."

Romilla clapped her hands and sighed. "The prince always rescues the princess," she explained to her younger brothers.

"Right," Papwa said. "Then Lord Rama and Sitaji returned to his kingdom – along with his brother Lakshmana of course. The people were so happy to have the three back, and so proud that Lord Rama had killed the wicked king, they welcomed them by lighting rows of clay lamps to guide the way. Oil lamps were lit in each house and there were huge firework displays, just like now. Lord Rama became king and everyone was very happy. So much feasting and celebrations there were!"

"And sweeties," Dennis said happily. His fingers sticky from a *jalebi* he'd already lost interest in, but refused to part with.

"I never thought you paid so much attention to my stories when you were a boy, *beta*." Ma smiled. "All your Pa was interested in was golf this, golf that!" Ma grumbled, but everyone knew she was only pretending to be displeased.

"That's because my Pa's a champion," Romilla said with a pleased smile.

"Champion, champion," Dennis shouted as he jumped off his father's lap to race through the house.

"Next time not so many sweets, Papwa, right?" Suminthra teased.

"Right, Mummy," Papwa said, grinning and shaking his head to show Romilla and Beepraj that he did not really agree.

Less than a week later, Baby was dead. Papwa knew that his feeling of hopelessness had been there for a reason. Never before had he felt this depth of grief. Not even when his own Pa had died. He'd been too young to appreciate fully how his father's death would affect his family. At the time, he'd thought it the greatest injustice to lose the father he'd loved so much and who'd loved him unreservedly so young. Now he knew the truth about injustice. A father should not outlive his son. Even the Hindu funeral rituals were predicated around a son doing them for his father. And if Papwa's grief was unbearable, Suminthra was inconsolable. Papwa did not have the words to comfort her.

Golf was Papwa's salvation. While it did not totally eradicate his grief, his friends knew that in order for the healing to begin, Papwa had to return to the golf course. For weeks he'd isolated himself, refusing to see anyone outside of work. His clubs were banished to a corner of the front room, an admonishing reminder of all the time he'd spent away from his family.

"But golf is what you do," Suminthra said, when Papwa told Louis that he did not think that he'd see the way clear to defend his Non-European Natal Open title.

"You have to, Pops," Louis protested.

A small, ugly part of Papwa wondered whether Louis was talking in his capacity as Papwa's manager or whether he was talking as the chairman of the Natal Golf Association and joint secretary of the South

African Non-European Golf Association. In addition to these offices, having discovered within himself a flair for administration, Louis was now contemplating going after the position of chair of the non-racial South African Soccer League. Louis had always been as involved in soccer as he'd been in golf, serving as the chairman of the South African Indian Football Association, a post from which he'd resigned after a controversy regarding his idea of introducing paid soccer. Papwa wondered whether Louis's other interests would leave him without a manager soon. One day he'd have to ask Louis about that.

On Christmas Day, Papwa had what he described as one the best rounds of his life. It was the opening day of the Non-European Natal Open, the second round, played in mist and rain on Kloof Golf Course. Papwa hit six birdies to achieve 67 – five under par – and in so doing, obliterated Harold Henning's course record of 68. He built up such a large lead on the first day that though his nearest rival, Transvaal's Joe Semenyane, brought out his best game on the second day of play, Papwa, with a score of 290, won the tournament by eight strokes. Since Papwa was a member of the British PGA, his new course record stood.

A few days after the Natal Non-European Open, Papwa travelled to Port Elizabeth, the city that had welcomed him so warmly with a dinner dance nearly two years before. The 1963 Non-European South African Open championship was being contested at Walmer Country Club, a traditionally white course. Ismail Chowglay from the Western Province was the defending champion. Chowglay began strongly, scoring 74 after the first round, which equalled the course record at the time. However, Papwa gained the lead after the second round and maintained it, thanks to his deadly combination of chipping and putting. By the end of the third round, Papwa led Chowglay by three strokes, but concluded the tournament to best Chowglay by thirteen strokes, taking the win with a final score of 301. Papwa and the other placed golfers were presented their prizes, sponsored by Gordon's Gin, at a mayoral reception in the Feather Market Hall. The prize-giving was attended by a host of white dignitaries, many of whom commended the players' etiquette and behaviour.

Soon after Papwa returned to Durban, he received word that, finally, he was being allowed to play in the white Natal Open. Banking on the permission he'd received when he'd entered the white South African Open, the white-only Natal Golfer's Union had decided not to approach the Minister of Community Development to approve Papwa's playing in the whites-only provincial tournament. Still shaken by the death of his son, but buoyed by his recent wins, Papwa did not know what to expect. He also knew that acceptance given one day, could be a totally different matter on another.

THIRTY-FIVE

Suminthra watched as Papwa placed the checked tie around his neck. He frowned as he struggled to fold it without the benefit of a mirror. "Come here, *Kanna*, let me do it," she said softly, reluctant to wake the sleeping children. They'd fuss if they woke to find their father gone before the big day, but they'd fuss more if they woke while he got ready. Romilla was at that age where she wanted to accompany her Papa everywhere. She refused to believe her mother and *Aji* when they said that little girls could not go watch golf.

Tilting his head in the direction of the children on the bed, Papwa placed a finger in front of his mouth. Suminthra smiled, and placing a hand on her husband's arm, steered him toward the kitchen. Water boiled in a pot on the stove. As Papwa donned the rest of his attire, Suminthra busied herself making his tea. Sandwiches for lunch had been prepared the night before. She wished she'd packed lunch for him yesterday, but sometimes when she did so, Papwa would bring the sandwiches home uneaten, though his tea flask at least, would be empty. Last night, Papwa had told her about how he'd had to eat with Louis in the car, since all that the permit allowed was for him to play on the course. The couple who'd had no interest in politics was learning more than they ever wanted to know about the government's rules and laws.

"I don't like it," Suminthra said as she handed him his first cup of tea for the day.

"Oh my dear, what can we do?" Papwa answered her, immediately knowing what she was talking about in the manner of one long-married.

"It's not right," Suminthra said softly as she rubbed her stomach.

She was seven months pregnant and feeling the strain and tension she always felt when her Papwa was off to play in an important tournament. "It's not right the way they treat you."

"Oh, *Kanna*, what can we do? If I win it will be a good thing for the entire family, especially this little one," he said, placing his hands over his wife's. "I'm lucky they're allowing me to play. I wasn't sure they would, you know."

"You should always be allowed to play!" Suminthra said urgently. "It's not right that they toy with you like this."

"Hush, little one," Papwa said. "Don't get upset now, you'll wake the children."

"They'll be disappointed if you leave without saying goodbye. Romilla especially thinks she's your good luck charm."

Papwa smiled at his wife. He opened the front door and took his tea outside. The morning was uncharacteristically cold and windy. The sky was streaked with grey clouds, not heavy yet, but they could either swell or blow away to nothing, Papwa wasn't certain. He cupped his hands around the cream enamel mug, willing them to warm. When the mug was emptied, he pulled his cardigan closer, remembering his own father's actions so long ago and went back inside the house. Ma and the children should be awake by now and his lift would arrive soon.

Louis kept up a constant patter as he drove, but Papwa was in no mood to talk. Sometimes Papwa was like that before he played, preferring silence to gather his thoughts and prepare himself mentally for the rounds ahead.

"Looks like rain," Louis said idly.

Papwa cracked the window and sniffed the air. He caught the faint ammonia odour that presaged rain in Durban.

"Serve them right if you win and it rains," Louis said.

Papwa wasn't sure what he meant, but he was not in the habit of jinxing himself by talking about winning before he set foot on the green. "Hush, Louis," he admonished. "Don't say such things."

"Yes I know, Pops, I forget what you're like with all your superstitions and whatnot. But mark my words: it will embarrass the government if you win. Perhaps they'll even have to rethink their stupid laws. Look where we are today – the first Indian to play in the competition and we, you and I, we made it happen. There are more competitions. If you win this one, it could force their hand."

"For bad or good, Louis," Papwa pointed out. "But I can't think about that now. I need to prepare myself for the game. You know that."

"I'll leave you alone for now then, but think about what I said," Louis said.

Grateful for Louis's eventual silence, Papwa concentrated on the road. It was one with which he was much familiar, from the days when he'd contested caddie matches at the Durban Country Club. It was very different to be playing here as a contender, not as a caddie. Yet in many ways, it was as it had been then too. Even as a contender, he felt as out of place as he'd always been.

"They call that style of building Cape Dutch," Louis said when they drove from the club's gates towards the imposing clubhouse with its twin curving stone stairways leading to an expansive veranda and another set of stone steps – none of which Papwa had ever ventured a foot upon. Papwa had always found the façade of the clubhouse to be beautiful, but uninviting. How could it be anything but?

"This club was built because Royal Durban, the *larney* club at the time, was built on too-low ground and the course would become waterlogged in heavy rain. Do you know that the winner of the SA Open in 1919, I think it was Horne, took 320 strokes to win the title?" Louis laughed. "And that on a course with a par of 72!"

Papwa shook his head. He had never heard the story, had never heard of a golfer by the name of Horne. Louis knew so much about golf and other things. He never passed up on a chance to teach him something. Papwa thought, not for the first time, how strange it was that Louis had not pursued a teaching career as so many others in his family had.

Papwa knew that he and his kind were not welcomed at the club, except as workers. He accepted this fact as one more reality of his life and the country into which he'd been born. It had never been his wish to walk up those imposing steps and pass through the gleaming glass and dark wood doors. He was not a confrontational man. Well, not usually. He stifled a laugh. The one day he'd behaved out of character, the day that rude man had played with Master Graham and the others and he'd walked away, that had been a day when confrontation had changed everything. And now look where he was.

Louis turned to look at him. "Are you ready, Pops?"

Papwa nodded and then smiled. He felt relaxed, confident, he realised. He'd played this course many times before during the caddie tournaments so many Mondays ago. It was reassuring to be contesting this important tournament on the familiar greens. Two days ago, when he'd lined up with the more than one hundred white players in the field, he'd proven to everyone, even himself, that he deserved to be there. Today, on the third and final day, less than half the starting field would tee off. He was one of them and he was ready.

He'd been ready yesterday; he'd been ready the day before. Fishy and the rest would say he'd been ready since he'd first traversed this course during those early caddies' matches. And just like then – there they were, lined up to watch him play. Fishy, Gopaul, Jayendra and Raj stood out in the crowd of strangers and familiar faces. "Do us proud, Pops," they called out. Doffing his cap and tipping it in their direction, Papwa acknowledged his supporters' well wishes.

"You're building an army," Caddie Master had said on the first day. "An Indian Army," Raj had agreed. Raj had brought his two young sons to watch the tournament every day, and Papwa felt a twinge of regret. Had he been wrong to insist his family stay at home while he played?

Just like the previous two days, as the day progressed, Papwa's name edged up the leaderboard. By the time they reached the final round, the weather that had turned progressively worse since morning was miserable and foul, so bad that the remaining players struggled to stand upright. Their clothes were wet, their grips slippery and visibility poor as the wind and rain continued to crash against the fairway. Spectators huddled under umbrellas, hats, pulled their jackets up over their heads, sheltered under folded and sopping newspapers. Despite the bleakness of the day, the mood of Papwa's Indian Army was buoyant and bright.

"He's playing like it's a clear day," Gopaul said. "As if the rain, this wind, don't exist."

"Papwa studies the weather; always has," Raj agreed. "He once told me that everything in golf follows the sun; as the sun moves, the grass moves. It's all nuance, you see. Even though the sky is so dark, I'm sure Pops knows exactly where the sun is, hidden behind these clouds."

"Shut up, Raj," Fishy joshed. "We all know that. Let's watch the man play. I have the feeling our friend's about to make history."

Pursing his lips as they focused on their friend through the pelting rain, Raj nodded, silenced for once by a bigger truth. But Raj, being Raj, could not stay silent long. "They'll say it's a watered-down field if he wins. Or that he got lucky."

"How can they say that? Jayendra demanded. "You've got your Denis Hutchinson. You've got your Harold Henning – South African Open champion and all. You've got Bobby Verwey. Hell, you've even got Bobby Locke – old, but still good. The starting field was full of top competition, all hundred-odd of them and only one brown face amongst them!"

"I'm not arguing with you Jay," Raj said, waving his palms in front of his torso. "I'm just saying what *they* will say. And that's if they say anything. SABC won't even broadcast the tournament because our boy's playing."

"Bunch of stooges, that's what," Jayendra spat. "Nothing but racist lackeys."

Later, Papwa would not be able to recall sinking the putt that won the competition for him. Golf shots had a habit of blurring into each other and sometimes when he played, he went into a zone wherein he shut off all other distractions. When he was in this space, he played golf one shot at a time. He'd learned that worked best. The record books would state that Sewsunker "Papwa" Sewgolum won the 1963 Natal Open with a score of 293. They'd state further that Papwa parred the final hole, a par-four, to clinch the title by one stroke over runners-up Denis Hutchinson, current holder of the South African Masters title, and Bobby Verwey, who was placed third.

What Papwa could recall was the dense roar of the crowd, loud and booming above the rain. He remembered being rushed and borne aloft by the crowd, carried towards the clubhouse where he'd idled outside in a state of bemusement, until Louis came over to remind him that he should get ready for the prize-giving. He remembered the rain, but the rain had been a constant from early on, clearing only momentarily throughout the day. In time he would marvel at how his had been a wet win. He'd laugh about it then, thinking back fondly to his first British

Open and the bitter-cold Scottish winds and rain that had bested the amateur he'd been then.

Odd details stuck out when he forced himself to think of what happened. He remembered changing into his good suit in the car and wishing that he'd had a chance to shower like the other men. For so long, Indians had been made aware of the smells of their bodies – the joke went that all the curry they ate was excreted sourly through their skin – and Papwa had always been sensitive lest he offend.

Years ago, during his first overseas trip, Master Graham had insisted he wash his clothes every night. Without Ma or Suminthra to do so for him, he'd had no choice but to learn how to keep his clothing clean. He remembered the vitamin pills Master Graham insisted he take. It was only later that Louis said that those were not tablets, but sweets to make his breath smell fresher. He remembered the crowds crushing against Louis' car, but the crowds afforded him a degree of privacy too. The people swelling around them were his people. Privately, it would always make him feel somewhat diminished whenever one of the white gents saw him changing in the car or exiting the caddies' quarters at tournaments, but this was only his second white tournament and so he had not yet begun to feel so.

He remembered slicking back his hair with the ivory fine-toothed comb he kept in a pocket of his suit, checking his reflection in a rain-rippled car window once he'd gotten out. As they stood there waiting for the other men to finish their showers, Louis had straightened his tie for him, and Papwa remembered thinking how it felt tight enough to choke. Louis pointed to a group of men huddling in a corner of the terrace – club officials and organisers, he'd said. Dazed by his win, Papwa had not been paying attention. His gaze had drifted instead to the grinning Indian wait staff as they arranged trophies on a trestle table; the cloth covering it was already darkened with rain.

Dreamily, he'd made his way over to the table by the caravan when his name was called. A Mr Bell from the liquor company sponsors awarded his prize. Papwa already knew that the prize-winner's cheque was for R800 and he'd been thinking of the ways he'd spend the money. Perhaps he'd be able to cut down on his hours at the factory; be able to practise for more than one full day a week. The terrace was on the North side of the club, with a view of the first and last holes. For once,

Papwa was not cowed by the imposing clubhouse, the members and the officials. Then the cheque was handed over, the trophy was handed over, and Papwa beamed. Clustered around him, his army was a jubilant mass, roaring with pleasure and pride. Some thrust hands out at him to shake while others lugged arms around his shoulders, patted his back, his arms, grabbed at his jacket. The children would have been afraid Papwa thought, but how he wished that they and Suminthra had been here to share his joy.

He'd won bigger competitions before, but this one, in his home city, was different, special. He was not interested in what people were saying: about his win being one for the record books. How not only was he the first person of colour to compete in the white man's Natal Open, he was the first person of colour to win it! He was not interested in such things and was only happy he'd won. After all, a player didn't think of making history when he stepped out on the course: he thought of winning.

Once Papwa's prize was handed over, the four other prize-winners – the first five were always awarded their prizes in the Natal Open – went inside to receive their rewards. The rain had come down harder, or perhaps its intensity was no different to what it had been all day. The Indian Army began to disperse and it was only then that Papwa heard the grumbling: why hadn't their hero Papwa received his prize in the clubhouse out of the rain and cold with the other players? Papwa was the best; he'd beaten them all. Why had he been treated like that?

Clutching his rain-spattered jacket around him with one hand, his trophy in the other as he walked to the car, Papwa told himself that it did not matter. Winning was what important, not where he received his award.

THIRTY-SIX

It mattered to Louis. More so, he was livid. It was great and well that Papwa had won the tournament, but that's what he'd been saying all along: that the humble man from Riverside had it in him to beat the best players white South Africa had to offer. And he, Louis, had helped make it happen. For now, even that was not important.

"That was an insult; the way they handed over the prize to you in the pouring rain, like they couldn't wait to get rid of you. And then *they* all trooped inside to bolt down their whiskies and brandies in the warm, dry club, while we were left there without so much as a by-your-leave!"

Louis exhaled the bitterness he felt on Papwa's behalf. After all this time, they weren't quite friends. Sometimes he thought it a wasted opportunity for Papwa to have all that skill. It was uncanny. If Papwa were more erudite, he could have been a symbol for the struggle against apartheid in sport. Sometimes Louis wondered whether the man understood politics at all. Whenever he raised the subject, Papwa would nod knowledgeably, but would look for ways to turn the conversation around. Even now, Papwa was silent, not responding to his manager's tirade at all.

Louis turned, averting his eyes from the road to assess Papwa's mood. "Doesn't it bother you the way they treated you?" he asked after a while.

Papwa sighed. "I was so excited to win. That was all I could think about: how Suminthra would add the trophy to the shelves with the rest of them; Ma's blessings and praise; the children . . . They're young yes, but the whole family celebrates when I win. Romilla especially is so proud of her daddy. I wish she could have been there to see it. And my father, all those years ago when he carved that club out of that tree branch, did he ever dream that I would win the Natal Open? He knew about this competition you know, though he didn't know much about golf. Everyone knew about the Natal Open."

It was Louis's turn to sigh. "People aren't going to leave this alone, Papwa. You mark my words. Even if they don't report on it in South Africa, the press is going to write about it. It's not every day an Indian from Durban gets to show these whites a thing or two. DF Malan must be turning in his grave! Verwoerd too, will not be too pleased."

"I told you that this would be your year," Ma said, beaming when Papwa arrived home with his trophy and the cheque. "Give the trophy here, let me feel."

Papwa placed the trophy on the kitchen table and guided Ma's hands to it. She ran her age-smoothed fingers over the shiny metal surface. "So big," she said. "And money too! How much *beta*?"

Papwa told her the number on the cheque and Ma clucked in admiration. "One day you leave that factory eh boy and be a big man, buy a big car with all this golf-golf business and all!" Ma's face was all teeth, the gold insets sparkling under the glow of the kitchen light.

"I told you, *beta*!" Ma insisted again. "At the start of the year, remember?" Though it usually fell during October or November, the family had always considered *Diwali* to be the real start to the year.

Papwa looked at Suminthra's face, her reddened cheeks and the bright, pained expression in her eyes. He felt the same way. The past few months had been the hardest they'd ever had to deal with as a family. Losing Baby had been the worst thing that had happened to them.

"Yes Ma," Papwa answered dutifully. "You said it was going to be my year." He tried to smile, but his teeth were bared into a grim caricature of what he'd been aiming for.

By the next morning, the press had picked up the story. Louis had been right about that. And Louis being Louis, he came over a few days later to remind Papwa of the fact. Papwa was surprised it had taken that long, but his manager was a busy man and getting busier by the day.

"Listen here, Pops," Louis said. He waved a sheath of newspaper cuttings in Papwa's face; then cleared his throat before continuing.

It was an affectation that Papwa knew well. It meant that Louis had much to say.

"Sit down, Louis," Papwa said as he himself took a seat at the old kitchen table topped with a green, marbled-pattern Formica that Suminthra kept pristine for guests. "My wife will make you a cup of tea."

"You don't have anything stronger, hey, Pops?" Louis asked. "You might need it with what I have to tell you. It will make your head spin!"

Papwa shook his head. Suminthra did not approve of drinking in the house and out of deference to her and her belly swollen round and high with his child, he decided to abstain.

Louis shrugged and repeated his opening salvo. "Listen here: listen to what the newspapers are saying about you. Was I right or was I right?"

"You were right, Louis," Papwa answered, knowing that Louis wouldn't continue until Papwa had agreed with him. "What are they saying?"

"First the good news; you've made all the local papers and you were even in some of the overseas newspapers, I heard. Everyone's talking about you and how they made you accept your prize in the rain."

"Yes," Papwa answered.

Louis wasn't sure whether Papwa's response was a question or a statement. He continued anyway. "Listen to what the *POST* said, they called it 'The Glory and the Shame'. Glory because you won the competition above one hundred and thirteen white players; shame because they made you accept your prize in the rain."

"I know. One of the men here showed me," Papwa said. "He read me the article."

"Yes, it's in the scrap-book and all," Suminthra said. She'd been standing quietly, observing the men as they spoke. "I save all Papwa's clippings people give me. My Romilla is a great help!"

"It's not only the *POST*, Pops. We're talking national newspapers, overseas newspapers and magazines. Not to mention all the letters the newspapers are receiving, letters from ordinary people, ashamed at what was done to you. It's not only the government and its ridiculous laws; many people are disgusted that the club's officials and the Open's organisers saw fit to treat you that way. And the SABC's decision not to broadcast the results has been condemned too."

Louis drew a long breath, trying to calm himself down. His doctor had warmed him about his blood pressure and about not getting overly excited. Papwa waited for Louis to continue, fascinated by what he was telling him.

"... not that the government's backing down mind you, one of this government's ministers, I can't recall which one, maybe it was De Klerk or maybe it was that Frank Waring fellow, has hinted that there'll be an investigation and possible action against you since he's claiming you didn't have a permit from the Group Areas Board to play on the course. Oh, I got it," Louis said, raising the heel of a palm to his head, "it was Piet Botha, the one they call PW. They even discussed your win in their parliament, you know?"

THIRTY-SEVEN

Cradling the newly born Rajen in her arms, Suminthra hummed softly to calm the grousing baby. Papwa sat on the bed next to her, one of his fingers clenched tightly in his infant son's fist. The boy would never be a replacement for his late brother, but his birth had lessened the pain of Baby's death for the entire family. While the world had been scandalising about the prize-giving in the rain, Papwa and Suminthra had been preparing to welcome their new son into the world.

"Perhaps this is the son I shall teach to play golf," Papwa whispered to his wife.

The infant opened his eyes; a liquid mix of greens and greys that would in time darken to brown as the other children's had.

Suminthra smiled, not sure whether this would be a good or a bad thing. "I don't think Dennis will be happy with that," she said instead. "Romilla too, she more than any of the others, wants to learn how to play golf!"

"Times are changing; I have a lady caddie now," Papwa conceded. "Perhaps I shall teach our daughter to play after all!"

Suminthra frowned at the reminder of Papwa's new caddie, but chose not to air her feelings on that matter. This was a happy time; her Papwa was home with his family where he belonged. Later in the year, he would be going overseas to play in the tournaments there. Louis seemed convinced that this time they'd be able to raise adequate funds for this to happen and the couple chose to believe that he'd come through. Who knew, perhaps her husband would come home with the copy of the Dutch Open trophy for a third time (Papwa had told her that they kept the original in Holland), or perhaps his luck would be better in the British Open? The lady caddie would stay behind in Durban. Not that she had any reason to doubt her husband, mind you. Suminthra reassured herself. Her Papwa was a good husband and father. If only he didn't have to travel so much to play.

"It's because of the trophies, I think," Suminthra said. "When Romilla helps me polish them, she talks about one day winning trophies of her own! Yes, times are changing. It is a good thing, I suppose."

Times were changing, or so Papwa chose to believe. A few weeks after the birth of his son, and a month or two after the prize-giving in the rain, Louis drove him once more to the gabled majesty that was the Durban Country Club – to participate in yet another of the white man's tournaments, the 1963 South African Open. Papwa had been one of two non-white golfers to enter. While Papwa had been accepted to play, William Manie's application had been denied. In a statement on their decision, the South African Golfers' Union acknowledged that Papwa had been granted entry due to his outstanding qualifications.

"It's similar to what old Senator de Klerk said when they allowed you to play in the first South African Open, remember?" Louis said. "That you were 'a most exceptional case'."

Papwa smiled weakly, embarrassed that he out of so many other competent players had been singled out. It wasn't right, but he'd play on behalf of all of them, show the white golfing fraternity what a man with a brown skin was capable of. Not that he was being political, Papwa told himself. Some things were a matter of pride.

"But I must warn you, De Klerk said not so long ago that if the Golfers' Union accepts your entry then his government will have to tighten up the laws to keep white sport white. No racial mixing on the sports field and all that rubbish!"

This time Papwa was not intimidated when he and Louis drove up to the club on the first day. He wondered whether he was imagining it, or whether the managers of the club were abashed to see him. He'd heard that the club had sought legal advice before going ahead with the prize-giving the last time. It was for this reason – the legal advice – that his winner's cheque and trophy had been hastily handed over in the pouring rain, whilst the four runners up had received theirs in the clubhouse. He, Papwa, had been forced to skulk away as if by winning he'd done something wrong, while the white men had celebrated late into the night. It was the Group Areas Act, they'd said.

"Nothing against you, Pops."

To have let him inside the clubhouse with the booze and the white patrons would have been to break the law. It all went back to the ruling with those soccer players on the non-racial team who'd been caught playing soccer together in an Indian area. They'd had their charges for contravening the Group Areas Act dropped since they hadn't socialised together after their match. The rulings regarding Papwa's own permits had played a part too for that matter. He was allowed to occupy the field of play – the golf course – but not the clubhouse. Therein lay the difference, these stupid government laws. No hard feelings, right?

Right.

No, it was best not to dwell on such matters. He needed to get his mind on the game. The Indian staff greeted him by name as he walked past the clubhouse to the first tee. A sparkling blue swimming pool glittered a deceptive invitation. The sea shimmered in the near distance, the early morning sun catching it just so. Monkeys scampered and hollered in the trees while his army of supporters were out in full force. Papwa was pleased.

The first day of the tournament Papwa excelled. By the final day, his army, the media and even the white spectators, many of whom shouted Papwa's name and clamoured for his autograph at the end of the day's play, were saying that Papwa was about to do the impossible: become the first person of colour to win the white South African Open. Many didn't want to consider what the government would do next. If winning the Natal Open had caused such uproar, imagine if he should win the national event?

Papwa was a contender until the last hole. Inexplicably for the chipping and putting master, he missed a five-meter putt on the eighteenth hole. With a score of 281, twenty-three year old Retief Waltman won the 1963 South African, beating Papwa's score of 282, to second place. A single stroke had decided the title, and with it, Papwa's chance to play in the US Masters championship, as intimated when his appearance on the "Wonderful World of Golf" fell through. Papwa had played against Retief before – two years ago at the first white South

African Open in which he'd been allowed to play. The young man had won that too. They were scary this new crop of young, hungry players, as eager to win and prove themselves as he was. He'd been that boy once too, he thought wryly, casting his mind back to his first win at the age of sixteen. He'd beaten grown men then. Had he perhaps taken too much pride in that fact? Louis had a saying when he believed people brought their problems upon themselves: something to do with chickens coming home to roost. Papwa sincerely hoped that this was not the case.

Papwa's one consolation was that the Papwa Trust Fund had enough money in its coffers to send him overseas on his European tour. What a story the fundraising had been! Papwa had played in exhibition matches around Durban. Some of his good friends had gone around door-to-door to collect money from his supporters in Riverside and other Indian areas. Even schoolchildren had assisted. Papwa smiled at the idea of young children Romilla's age, adding their pennies and *tickeys* to the money collected from teachers and principals.

"You're an inspiration to children," Louis had explained when he'd first mooted the idea. "They look up to you and think that one day they too can compete successfully against whites. Don't forget that."

Yes, there might be more money to be made from an American tour, everyone knew that's where the money was, but Europe and England were more familiar to him. After two prior trips, he knew what to expect. He'd no longer be the green golfer he'd been during that first trip with Graham. Playing in the white tournaments, he'd made friends with some of the other South African golfers too; it would be nice to have a few friendly faces around. Look how well Gary had treated him in Scotland all those years ago and all!

When Papwa left for Europe, a small crowd saw him off: his family, Raj, Gopaul and them from his caddying days, a few members of the Durban Indian Golf Club and a handful of well-wishers from the community.

"There are always more people when you return, *Kanna*," Suminthra remarked as Papwa surveyed the crowd.

For her sake, Papwa pretended that he was concerned about the sparseness of the crowd, proof of his waning popularity, but in actual fact, his eyes had fixed on two men in heavy suits – too warm for

Durban in the middle of June – furtively watching from the edges of the gathering.

"You can tell an Afrikaner from a mile away," Jayendra said, twirling a make-believe moustache in front of his face. He'd noticed the direction of his friend's furtive gaze.

"You must be careful, Pops," Raj cautioned. "You have to expect the government to get its stooges to watch you now that you've embarrassed them so."

"I –" Papwa tried to protest, but Raj cut in.

"Yes, we know you didn't mean to, but fact remains, you did. What did that Helen Suzman lady say in parliament again?" Raj turned to Jayendra for confirmation.

"That Papwa receiving his prize in the rain set the true image of South Africa overseas," Jayendra replied. "Despite what they'll have foreigners believe about 'Sunny South Africa'."

Overhearing the conversation, Louis walked over and placed a heavy hand on Papwa's shoulder. "I believe the Security Branch has been watching him," Louis told Papwa's friends, referring to the special branch of the South African Police. After what took place in Sharpeville the Security Branch had been tasked by Minister BJ Vorster, the Minister of Justice, to tackle and detain suspected opponents of apartheid. Very often their methods were cruel and there had been rumours of torture.

"They've been observing him for a long time now," Louis continued. "On and off since the Dutch Open, if you ask me, and more so since the first SA Open he played in. They watched us like hawks then; careful we didn't overstep any mark or take any liberties over and above. Now that he's won the Natal Open and come second in the nationals, I've been expecting it to get worse – the surveillance. Those two are nothing," he said, tilting his head in the direction of the two men. "Sometimes there's four, five, six of them, sweating in their suits, their faces burnt red like beetroot that's been boiled too long. Can't handle Durban's heat is what!"

"Serves them right, bloody pigs!" Fishy said, with bright, mischievous eyes.

No one laughed.

THIRTY-EIGHT

The highlight of Papwa's 1963 European campaign was playing in the British Open in which he finished thirteenth – ahead of several renowned golfers of the time, amongst them Arnold Palmer, the great American player and that year's defending champion. Papwa's success, though short of his own ambitions, prompted the New Yorker's Herbert Warren Wind to write: "I have an idea that it will be only a matter of time now before a major title falls to the world's greatest cross-handed golfer, Sewsunker Sewgolum."

The Hague Golf Course was once more the venue of the Dutch Open that year, but Papwa left disappointed, dismaying the crowd who cheered on the two-time winner and tournament darling. The story of the ignominious prize-giving had reached Holland a few months before. Retief Waltman, buoyed by his South African Open victory snatched the title with a score of 279, to Papwa's down-the-field 289.

Papwa had a worse showing in the German Open which saw him being disqualified for being late on the tee. He'd been suffering ill health then, plagued by throat and back ailments intermittently during his tour.

All in all, for the two months he was away, Papwa netted R300, most of which was from his placing in the British Open. Of this sum, R50 was spent on medical treatment, while the tour itself had cost more than R2,000. Louis, the chairman, and the other trustees of the Papwa Trust decided to dissolve the fund. A balance of R1,000 remained – money which was to be allocated to buying Papwa and his family a new home. This did not come to pass.

Soon after the dissolution of the Papwa Trust Fund, Louis informed Papwa that he could no longer manage his career. Louis's own work in the trade union had become more demanding – he'd recently returned from an international labour conference and remained heavily involved in golf administration, not to mention his interests in soccer. But this was not an excuse, mind you, he assured Papwa. Neither man mentioned whether the two year-old scandal of the fund's accounting had played any part in Louis's decision. A small, insecure part of Papwa wondered whether Louis believed that Papwa's days of winning were behind him. Perhaps if he'd won the Dutch Open again? After all, it was only once he'd won the tournament for the first time that Louis had spoken about helping him out with his career, and how together, they were going to make history.

A few days later, one of Papwa's friends introduced him to Fred Paul, an insurance salesman. Though Louis had publicly expressed confidence in Papwa's ability to manage his career on his own, everyone knew this was not true. Over the years, Papwa's writing skills had not improved much beyond the ability to sign his name and write down numbers on a scorecard. Someone needed to write to tournament organisers and the relevant authorities seeking permissions for Papwa to play; entry forms needed to be completed; legalese deciphered; monies disbursed; and the various other administrative tasks necessary to maintain the momentum of Papwa's golfing career had to be managed.

Though FM, as he preferred to be known, professed to have little interest in golf, he saw in Papwa a man in need of assistance and agreed to take on the role of his manager – despite a heavy work schedule of his own. One of his first tasks was to enter Papwa in the South African Open due to be played in Bloemfontein at the end of that year – 1963.

FM succeeded in this task. By mid-November, the newspapers announced that Papwa and Ismail Chowglay had both been accepted to compete in the white South African Open. They had not been the only players of colour to enter the tournament, but given Papwa's profile and Ismail's ascendant star – after beating Papwa in the Non-European South African Open, Ismail toured Europe in 1961 and had played in the British Open three times – they were the hardest to deny of all black comers. Of course, the newspapers made certain to mention, Papwa's and Ismail's participation remained contingent on government approval and then there was the matter, pertinent for Papwa at least, of Indians not being allowed to remain in Bloemfontein for longer than twenty-four hours.

Papwa was granted permission to stay in Bloemfontein for the three-day duration of the tournament. However, with the tacit threat of an undercover police presence, the hosting club made sure to follow the letter of the law regarding fraternisation and the almighty Group Areas Act. Papwa and Chowglay were granted a tent as a dressing room, and here too they ate and rested between rounds. These makeshift quarters were replaced by a caravan when the international press pointed out the discrepancies between the accommodations provided for the two non-white players and the rest of the field.

That year's field was top-notch, counting Gary Player, Harold Henning and New Zealand's Bob Charles, winner of that year's British Open, amongst the contenders. However, it was nineteen-year-old Allan Henning, younger brother of Harold, who took the title with a score of 278. Papwa finished three strokes behind Allan and settled for third place, which he shared with Gary Player and Bob Charles.

Months later, Papwa's good, but not good enough performance in the second South African Open of the 1963 thwarted his hopes of playing in the prestigious Carling World Cup tournament in Detroit. Initially, after claiming the Natal Open and his near victory in the South African Open, Papwa had been advised by the South African PGA that he would be the first alternate if one of the three players already chosen to represent the country in the American tournament – Trevor Wilkes, Bobby Verwey and Cedric Amm – were for some reason unavailable to play. However, after Allan Henning's win in Bloemfontein, he replaced Trevor Wilkes on the team, with Wilkes named the first alternate. Papwa was relegated to second alternate.

Media speculation cited "unconfirmed reports" that the organisers of the Carling World Cup were unhappy with the selection process. It was said that the organisers had instructed the South African PGA to select players based on the results of the 1963 Natal Open and first South African Open of that year. Were sinister forces afoot? Although the second national Open had taken place in December 1963, no tournament took place in 1964. Official fixtures for the South African event state that there was no 1964 South African Open due to the two events the previous year. Had Papwa scored higher in the latter event, it was understood that he'd have been automatically included in the team.

By the time his relegation was being discussed in the press and in caddies' rooms and on the golf courses of South Africa, Papwa had already left Durban for England. In addition to Papwa's family, only five people, including a photographer and journalist had been at Louis Botha Airport to see him off. Remembering the crowds of earlier years, the thought that the constant Security Branch presence that shadowed him whenever he was in the public eye, had deterred his supporters and friends flickered across Papwa's consciousness. "It doesn't matter," he told himself. "I don't play golf to be popular." Papwa was honest enough with himself to recognise a slight untruth in his reasoning.

As usual, Papwa played in a number of tournaments in Britain, including the British Open. He then travelled to Holland, where in Eindhoven he won the Dutch Open for a third time. With a score of 275, he defeated a number of established and rising South African golfing stars: Harold Henning, Brian Wilkes and Denis Hutchinson amongst others. Unfortunately, Papwa's health continued to plague him as it often did when he travelled to the Northern Hemisphere. Even at the height of the European summer, temperatures didn't come close to Natal's tropical winter warmth and Papwa found it unbearably cold. Eventually, his struggles with the jaundice he was unable to shake completely brought his 1964 tour to a premature end.

"So they've finally kicked South Africa out of the Olympics, hey?" Raj said, waiting for an opening. One of the ways he did this was by posing statements like a question.

"Hmm," Fishy said, refusing to give Raj the gap he was looking for.

It was a beautiful day – balmy, breezy, bright – the kind of day for which Durban was renowned. At the start of that month, Papwa had taken up full-time employment at Springfield Golf Course as the club's professional. This was the long-promised position first discussed in the aftermath of his first Dutch Open win. Making the most of the weather, Fishy, Raj and Gopaul had joined him for a few friendly rounds.

"It's just like the old days, the four of us together," Fishy said.

The friends had not seen much of each other in the months since

Papwa's return from Europe. Work and family commitments had often stood in the way of the other men who at one time had been almost as ardent golfers as Papwa himself – if without his tremendous skill.

"Except that Jay's not here," Gopaul corrected.

Jayendra was becoming increasingly involved in the anti-apartheid movement. Papwa had heard the news from Fishy, who still lived in the area. To be seen too frequently in the company of Papwa Sewgolum, the man who'd caused so many problems for the government after the whole prize-giving in the rain incident, was to call unwelcome attention to oneself. Papwa knew this, though he missed his friend. As to what kinds of things Jayendra was involved in, Papwa preferred not to know. Along with many of Durban's Indian community, Papwa was still reeling from the news about Suliman Saloojee, a member of the Transvaal Indian Congress, who'd died under mysterious circumstances while under arrest. Government said he'd thrown himself from a window on the seventh floor of the Security Branch headquarters, refusing to betray his comrades. People said, "Thrown himself out, my foot, more likely pushed out by those pigs!"

Papwa worried about Jayendra. He'd been accosted by Security Branch men enough times to wonder when the intimidation and comments about a "Coolie knowing his place" would veer into something worse than rude words and veiled threats. A man's fortunes could change like that.

As if divining his thoughts, Raj continued, undeterred by his friends' lack of response. "To think Brutus probably had to hear the news on Robben Island," he exclaimed.

From all the time he'd spent with Louis in the past, Papwa knew that the South African Non-Racial Committee – SAN-ROC – had been formed to fight against discrimination in sport and to lobby for South Africa's non-racial sports bodies to be recognised internationally. The organisation had replaced the South African Sports Association, which had drawn too much negative government attention. One of SAN-ROC's main goals had been to get South Africa barred from the Tokyo Games, and now they'd accomplished that aim. Last year the International Olympic Committee had given South Africa's Olympic Committee an end-of-year deadline and ultimatum: abolish apartheid in sport or face being barred from the Games.

"They tried to prevent SAN-ROC from putting its case forward," Gopaul said.

"Yes," Raj agreed. "Refused Brutus a passport and placed him under strict banning orders. They wanted to stop anyone going to the meeting in Baden-Baden. They can't stand for the lie to be exposed." The lie being that the South African Olympic Committee's policy was non-racial and that they neither supported nor practised discrimination.

"Of course it's a lie!" Gopaul picked up the slack caused by Jayendra's absence. Papwa was surprised. He'd not been aware that this friend of his was so clued up about the politics of sport.

Raj beamed at Gopaul in approval. "Yes, Senator de Klerk has made it clear time and time again that the government will not allow non-racial sports teams. That's their policy and they'll stick with it. No matter what the rest of the world has to say about it."

"Not that everyone disagrees with these racist policies, mind you," Gopaul offered.

"Yes, like that Stanley Rous fellow," Raj said, referring to Sir Stanley Rous, who'd become president of the international soccer federation a few days after South Africa had first been suspended from the body in 1961. Championing South Africa's inclusion, Rous insisted that FIFA should stand aloof from political involvement. Rous had visited South Africa in January 1963, and following that he had recommended the lifting of the suspension, stating that football in South Africa would not survive otherwise.

"*Sir* Stanley to you and me." Fishy wiggled a finger in front of Raj's face.

"Sir Stanley might have succeeded in overturning the suspension last year, but now FIFA's also suspended South Africa. For good, this time, I think."

"Such decisions are only going to make this government more hardheaded than it already is. Papwa, my friend, you have to prepare yourself for worse times ahead. I can feel it in my bones," Fishy said, with an uncharacteristic seriousness.

"Look what happened to poor Mr Brutus," Raj said. "Banned, arrested, shot in the back; then to add insult to injury, he had to lie there in the street bleeding until they sent the 'proper' ambulance for him. A white ambulance showed up first you know? But they sent it away, all because of the colour of Dennis's skin. Man could have died!"

Papwa shivered beneath his thin clothing. The day had been so warm and clear only minutes before.

THIRTY-NINE

"My playing's off," Papwa said as he readied himself for the first day of the white Natal Open of 1965.

"Think positively, *Kanna*," Suminthra said as she massaged the muscles of her husband's neck. "You, yourself, have told me that a man can play good golf one day and poorly the next. You must try to play good golf today; one hole at a time."

Papwa smiled broadly to hear his opinions being echoed by his wife. Though Suminthra knew little about golf beyond the basics, she listened attentively when Papwa returned home after each game – be it a titled tournament for high stakes, or a pick-up round or two with his friends.

Suminthra knew that her Papwa had not been playing too well. In the Natal Non-European championship played at Kloof Country Club at the beginning of the year, he'd lost the tournament he'd come to dominate by scoring 294 to the 22-year old winner, former Kloof caddie Ramduth Rajdaw's 293. Papwa had held the title for the past eight years and Suminthra was sure it pained him to lose it, though Papwa had accepted the defeat with his usual good nature. It had hurt Suminthra when a neighbour read to her what one of the newspapers was saying about Papwa after this loss: that he lacked the fighting qualities needed for competing on a professional level. Instead the article had called for opportunities for other black golfers to play overseas, players like that Rajdaw boy and Simon "Cox" Hlapo whom she knew from Papwa's stories.

Papwa's defeat at the hands of the Rajdaw boy would have further implications: it smashed the myth of an unbeatable player on the black golfing circuit. Indeed, though many spoke about "playing for second place", there was a growing contingent of black golfers eager to beat the master at his game. Ismail Chowglay was widely believed to be equal to or better than Papwa. Vincent Tshabalala was another hungry lion and during the 1965 South African Non-European Open, all three had come together on the East London Golf Course in a thrilling battle for ascendancy.

By lunch time on the last day, Papwa had a one-stroke lead over Vincent, with Ismail and another player, Ramphal Tiney, close behind. Playing systematic golf, Vincent took over the lead between the tenth and sixteenth holes. However, he chipped badly at the sixteenth hole, once more levelling the score with Papwa. The mixed crowd of spectators had been cheering every stroke played by the leaders, and were already predicting that Vincent would snatch the title from defending champion, Papwa. Forced to bring his best game, Papwa played brilliantly. Vincent did too. At the final hole, Vincent, who was up first, sunk an eight-foot putt. Silently, Vincent watched as Papwa sunk his ball from six feet away to tie. Talk of a playoff was abandoned when the organisers were unable to contact the Minister of Bantu Affairs for permission to play on the course one day longer. Besides which, Papwa could not stay: he was expected in Cape Town in a few days' time to play in the white South African Open.

Here his performance had been even grimmer. After the expense of travelling there from East London, a sprained wrist had put Papwa out of the money. He finished in eleventh place – just out of the prizes awarded to the top ten finishers – with a score of 287. Gary Player, with a gross aggregate of 273, placed first, three strokes ahead of runner up John Hayes. In addition to the wrist injury, which curtailed his play, Papwa felt that his putting had been off. He'd missed about five putts to loud groans from the audience. "I had back luck," Papwa told reporters afterwards, "but I have no excuses."

As he prepared to leave his home, trying to clear his head for the rounds ahead, Papwa wondered about his luck. Suminthra's reminder about playing well one day and poorly the next had come at just the right time.

He turned to kiss her goodbye in an uncharacteristic show of affection. Theirs was a stoic marriage of little gestures and comforting words.

Confirming his thoughts, Suminthra straightened Papwa's tie once their embrace ended. She'd always fiddle with his appearance before he left the house. Sometimes he expected her to slick down his hair with spit-wetted fingers as she did for their children. "There, all ready," she said. FM had arrived and the older children were already lined up at the gate to see their father off and to wish him luck.

Handing him his flask of tea, Suminthra declined to mention as she'd done two years ago in preparation for the same tournament, how unfair the rules were that forced Papwa to change in the car and take his meals with the caddies and waiters of the club. The weather was good; she hoped it would remain so for the next few days. Should her Papwa win, clear skies meant he would not have to be humiliated at what should be a time of celebration.

"Oh well, at least they're allowing you to play ... Play well and may Lord Ganesha guide you during the day," Suminthra said instead.

The couple had not been sure that the government would allow Papwa entry into the white tournament that year. As usual, there'd been much speculation – in the neighbourhood and in the press. When it seemed that Papwa would be denied admission, the media had approached Gary Player for comment.

"I'm disappointed in Gary," Suminthra said, not sure whether she should continue. She did want to affect Papwa's feelings for his friend. "He should have voiced his disapproval of the government's policies more strongly. For a man like that to say nothing means he supports them. Ask anyone."

"He said that he was disappointed that they weren't allowing me to play," Papwa pointed out.

"Let's see how he feels at the end of these three days," Suminthra said, an inscrutable smile brightening her face.

"We'll see," Papwa replied, with a smile to match hers. They lingered for a moment more, before FM coughed apologetically and said that it was time to go.

In the years since they'd first met on that wet, cold golf course in Scotland, Gary had racked up tournament wins: most recently, the 1963 Australian Open, the 1963 and 1964 South African Masters, the San Diego Open, the '500' Festival Open and the Pensacola Open in America. Gary had also won three Major tournaments by then: the British Open of 1959, the 1961 US Masters and the 1962 PGA Championship. This was the first time that Gary and Papwa would be playing alongside each other at the Natal Open. Having won the tournament in 1963, Papwa had one Natal Open title to Gary's four wins in 1958, 1959, 1960 and 1962.

On the first day of the tournament, Papwa played journeyman style golf – competent, but not exceptional. It was enough to keep him within sight of the day's leaders. Harold Henning and Gary Player were already showing their mettle. Papwa had the feeling that one of them was the man he'd need to beat in order to claim the title as his own.

The second day went better. Papwa ate his meals with the caddies. During breaks he drank the sweet tea and munched the biscuits and bananas Suminthra had packed in for him. Steadily, Indian faces infiltrated the ranks of the spectators – Papwa's Indian Army, the stalwart few strengthened by ordinary Indians anxious to see one of their own take on the white man at the game they regarded as their exclusive preserve.

"It's a matter of pride, Indian pride; black pride too," Jayendra had said in passing, keeping in step as Papwa walked from one hole to the tee-box of the next. Papwa smiled, happy to see his friend. For a day or two, Jayendra could be just another face in the crowd and Papwa would not have to worry about his friend and the eyes that watched him.

By the third and final day, Papwa had edged up the board to be one of the tournament leaders. He and Gary were thus paired to play in the final rounds. Sensing a battle between white South Africa's favourite sporting son and their hometown hero, Durban's Indians surged to the whites-only course in droves. Off the course, Papwa, like many of his supporters, was disadvantaged in so many ways. The golf course was the one place that allowed him a chance to equalise. If Papwa were to beat Gary and win the title once more, his loyal supporters wanted to be there to witness it. Many of Papwa's supporters were not necessarily golfers and only a few were aware of the strict rules governing one's behaviour on a golf course. Others, a small minority, yes, but enough to cause problems, were indifferent to the rules of the game. This "hooligan" element rankled Gary and unsettled his game. They disrupted Papwa's concentration too.

Going into the final round, Gary led by two strokes. He picked up another stroke to lead by three after a magnificent drive that saw him scoring a birdie to Papwa's four. Trouble found Gary on the third hole, when his ball landed in a small stand of trees. The ball was not found within the allotted five minutes and Gary was forced back to the tee to play a second drive. This snafu meant that Gary scored eight for the hole to Papwa's even-par five. Now the players were on equal standing. As they progressed, matching each other stroke for stroke, Gary began to complain about being "put off" by talking and jostling when he was lining up vital putts. In addition, several spectators, oblivious to the etiquette of golf, were seen running across fairways and encroaching on the greens; some even refused to heed the marshals' warnings when confronted.

The fourteenth hole was another turning point in the competition. It was here that Gary and Papwa received word that Harold Henning had returned to the clubhouse with a score of 71 for a total of 286. Unless they picked up two shots in the next five holes, Harold would be the winner. Inspired, Papwa shot an eagle on the par-five fourteenth hole. There would be no looking back for him.

At the eighteenth hole, speculation was rife that the two golfers would tie. Gary's drive landed on the green and it appeared likely that the seasoned golfer would score an eagle. Papwa's ball had landed in the bunker at the right of the green. Calmly, and ignoring Gary's grumbles and the protests of the marshals as they tried to maintain order over the crowd that had by that time swelled to seven thousand, ignoring everyone and everything around him but the ball and his club, the sun and the wind, Papwa chipped his ball to the edge of the green. "I've always liked playing in sand," he whispered to himself. Swinging gently into the shot, he chipped again. This time, the ball landed within a few feet of the hole. Smoothly, Papwa chipped it into the cup.

Gary was not as lucky. His putt for the eagle from the edge of the green curled to the right. Papwa finished the round with a grand aggregate of 285 to Gary's and Harold Henning's totals of 286. Like so many tournaments in which he'd played, one stroke had made all the difference; this this time in Papwa's favour. Truculent to the last,

Gary queried the scores on Papwa's card, but the marshals ruled it in order. Then, summoning the grace that had deserted him earlier, Gary congratulated the victor and told the assembled press that Papwa had "chipped like a man from Mars."

Happily, the weather was clear and the prize-giving could be held outside without attracting attention. The organisers breathed a sigh of relief, thanking the weather gods for their benevolence. Papwa beamed broadly when he was presented with the winner's trophy. Whatever words he uttered, were drowned out by the crowd's roar. All the white bigwigs were inside the clubhouse and on their first drinks when the organisers realised that in their agitation and relief, Papwa had not been awarded his winner's cheque. Papwa was hastily summoned and made to wait outside on the veranda before the cheque was passed through an opened window. In this way, Papwa's victory of the Natal Open was once more tainted. "The sour and the sweet," Papwa intoned under his breath, a painful smile plastered on his face for his clamouring fans.

Notwithstanding the SABC's refusal to broadcast mixed sports, news of Papwa's win had already made it onto the streets of Riverside by the time FM's car neared the Sewgolum home. Friends and neighbours thronged outside in a mood of defiant revelry. FM blasted his hooter to punctuate Papwa's victorious return. Standing at the gate, his children formed a wriggling guard of honour, kept in check by a stern word or two from Ma. Romilla raced inside with the trophy she'd cajoled her father into handing over as soon as he'd alighted the car. Standing on a chair, she made space on a shelf directly opposite the front door. Here, the new trophy took pride of place amidst so many others. Suminthra smiled as Papwa handed over the cheque for her safe-keeping; the younger children searched Papwa's pockets for the sweets and other treats the returning hero had brought home. Pre-empting her husband's triumph, Suminthra had cooked a feast fit for kings. Papwa, FM and a handful of his closest friends sat down to the meal.

It was the other men, and not Papwa who regaled Papwa's family with a play-by-play recount of his victory. Papwa was subdued; more so than he'd been after the disastrous prize-giving in the rain. "My Papwa must be exhausted," Suminthra told herself. "Winning this competition is old hat to him now." She smiled fondly as she bustled about feeding the men and clearing glasses and dishes away.

Once the children had been put to bed and Ma and Suminthra too had retired for the night, Papwa joined his friends and an exuberant crowd of supporters in town to celebrate his victory. This, here, is how a win should be celebrated, Papwa thought to himself, with family first and then friends and fans. Forget the club and their stupid rules. Or was it the government's rules? Papwa couldn't care less. Pretty girls hung onto his every word, others asked him to dance. Strangers insisted on the honour of buying him a drink. Amongst his own people, Papwa was indeed king for the day.

FORTY

By and large, the press reacted positively to Papwa's win, painting the battle between him and Gary as one between a David and a Goliath. As unstinting as the press were in their praise, most articles made mention of the unruly element within the gallery. Papwa was not overly worried. As with his first Dutch Open win, his defeat of Gary opened up a trickle of support: new sponsors came on board, while his existing sponsors remitted bonuses for his win. Well-wishers sent small donations, cash and otherwise, like the radiogram gifted by the grateful Indian community of Greytown, some 150 kilometres away from Durban.

"You should be worried Papwa," FM warned, reading aloud from that day's *POST.* "Listen to what that 'Corona' fellow has to say. 'The ignorance of etiquette by a small group of hooligans should not jeopardise the great challenge of our sole representative in BIG golf. There was nothing wrong with the jubilation and hysteria when Papwa won the Natal Open for the second time. It was a natural and spontaneous reaction.'"

"That's good, right?" Papwa asked.

"Yes, it's good, but then he says that you could possibly be blamed or barred because of how your supporters behaved. You know this government will use any excuse."

"If you say so, FM," Papwa replied, his mind on other matters. "But I've already been accepted to play in the PGA Championships, so I don't know what they can do."

Days later, Papwa received his answer when the government issued a proclamation under the Group Areas Act which effectively banned mixed sporting audiences. In terms of the proclamation dated 12 February 1965, the Group Areas Act was to be applied to all public places of recreation, including theatres, concerts and public sporting events. Venues in white areas could not be frequented by non-whites and vice versa. Even if Papwa were granted permission to play in whites-only tournaments in the future, a fact very much in doubt at this stage, he'd have to do so without the support of his Indian Army.

Then, during April 1965, the tensions that had simmered between Papwa and Louis ever since they'd parted ways, boiled over into an ugly spat played out in the press. Papwa had been quoted criticising the lackadaisical organisation and paltry purses of the Non-European tournaments. Both, it must be said, were valid arguments. While planning suffered the whims of a capricious government, as liable to grant approvals as not, and as such were beyond the control of organisers, the prize money on offer was indeed low and a mere fraction of what could be earned on the white South African golfing circuit. Coming in the wake of his victories in two Non-European tournaments – the Griqualand West Open and the Transvaal Open, the latter which he won by an astonishing twenty-two strokes – Papwa knew all too well of which he spoke. Both tournaments required that he travel there, and with attendant costs, the prize money he earned yielded very little profit.

Not one to accept criticism calmly, Louis, by now the president of the Natal Golf Association, a black body, slammed back at Papwa in a letter to the press. Papwa responded in a letter drafted by FM, in which he furnished numerous examples of organisational glitches. Papwa's funds were at a new low then, which might have prompted him to comment in the first place. It was not long before Papwa announced that he would not be travelling to Europe to defend his Dutch Open title.

This was not the end of the feud between Louis and Papwa.

"What do you mean he's saying that I neglected my coaching duties?" Papwa asked as FM read the letter he'd received from Louis in his capacity as chairperson of the Durban Golf Club – the erstwhile Durban Indian Golf Club. The name change reflected Louis's aims for making Natal golf more inclusive than it had been before.

"He says that you're only interested in coaching people who can already play," FM sighed.

"But I coach whoever asks me," Papwa said.

"Yes, I know Papwa, but Louis has a bee in his bonnet about this. Don't worry, I'll send a reply."

Again, this was not the end of the matter. Papwa was then asked to provide the names of people he'd coached. The handful of names he supplied was deemed not enough. Nor was his promise to coach on Wednesday afternoons and Saturday mornings for a fee of R1.50 an hour. FM came to tell him the news.

"They're now saying that they've had to get other golfers to take over your coaching; professionals willing to work for free." FM tried to impart the news gently. "I'm sorry Papwa, but it looks like they want you out, even though you're supposed to be the club's pro."

"They or Louis?" Papwa asked.

"Doesn't matter; seems it's the same thing," FM answered.

"This is a great insult to me, my friend," Papwa said under his breath, but FM heard him.

"Yes, my brother. Can you now understand why they say you should keep your friends close and yours enemies closer?"

"But Louis and I are not enemies," Papwa protested. The words tasted false and sour on his tongue.

Papwa had other worries, but as usual, he kept them close to his chest. At the beginning of September, seven months after he'd beaten Gary to win the 1965 Natal Open, a speech at the newly-built Loskop Dam on the Olifants River near Groblersdal in the Transvaal, would have far-reaching implications for Papwa's golfing future. Prime Minister Verwoerd, the man responsible for the speech, was inaugurating the dam. Around the same time, in New Zealand, the Springboks were concluding their rugby tour against the All Blacks. Once again, it was up to FM to explain the ramifications of Verwoerd's speech. With the exception of Fishy, Papwa hadn't seen his friends from his Beachwood days in months.

"Verwoerd said that he will not judge another country's customs and that if the All Blacks want to have Maoris on their team, that's their business." FM said.

"That's good, right?" Papwa asked.

FM felt a rush of pity for the other man. He knew that Papwa had a naïve optimism that things would eventually work out in his favour. FM knew the government's intransigence, especially Verwoerd's, when it came to matters of racial integration and relaxing their draconian laws. "No, Papwa, it's not good. Hear me out first." He explained that Verwoerd had only prefaced his speech that way and was in fact sending a subtle warning that when the All Blacks next played in South Africa, they would be expected to respect South Africa's customs. "In other words, no Maoris will be allowed to play in South Africa."

"Oh," Papwa said, at a loss.

"And remember what De Klerk said in '63: if the government's sporting policies are not complied with, then they'll introduce laws to make their stance regarding mixed-race sport clear. Here in South Africa and when they send teams overseas. And you can't forget, after you won the Natal Open that year, De Klerk also spelled out the Nats' sporting policy – separate governing bodies for each race in each sport; no mixed teams to represent South Africa, no mixed teams from other countries to play here; and of course, white associations to be in charge of each code with their players and their players alone, representing this country overseas. Many people believe that it is because of you and your supporters that the government is taking such a hard line."

Papwa looked at FM aghast.

"But I have no interest in politics, I never say anything political. Even after they gave me my prize in the rain, I kept quiet. When I am overseas, I never say one bad word against the government."

"I know this, Papwa, maybe even the government knows this, but you know what? It doesn't matter. You're a symbol. And when you beat Gary Player, beat the best golfer this country can boast of, you sent out a message, the message that maybe whites aren't automatically better than you and I are. They can't have it. Gary is their blue-eyed boy, maybe if it was someone else, maybe not. Now they see you as a troublemaker. They just don't understand how it can be, how you, a nobody from Riverside – no offence, Papwa – can beat their man."

"But Gary is my friend." Papwa stopped and thought about his statement before protesting further. Suddenly, he remembered what Gary had said when asked to comment on his first Natal Open win back in '63. "He's damning you with faint praise," Louis had said at the time. "Says your grip restricts your follow-through and therefore your length, but you have good nerves and a good short game."

Some of the other South African players had had better things to say. In the same article, Sid Brews had said that Papwa deserved to be classed as one of the best golfers in the country. He'd defended Papwa's right to play by stating that "the idea of an open is to allow the best players to compete against one another." Papwa remembered every one of Mr Brews's words. Even Reg Taylor, a member of South Africa's golf team at the time and a man Papwa did not know that well, had said that he, Papwa, had proven himself to be a talented sportsman and a gentleman both in his win and in his handling of the humiliating prize-giving. Come to think about it, perhaps Gary was not such a good friend to him after all? Still, Papwa chose to believe in the other man's integrity. Friends looked out for one another. It had always been that way with his old friends even if they didn't see as much of each other as in the past.

"I have an idea. We don't need to ask Gary, but what if we asked his manager for help?" Papwa suggested.

The newspapers had been full of stories of Gary's success and there was always a helpful neighbour or acquaintance willing to share the news with Papwa. In June, Gary had won the US Open at Bellerive Country Club in St. Louis, Missouri, becoming the first foreign-born player to do so since 1927. He netted $26,000 for the win. Gary had so much money, that during the prize-giving of that tournament, he'd announced that he would only be keeping $1,000 of the prize money. He intended to return $25,000 to the US Golfer's Association, with one fifth going to cancer relief work and the balance, some $20,000, to be spent on the promotion of junior golf. Gary could well afford his largesse: by the time 1965 ended, he would add Canada's NTL Challenge Cup, the World Cup individual and team events, the Australian Open, the World Match Play Tournament, the World Series of Golf and the South African Open to his list of victories for the year.

Papwa would not admit it to anyone, but sometimes he felt a galling bitterness when he thought of the money Gary was making – so much money that he could afford to give a fortune away – compared to the slim pickings he, Papwa, eked out on the Non-European circuit and the few whites-only tournaments in which he was allowed to play. A man like Gary would never have to humble himself for the chance to earn R1.50 an hour trying to teach novices and amateurs the professional game at a club that no longer wanted him!

Nor had it helped matters when people made comments like how Papwa was Gary's equal on the course. If anything, it made it worse, but a man would become despondent if he thought that way. It would be enough to make a man want to break his clubs and give up the game altogether. No, he did not have that luxury, Papwa admonished himself. A man had to support his family and how would he do so if not by golf? No, if so many others recognised Papwa's ability relative to Gary's, surely it was likely that the other man's manager would too? What was it that Fishy had said when he'd first planted the seed in Papwa's mind weeks ago? That it made good business sense for a man like that Mr McCormack to have another player of Gary's calibre on his books.

"I'll write a letter to Mr McCormack," FM replied, sucking on a pencil. "I doubt that he'll be willing to represent you, he already has Arnold Palmer and Jack Nicklaus on his books, besides Gary. He's said to be very particular, but I'll see what we can do. Maybe he can help out with money to get you to play in the States. You know that's where the big money is and perhaps it is time for you to look outside of South Africa if you are to have any hope of making a living from golf! Anyway, at least you still have your job until then."

"Yes, my job, Papwa answered uncertainly. His job as the club pro still hung in the balance. For the moment though, he could not worry about that too.

In November 1965, FM announced that Papwa had already taken time off work to prepare for a number of tournaments in the months ahead. According to FM, Papwa was being supported by well-wishers who were "contributing towards his upkeep during training." FM added that Papwa had already been entered into a big sponsored tournament – the General Motors Tournament – to be staged in Port Elizabeth during January the following year. Confidently, he named the tournaments that made up the South African Tour circuit and promised that Papwa would play in them in the forthcoming season.

FM's statement was more than bravado, or the opening gambit in his bid on Papwa's behalf to gain admission into the white tournaments. Earlier that year, he and Papwa had received word about the richest tournament in the world at the time: the Carling World Golf Championship. Sponsored by the Carling Brewing Company of Cleveland in the USA, the tournament had evolved from the Carling Open, initially staged in Cleveland, but which had been extended to cities in which the rapidly expanding company was building breweries. The Carling Open earned a spot on the US PGA circuit, but in order to differentiate the competition from others, a decision was made to offer the largest purse in golf for which the best professional golfers (and the occasional amateur) from all the golfing countries in the world would compete.

Entry would be decided on the basis of a points system with players in the various world regions earning a number of points for their placement in a number of recognised competitions. Aware of South Africa's stance regarding mixed competitions, the organisers deemed it necessary to include the North African and Middle Eastern countries with Europe and allow South Africa to form its own zone. In South Africa, the qualifying tournaments were: the General Motors Tournament, the Dunlop Masters, the South African Open, the Transvaal Open and the Natal Open.

The winner's share of the $200,000 Carling World Golf Championship purse was $35,000 – with generous cash prizes for those who placed. Almost half of the approximately 150-strong field were guaranteed cash awards of some sort. With such riches at stake, Papwa was determined to be counted amongst the five South African contenders.

FORTY-ONE

"I'm afraid I have some bad news for you," FM said, putting his keys down on the battered kitchen table of the Sewgolum home.

"Bad news?" Papwa asked.

"It's about the Natal Open."

Papwa had already played in the Non-European Natal Open and in so doing, had reclaimed his title from Ramduth Rajdaw, the previous year's winner. Despite beating runner up, David "Locke" Motati, by five strokes, *POST* summed up his performance as follows: "There were streaks of brilliance by the maestro Papwa. But on the whole, from this showing he will have to put in some eight hours of practice per day if he is to be in the hunt against top golfers in the White circuit."

FM could only be referring to the other one, the white one.

"What about the Natal Open?" Papwa asked. He had not for one minute worried that anything could go wrong with his entry. He was the defending champion after all, and the South African Golfers' Union knew that he needed to compete in the event in order to earn points towards playing in the Carling World Golf Championship.

In order to earn those coveted qualifying points, Papwa had scaled down his commitments on the non-European circuit, though he'd played as many matches as possible, which he considered practice for the more challenging South African tour. In November 1965, for instance, he'd won the Griqualand West Open title for the fifth time, beating Simon "Cox" Nhlapo into second place by five strokes. Papwa's gross aggregate for this tournament had been 281 – eleven strokes under par on the Kimberley Golf Course. And he'd won the Thunderbird Classic in December. Held at the Springfield course in bad weather, with the last round played under downpour conditions, he'd beaten his nearest rival by five strokes to claim his share of the R500 purse. During the prize-giving, one of the sponsors, Leslie de Vos, announced that he and his friends would donate R50 towards a fund to send Papwa overseas. Such funds would be much needed, since Papwa had in the meantime been relieved of his position as club pro. Yet Papwa was confident. Despite not participating in all tournaments, he'd ended third on the South Africa tour's Order of Merit for the 1964/65 season – behind Gary Player and Harold Henning. His gross earnings for the season were R1,448.

In pursuit of a bigger reward, Papwa had been so committed to gathering points and not prize money, that for the first time in a long time, he'd decided to sit out of the Non-European South African Open, which was held in Bloemfontein and won by David "Locke" Motati from the Transvaal. Everyone said that if he'd entered he'd have won, but Papwa did not want to deny the younger player his victory.

"They're saying you need to apply to enter the tournament, Papwa," FM said.

"The Natal Open, they want me to get a permit?" Papwa asked.

"Yes. I think it's because of what Verwoerd said at that dam opening."

"So we apply," Papwa said.

Days later, FM delivered the response to Papwa's application.

"So sorry, brother, but seems they're turning you down."

"Who's turning me down?"

"Government; they're refusing to allow you to 'occupy' the Royal Durban Golf Club for the Natal Open Championship. You know, if you can't occupy, you can't play."

"But I played at Royal Durban before. I am the defending champ, FM. How can they do this?"

FM shrugged, not daring to meet Papwa's eyes. What could he say? He did not have the answer to Papwa's questions other than that the government's laws were fickle and unfathomable.

FM's unvoiced answer would have been as good as any. Days after refusing Papwa's permit, the Minister of Planning indicated that he would permit Papwa to play in the 1966 Natal Open after all. Non-white spectators would be allowed to attend too – subject to separate entrances and payment of an entrance fee. Even with a watchful government and security presence, the separation of the gallery did not work in practice during the tournament. White and black spectators mingled freely and without friction. This time around, Gary won the title and Papwa finished fourth – behind Cobie le Grange and Britain's Tommy Horton respectively, and six strokes behind the winner.

Papwa had been playing under severe mental strain, brought about by the uncertainty about whether he'd be allowed to play in the tournaments he'd entered – tournaments in which he desperately needed to prove himself if he had any hopes of making it to Royal Birkdale Golf Club in Southport, England, where the Carling World Golf Championship would be contested in August that year.

"More bad news, I'm afraid, brother." A letter fluttered from FM's hands.

"What now?" Papwa asked, afraid to hear what FM had to say. These days his stomach was in knots, not knowing if he'd receive the permissions he needed or not, not knowing who was watching.

"It's the Western Province Open; they're banning you from playing."

"Banning me?"

"You know what they said after Natal. You can play in tournaments you've played in before."

"I don't understand –"

"Don't worry about this now, Papwa, we'll sort it out later," FM tried to reassure Papwa. "All you should think about is the PGA now, one tournament at a time, right?"

"Right," Papwa said trying to drum up a semblance of enthusiasm for his manager's sake.

FM was worried too. Not too long ago, he and Papwa had been escorted to the Security Branch offices for a "chat." Once there, the two men had been separated. At first the interview had begun cordially enough, if one could get beyond the fact that they'd been brought there in the first place, and under duress too.

"Why are you applying for permits on Papwa's behalf when you know it's against government policy?" his interrogator had asked casually, as if he was inquiring about the time or seeking confirmation that the weather was indeed lovely.

"Golf is what Papwa does; he needs to earn a living," FM found himself stating again and again.

The man behind the desk had not been amused. "You and that boy are trouble makers, boy," he'd wagged his thick fingers, pale, like uncooked sausages, in FM's face.

"We're not trying to make trouble sir. I'm an insurance agent, I'm just trying to help Papwa," he'd said in his defence; anything to get out of there. If they want to get rid of us, they can, FM thought, squirming around to see the window and its view outside. No one would see us fall. They were on one of the top floors. Just like Saloojee, he thought, wondering if this was the building from which the man had been flung. No, that had happened in Johannesburg; perhaps it's different here in Durban.

After hours of answering the same questions, FM and Papwa were released.

Was he crazy to keep on doing this? FM asked himself.

"I must be," FM said aloud. Not for the first time he wondered who of them was the most misguided: Papwa for thinking they'd let him play, or he, for fostering those notions?

"What was that?" Papwa asked now. "The PGA?"

"Nothing, brother. Get some rest, we leave tomorrow morning bright and early!"

Putting his concerns aside, Papwa competed in the South African PGA Tournament in Germiston amidst strict scrutiny to ensure that the mixed crowd did not, in fact, mix. Ultimately, Papwa's worries weighed heavily on his mind – this for a man known for his cool temperament and unruffled demeanour. He finished twelfth in the tournament with a score of 290 – eighteen strokes behind the winner, Harold Henning, on 272. Bob Charles, a left-handed golfer from New Zealand, was the runner up with a score of 278, while Gary Player on 279 placed third.

Immediately after the South African PGA, Papwa and FM flew to Cape Town, hoping to convince the Minister of Planning and Development, Jan Haak, to relax the ban on Papwa playing in the Western Province Open in a face-to-face meeting. No meeting took place and the Western Province Open went ahead without Papwa. In a statement at the time, Haak reiterated that "no extension of mixed golf tournaments could be permitted."

While in Cape Town, Papwa and FM stayed with supporters as they often did when out of town. One night, loud and persistent knocking woke the household from its slumber. The dreaded security police had come for a visit. Barging into the room where Papwa was hurriedly trying to put on his clothes, three policemen demanded to know what Papwa was doing in Cape Town.

"I've come to play," he answered, still half-asleep. Was this a dream? The minister had not yet made his announcement, and Papwa truly believed that things would work in his favour.

"You're banned, boy. You're not allowed to play! Don't you know that?"

Papwa tried to explain that he was still awaiting the minister's final word on the matter.

"Have you seen all the trouble you're causing? Poor Papwa, 'the poorest professional golfer in the world,'" another derided. The press, both in South Africa and abroad had come to Papwa's defence when word of his banning had first leaked.

Pointing to Robben Island across the bay from District Six where they were staying, the third said with biting clarity, enunciating each word in accented English: "We know what to do with trouble-makers like you!"

The three men laughed as they stomped away. Papwa was too unnerved to go back to bed, expecting the men's return any time, but his host pointed out that government would be doing more harm than good if they were to arrest Papwa and that they were merely trying to intimidate him. Already there was speculation in the press that South Africa would be banned from the Carling World of Golf Championship on the basis of racial discrimination were Papwa refused entry into the qualifying tournaments.

A shaken Papwa and FM travelled directly from Cape Town to Port Elizabeth for the General Motors Tournament. Staged at Wedgewood Park Country Club outside of Port Elizabeth, the organisers provided Papwa with a caravan on the course in which he could change as well as sleep. The club was relatively deserted and the caravan located out of the way to provide Papwa with a degree of privacy that had been sorely lacking in other of the white tournaments in which he'd participated.

Papwa had always been a superstitious man. On the eve of the tournament, he and FM settled in for the night. Nervously he began supposing all kinds of nightmare scenarios in this secluded spot – scenes out of the B-grade horror movies popular at the time. FM decided that given the isolation of the club, perhaps it would be best if they found alternate accommodation, which they did, travelling to a non-white hotel in the city.

When they returned to the caravan the next morning, just as Papwa was about to open the caravan door, FM stopped him. "I smell gas," he warned. "I don't think you should open the door." When the club followed up the source of the gas smell, they discovered that the gas pipe leading to the fridge had been tampered with. Gas is a silent killer. Papwa was a habitual smoker and known to knock back a drink or two at night to relax him before a big tournament. "Imagine what would have happened if we hadn't left? We could have died." FM shook his head. "I don't think this was an accident, Papwa."

Papwa was not sure what to think. But as he teed off that morning, the partially severed pipe was all he could think about. Was it an accident, or was there a simple explanation for it? Could people really be out to kill him? Rattled by the experience, Papwa failed to make the cut.

Papwa knew that he could not allow himself to be deterred by the setbacks he'd faced during the month. It was hard to find the resolve to carry on, yes, but eventually Papwa rose to the occasion; bolstered by the dream of winning the Carling championship and all that money. Money that would change the lives of himself and his family in ways he could only imagine. All he knew was that circumstances could not be worse. They'd been forced to vacate the family home in order to make way for the Northern Freeway. Currently Ma, Suminthra and the children were staying in two rooms of a shared shack in Riverside. When Papwa was home, they were packed even tighter. So with his eye on the twin goals of vindication and wealth, he and FM travelled to Johannesburg where Papwa had been entered to take part in the Transvaal Open. Arriving at the Parkview Golf Club where the tournament was to be staged, Papwa heard that he had been denied permission to play. In addition, non-white spectators were banned from attending the event, which meant that Papwa was not allowed to watch his points slip further in the standings since the Transvaal Open was one of the qualifying tournaments for the Carling World of Golf Championship.

In a departure from the usual procedure, when FM entered Papwa into the Dunlop South African Masters tournament, he was told by the organisers that Papwa would have to apply for his own permit. Duly, Papwa and FM visited the Department of Indian Affairs in Durban. After the visit, Papwa's usual optimism was depleted and he prepared himself for another banning.

"I have a good feeling about this," FM disagreed. "Everything will work out, wait and see. I'll book you on Wednesday morning's plane." The tournament was scheduled to take place at the Zwartkops Country Club in Pretoria. "We must think positively."

Papwa had been denied entry into the 1964 Dunlop Masters, but in 1965 he'd been allowed to play when the tournament was staged at the Royal Durban Golf Club. Papwa had comported himself well then, scoring a gross aggregate of 287 to finish third in a tournament won by Denis Hutchinson on 281.

FM's intuition proved correct. Late Tuesday afternoon, FM received word that not only had Papwa been granted permission to play in the Masters, he would also be allowed to play in the South African Open in Houghton, Johannesburg the following week. Furthermore, the South African Golfers' Union telephoned on the morning of Papwa's flight with the news that the union itself would be seeking to have Papwa's ban lifted.

By the time he teed off at the Dunlop Masters tournament in Pretoria, Papwa was lying seventh on the world championship points table even after missing the Transvaal Open. But if Papwa hoped to make up points, it was not to be. He finished in eleventh place with a score of 286, ten strokes behind winner, Cedric Amm on 276.

Papwa's performance in the South African Open at Houghton Golf Club was not much better. In fact, it was much worse. Teeing off in a field of 148: 80 amateurs and 68 professionals, Papwa failed to qualify for the final two rounds. Defending champion and three-time South African Open winner Gary Player beat Harold Henning and Cobie le

Grange by one stroke to retain his title, scoring 278 to Henning's and Le Grange's 279.

The South African Open was the last tournament of the South African season. Shortly afterwards, government announced that it would be strictly enforcing the colour bar in golf. And should Papwa Sewgolum believe himself the exception to the rule, this was soon clarified: Papwa would be excluded from all "white" tournaments in future. When asked to comment on the developments, Gary Player, eerily echoing Papwa's previously voiced sentiments said, "I do not meddle in politics."

FORTY-TWO

After the disappointments and highlights of his campaign, which had included a trip to Rhodesia in April, where he'd triumphed at the Bata Bush Babes Tournament against all of South Africa's top players in Gwelo; claimed fifth place in the Dunlop Tournament in Bulawayo and placed eighth in the Flame Lily Tournament in Salisbury, Papwa was happy to be home, no matter how uncomfortable and precarious his living situation was at the time. During his campaign on the South African tour, Papwa's landlord informed him that the government had declared Riverside a whites-only area under the Group Areas Act. Ironically this was the same piece of legislation that had led to him receiving his prize in the rain and a loophole of which, had allowed him to "occupy" the golf course, but nowhere else, in the short years before his ban.

Papwa would have to move to an area set aside for Indians, but for today he promised himself, he would not worry about that. If he allowed himself to worry, he'd start obsessing about all his troubles, the foremost of which was whether he'd still be allowed to play in the Carling tournament despite his poor record. FM was trying to appeal to the organisers of the competition, and FM, being FM, was optimistic that concessions would be made since it was through no fault of his own that Papwa had been disallowed from playing in all the qualifying tournaments.

Dennis had struggled to adjust to the new living situation, so just like Pa used to when he was a boy, Papwa took Dennis on an outing to Grey Street to take his son's mind off their crowded rooms in a shack stuffed with newspapers to keep the elements out and where the rain dripped through the holes in the rusted tin roof. The little boy was excited to be spending time with his father. Papwa knew that the children missed him when he was away and a boy, especially, needed his father. He smiled at the fond memories of his own childhood conjured up by the chaotic markets with their colours and smells and the small stores crowded from floor to ceiling with a mixture of exotic and mundane goods. One day Dennis too would look back fondly on these times, Papwa hoped.

Dennis was darting in and out of the stores, begging his father for sweets and toys.

"You've already had sweets, *beta*," Papwa remonstrated. The boy's hands and face were sticky from the little balls of *gulab jamun*, fried bites of dough soaked in sugar syrup fragranced with rosewater, that he'd persuaded Papwa to buy him earlier.

Dennis smiled in acknowledgment. "I can have an ice-cream, then, Pa?" The boy walked in the direction of an ice-cream vendor peddling his wares. The day was hot and humid; Papwa thought that one icecream would not harm the boy. As long as it did not interfere with his eating his meal at home later, Suminthra would be none the wiser.

Papwa handed a few rand notes to the boy. "Get one for me too, son, chocolate, okay? We won't tell your Ma." He watched the boy scampering towards the ice-cream man standing by his cart.

From behind him, Papwa felt a heavy arm descend on his neck. Papwa tried to turn around to see who it was – he was often recognised in town and even now, people still stopped him to discuss some of his big wins or ask for an autograph. The hand held him in place.

"What will it take for you to learn your lesson, Mr Sewgolum?" His name sounded coarse and derisive emitted by the disembodied male voice.

Papwa stood frozen, unable to answer, remembering the voices of the policemen who had carted him off and interrogated him. But this was an Indian voice, a Durban accent, a man no doubt chosen because he could blend in on the busy street.

"How would you like it if it was your boy next? You're good at making boys, aren't you? One of your sons died, I believe. Would your wife forgive you if you lost another son? Or maybe a daughter? Romilla is thirteen, I believe."

Papwa tried to shake the hand loose.

"Leave my children alone!" he sputtered. "Your argument is not with them; it is with me."

"A man has to look after his children, all his children. Do you look after your children, Mr Sewgolum?"

Before Papwa could answer, the man's voice softened, but it was no less ominous. Dennis had returned with the ice-creams, licking leisurely on one of the dripping cones.

"Hello, *beta*," the voice said. 'You're a big boy, right? Take after your father?"

Beepraj smiled, unsure, but he had an appealing grin for everyone. He was too young to know of the evil in the world and even if that ignorance was dangerous, Papwa was glad for it.

"Look after your boy, Mr Sewgolum," the man said pleasantly, as he slowly released his hold on Papwa's neck. "Such a good boy and all!"

Papwa rushed towards Dennis and accepted the proffered cone. As soon as he knew his son was close, was safe, he turned around to see who the man was. Who belonged to that sinister voice, that heavy hand? He could not tell. Indian men were going about their business, streaming idly and purposefully in the busy market. It could have been anyone taller than he.

"Who that man was, Pa?" Dennis asked, unaware of the sour dread leaching from his father's pores. Through the heat of the day, Papwa felt chilled. His appetite for the frozen treat had vanished.

"No one, *beta*, just a man who saw me play once," Papwa answered after a few seconds.

"The time you won, Pa?" Dennis balanced on his heels and nodded, as if answering his own question.

"Yes, *beta*, the time I won."

Despite the banning, the threats and the intimidation, or perhaps because of it, Peter Louw, the secretary-general of the South African Non-European Golf Association, which along with the South African Golfer's Union and the PGA, had been campaigning on Papwa's behalf, received a letter from Howard R. Taylor, the director of the Carling

World Golf Championship, extending an invitation for Papwa to participate in the tournament that year. "Our action recognises the fact that Mr Sewgolum was unable to complete his qualifying programme through no fault of his own and that in the four qualifying tournaments in which he participated, he has made a very good showing," Taylor's letter stated. Urging for assistance in designing "a qualifying programme for next year which is equitable for all golfers," Taylor specified that Papwa's acceptance was for that year only and would not apply to succeeding years.

In July 1966, the Sewgolum family, including Ma, moved to Mobeni Heights in Chatsworth, a newly developed area consisting of eleven neighbourhoods, and a total of more than twenty thousand sub-economic and low-cost houses for exclusive Indian occupation. Some of their old neighbours in Riverside had pointed out that Chatsworth had been planned as buffer area between white residential areas and Umlazi, an African township. But for Papwa and his brood, it felt good to have a home of their own after living cheek-by-jowl in the shared house they'd moved to when they had to make way for the freeway.

Barely settled into his new home, Papwa left Durban for England along with the five other South African golfers who'd amassed enough points to play in the Carling World of Golf Championship. They were: Harold Henning, Cobie le Grange, Barry Franklin, Trevor Wilkes, Bobby Verwey and Denis Hutchinson. Papwa was feeling confident; the last time he'd played at Royal Birkdale was during the Dunlop Masters of 1964, where he'd failed to qualify due to ill health. "The weather conditions in that part of the world are usually bad at this time of the year. But having been there in 1964, I am sure I will be well acclimatised this time and will not let my supporters down. I will give a good account of myself," he told a journalist from the *POST*.

FM assured the sprinkling who'd gathered to see Papwa depart – Suminthra, wearing a darker-blue cardigan over her turquoise sari, the couple's children and a few close friends and golfing enthusiasts – that he believed Papwa would be amongst the eighty qualifiers for the tournament. "Papwa has been in constant practice in Durban and has been playing top class golf. I feel quite confident."

After Papwa had played in the first qualifying round, FM predicted that Papwa would finish in the top ten if he played with the same consistency. "And that would in itself be a proud record in such world company."

FM's intuition once more proved correct. Papwa placed sixth in the tournament won by Australian professional golfer, Bruce Devlin. But Papwa did not wait to see the outcome of the tournament. After completing his final round on Saturday afternoon, he raced to catch the early evening plane back to South African. Trevor Wilkes, his South African team-mate accompanied him on his return journey. Due to two ties in the earlier placings, Papwa was only paid out for eighth place, earning approximately R2,500 before tax. Though not the main prize, it remained a fortune by Papwa's standards.

Flushed with Papwa's success, FM announced that Papwa would be seeking to play on the American circuit for the 1967 season. "It is clear that Papwa could exist as a professional golfer on the South African white circuit (he was allowed to play in some matches last year) and on the overseas circuits. Purses offered on the non-white circuit do not even cover travelling and hotel expenses at most times," FM explained.

Were Papwa to win each of the Non-European and Rhodesian tournaments, these would not garner him enough funds to sustain himself and his family. It made sense for Papwa to look further afield. This was not an ideal situation for a man who hated travelling, hampered by his inability to read and write. This state of affairs was compounded when he travelled in a foreign country, but a man had to do whatever it took to support his family or he could not call himself a man, Papwa reasoned. That's what Pa had always said.

FORTY-THREE

Two days after Papwa's return from England, the second assassination attempt on Prime Minister, HF Verwoerd succeeded. Verwoerd was stabbed in the House of Assembly in Cape Town by a white parliamentary messenger, Dimitri Tsafendas. It was said that the prime minister had been about to deliver a speech containing important policy announcements. The date was 6 September 1966.

At the time of Verwoerd's death, the National Party was more powerful than ever. In the general election held on 30 March that year, the party had won 126 of the 166 seats – some 58 percent of the votes cast. Moreover, the National Party had attracted substantial support from English voters, with the liberal Progressive Party suffering heavily at the polls. The country had experienced six boom years and from the beginning of the decade to the mid-1960s, the economy had been growing at an average of six percent. Even Verwoerd's detractors in the English press had taken note. On 31 July 1966, the *Rand Daily Mail* had written: "Dr Verwoerd has reached the peak of a remarkable career ... the nation is suffering from a surfeit of prosperity."

Needless to say, the prosperity was an unequal one.

When he was apprehended, Tsafendas claimed that he'd been motivated by the idea that poor white people needed more help. Later, during his trial, it emerged or was speculated that Tsafendas blamed a giant tapeworm inside of him that had compelled him to kill the prime minister. Tsafendas was deemed insane and so escaped the death penalty. He was declared a "state president's patient" – a person who due to mental illness or defect, is not criminally responsible for his acts. Instead of being committed to a mental institute, Tsafendas was sentenced to solitary confinement at the Pretoria Central Prison, where he was held on death row.

Within days of Verwoerd's death, the National Party Caucus gathered to elect a successor. BJ Vorster, the Minister of Justice since 1961, and to whose portfolio Prisons had been added in 1966, was named the new leader of the party and thus Prime Minister of the Republic of South Africa. As Justice Minister, Vorster had been responsible for the government's response to Sharpeville. Measures introduced under his direction included passing security laws that had only been used during times of emergency into permanent legislation. Now government had the right to detain suspects without charge for a period that ranged from 90 days in 1963, to 180 days in 1965. By 1967, suspects could be detained without charge indefinitely with judicial sanction. It is little wonder that interrogation, torture, and even deaths during incarceration increased during this time.

"I hear Vorster's a keen golfer," FM said. "Plays with Gary Player too, they say."

"Perhaps we can write to him and plead my case," Papwa suggested. Perhaps then I can go back to playing in the white tournaments."

"I don't know, Papwa. They seem pretty adamant about their laws," FM said, trying to convey his thoughts as gently as possible.

"But he's not Verwoerd," Papwa argued. "He has to be better than Verwoerd!"

"Yes, Papwa, I agree, he has to better than that Verwoerd," FM said after giving the matter some thought. "Anyone has to be better than Verwoerd, but don't forget what Vorster did as Justice Minister ... some pretty evil stuff."

"But there's no harm in trying." Papwa refused to be deterred.

"No, Papwa, there's no harm in trying." Extracting a pad of paper from the briefcase he carried around with him, FM carefully selected a pen from the same. "Now what are we going to say?"

"Tell him about my wife and children, how I have a family to support."

"Family's good," FM agreed. "We can put in your blind mother too, if you want."

"No, that's okay," Papwa said.

"Tell him that golf is all I know."

"Should I mention that you can't read or write?" FM asked.

"No, I don't think so."

"Agreed, we should stick to business. Like the tournaments you've played in and those you've won. Though I think they know all that," FM said.

"They had a file on me, right?" Papwa said. "I saw it that time at the Security Branch. Do you really think this will change his mind at all?"

"You can't think like that Papwa. Plus, this letter was your idea, right?"

"Right, okay, tell him that I never talk badly about the government. Here or overseas. Tell him how the banning's affected me financially and all."

"That's good," FM said. "It's really about you earning a living by doing what you know best."

"Appeal to him as one sportsman to another, one golfer to another."

"Well they do say that golf is a gentleman's game, right?"

"Right," Papwa agreed.

Vorster's reply to Papwa's letter was there for all to see. Soon after it was sent, the newspapers reported that not only was Papwa's banning order still in force, now white links too were closed to him.

Then in April 1967, Vorster spelled out a new sports policy in respect to the Olympic Games, tennis, cricket and rugby. In terms of this policy, South Africa would adhere to the IOC's strictures regarding national representation by a single team – if "there are any Coloured or Bantu good enough to compete." With regard to tennis, (white) South Africans could compete against black (international) teams at home and abroad. Foreign rugby and cricket teams would not be prescribed to in respect of whom they could select to play in South Africa and this would be left "to the sound judgement of the sports administrators in the country which is invited to South Africa." Vorster's measures were an attempt to preserve existing relations with the white Commonwealth nations. South Africa would not seek to establish cricketing relationships with the West Indies, Pakistan or India and rugby ties with the newly independent Kenya would be allowed to lapse. Vorster particularly hoped to lure the All Black team, who'd declined to play in South Africa in the wake of Verwoerd's Loskop Dam speech, back to the country where rugby was sacrosanct among a large portion of the white community – Afrikaners, certainly, but a significant number of English too followed rugby.

As for mixed sport within the country, there would be no mixed competitions no matter how good the participants may be. "In respect of this principle we are not prepared to compromise, we are not prepared to negotiate, and we are not prepared to make any concessions," Vorster insisted. He might have been talking specifically about Papwa, FM thought, wondering how he was going to break the new developments to his friend. Vorster had made it patently clear when announcing his policy that the tenets of apartheid would remain in force. "If there are persons who remotely think that ... dividing lines will now be broken down, then they are making a very big mistake," Vorster had said at the time.

Resigned, Papwa competed in a number of Non-European tournaments while making plans for his trip to America. In April he travelled to Rhodesia to take part in the circuit there. First up was the Flame Lily tournament, where Papwa finished down the field on a score of 300 to the 281 of winner, Englishman Brian Barnes. In the second event, won by Graham Henning on 282, Papwa tied for fourth with a score of 286. Then in the Dunlop Tournament, Papwa again tied for fourth place on 285 – far adrift from Graham Henning's winning score of 276. However, it was not all bad news as Papwa triumphed in the pro-am event held prior to the latter tournament.

No sooner had Papwa returned to South Africa, than he was packing his bags for India to take part in the relatively new (it was launched in 1964) Indian Open. The organisers had committed to paying all his expenses, bar the cost of his plane ticket. Given his Indian ancestry and the trials and humiliations he'd been subjected to by the South African government, Papwa was wildly popular in India and feted wherever he went.

When Papwa arrived at the Royal Calcutta Golf Club, where the tournament was being staged, the organisers were puzzled by his insistence that a South African flag be flown to reflect his nationality as with the flags of all other foreign contenders hoisted alongside India's tricolour pennant. The omission of the South African flag had been deliberate on the part of the organisers and they, along with many ordinary Indians, could not understand Papwa's loyalty to a flag and a country that had treated and continued to treat him so horrendously.

Several big names in international golf were included in the starting field, such as Australia's Peter Thomson and Guy Wolstenholme and Malcolm Gregson from England. However, it was a little-known Japanese player named Kenji Hosoishi who took the title, beating Malcolm Gregson to second place on play-offs. Papwa finished seventh, tied with Randall Vines and Barry Coxon on 295 – twelve strokes behind the winner.

Papwa's long-awaited US tour materialised after the Indian Open. He had a full itinerary and had been entered into the Dallas Open, the Texas Open, the Houston Open, the New Orleans Open and Oklahoma City Open. The Houston Open was his first event, but during the tournament, Papwa suffered a setback in health and decided to return home, much to his sponsors' chagrin. Upon his return, Papwa was hospitalised with duodenal ulcers.

In July 1967, Papwa travelled to England to compete in the British Open at Royal Liverpool Golf Club, Hoylake. He progressed through the qualifying stages, but did not make it into the final rounds. He came second in the Dutch Open, losing to English golfer Peter Townsend by a single shot, and fifth in the French Open, won by England's Bernard Hunt. Papwa's next international trip that year was to Canada, where he competed in the Carling World Open in Toronto. Here he failed to shine and did not make the cut with a first two rounds total of 152.

Shortly after his return from Canada, Papwa received a letter from the Royal Calcutta Golf Club, offering him the job as the club's professional. If he were to accept, he'd be the first Indian in the position since the club was first founded in 1829 to cater for the officers and merchants in the British Raj. FM came to discuss the matter with Papwa and Suminthra.

"It's a lot of money," FM pointed out the generous salary, multiple times more than Papwa could expect to make in South Africa. "You'll have your own house."

"We have a house here," Suminthra argued, "a good house."

"Royal Calcutta is a lovely golf course. The people were very kind to me there, *Kanna*," Papwa offered. "There is no such thing as 'European' or 'Non-European' in India."

"What about caste system? What about North and South?"

"It is here too," Papwa said.

"No, here there is rich and poor, black and white or white and Indian, what have you. But I was born here, husband. Our children were born here. Can you leave it all behind? Ma is old . . ."

The offer was rejected and the family remained where they were. Despite the government's ruling, FM believed that they'd relent sooner or later. The world was not happily accepting South Africa's idea of separate sports for separate races. Change would surely come sooner rather than later. Papwa told himself that he'd made the right decision and that he was happy with it.

FORTY-FOUR

Papwa was right about one thing, the world was in no great rush to accept Vorster's new sports policy – not the entire world at least. In 1966, the Organisation of African Unity, a powerful grouping aimed at fostering goals of freedom and dignity for African nations, had set up a Permanent Committee of African Sport. At its inaugural meeting, the committee passed a resolution to force South Africa's expulsion from the Olympic movement and other international sporting federations if South Africa failed to comply with IOC rules of non-racism.

South Africa might have been banned from the last Olympic Games in Tokyo, but after Vorster's policy announcement and further concessions by the South African National Olympic Committee, the IOC voted 38 to 27 in favour of inviting South Africa to the 1968 Olympic Games in Mexico City. Demonstrating the power of working together, in 1968, Algeria and Ethiopia along with some fifty countries and black members of the American team announced their intent to withdraw from the Mexico City Games in protest of South Africa's inclusion. The IOC held a new vote, the outcome of which was an overwhelming decision to retract South Africa's invitation.

Countries with longstanding ties to South Africa maintained their existing sporting and other relations with the apartheid state, tacitly agreeing to adhere to the country's sporting policy when touring South Africa. England was one such country. Matters came to a head however, when a Coloured batsman was included in the team to tour South Africa during 196869. The name of the batsman was Basil D'Oliviera, the same cricketer from Cape Town who'd left South Africa for Britain in

1960 after being denied a place on the Springbok team to tour England. D'Oliviera, or Dolly, as he was known to his fans, had progressed from playing in the minor league to playing senior county cricket and by the mid-1960s, was a strong contender to be included in the England team invited to play in South Africa.

At first, D'Oliviera's selection had been uncertain. He'd received British citizenship and in May 1966, was selected to play for England. On debut, D'Oliviera enjoyed a successful series against the West Indies, followed by another good series against India and Pakistan in 1967. He enjoyed a less stellar performance during the 1967-68 tour of the West Indies, but with the South African tour imminent, Dolly regrouped. He hit an impressive 87 in the first test of the of 1968 summer series against Australia. This match was the last in which D'Oliviera participated during The Ashes, a series of five tests between England and Australia, until the final test where he came on as a late substitution.

Knowing that his selection rode on his performance, Dolly played superbly – scoring 158, which helped England win the match and draw the series. In so doing, he topped the Test averages for the season. Selection for the South African tour should have been a *fait accompli*, but the Marylebone Cricket Club (MCC), the body responsible for choosing the English team, was very aware of Vorster's policy and presumably did not want to sour relations between the two countries. Basil D'Oliviera was omitted from the side due to tour South Africa.

A public outcry followed the contentious selection process. The MCC was castigated by Britain's labour government and by the media for attempting to appease the apartheid government. Noted anti-apartheid campaigner John Arlott of the *Guardian* newspaper wrote that the MCC had "never made a sadder, more dramatic or more potentially damaging selection." D'Oliviera, who remained calm and dignified throughout, received thousands of letters of support. It was clear that public opinion in Britain and the rest of the developed world had turned against the racist policies of the South African government and this incident was seen as a turning point in the tolerance for segregated sport, in South Africa and abroad. Consequently, when one of the originally selected players was injured and could not play, D'Oliviera was chosen as his replacement.

Vorster reacted to D'Oliviera's selection in the following manner:

"We are not prepared to accept a team thrust upon us by people whose interests are not the game, but to gain certain political objectives which they do not even attempt to hide. The team as constituted now is not the team of [England] but the team of the Anti-Apartheid Movement ..."

It is widely held that Vorster's stance on D'Oliviera was an attempt to placate the right-wing *verkrampte* (narrow) element within the National Party that rejected any deviation from the strict tenets of racial segregation as set out by Verwoerd in his time. Yet days after Vorster's incendiary announcement, newspapers around the world reported that Vorster himself had approved the inclusion of Maori players in the New Zealand All Black team due to tour South Africa in 1970. Citing the fact that Maoris had been included in previous All Black teams to play in South Africa, Vorster confirmed: "Similarly, there will again be players of this nature in the 1970 touring side. We will receive these players as in the past and give them our traditional welcome as in the past."

Why different rules for different nations? Pundits believed that Vorster was able to make a clear distinction between Maori players who were not born in South Africa, and D'Oliviera who was – satisfying his own views on foreign versus domestic players. The fact that D'Oliviera had since achieved British citizenship, made no difference in Vorster's mind; D'Oliviera was of mixed race and therefore unacceptable, lest other black South Africans think that they too could compete against white South Africans.

In the aftermath of the D'Oliviera affair, the Anti-Apartheid Movement, already active in the United Kingdom was thus able to speak with a louder voice when calling for the cancellation and cessation of tours involving a number of codes, not only cricket, and were able to mobilise greater public support demonstrations when these tours went ahead. Just as Papwa had put a human face to the realities of petty apartheid when he was forced to accept his prize in the rain, the affable and urbane D'Oliviera epitomised the lengths to which the South African government would go to achieve the collusion of foreign teams, and by extension nations, in perpetuating the prejudices that so many South Africans took for granted.

On 2 December 1968, the General Assembly of the United Nations called upon all its member states to suspend cultural, sporting, educational and other ties with the apartheid government and with South African organisations that practised apartheid. The UN Special Committee against Apartheid, which had met for the first time in 1963, also began to actively spread the message to boycott apartheid sport around the world.

These political changes had not impacted Papwa's life at all. Between 1968 and 1969, he restricted himself to playing in Non-European tournaments in South Africa and certain neighbouring countries. In 1968 he won the SA Non-European Open with a record 285 and set a course record of 69 when he won the Spa open in Swaziland. In April that year, he'd made the trip up north to play in the Rhodesian circuit where his fortunes were mixed. His third place tie in the Flame Lily Tournament and joint ninth in the Dunlop Masters were his greatest finishes during the trip this time. Papwa returned to Swaziland in July the following year. He participated in sponsored tournament in Mbabane played over 54 holes, carding 218 for the win to runner up Simon "Cox" Hlapo's 223.

By November 1969, FM considered that the wind had died down sufficiently to submit an application for Papwa to re-enter the white circuit. He began by entering Papwa into the white South African Open.

"I have a good feeling about this, brother, trust me," he winked. As much as Papwa wanted to, he could no longer trust FM's feelings. He tried to put on a brave face for Suminthra and the children, but he knew enough about government now to know how inflexible they were. The worldwide condemnation against apartheid would have no effect. Nor would they make concessions for Papwa, even if it meant that Gary Player would receive a better reception overseas. Gary didn't care – he was still allowed to do what he loved best. While he, Papwa, was condemned to spending his days and his talent on the non-European circuit, limited though it may be, and taking the few opportunities that came his way to try his hand further afield. What did it matter that he continued to dominate in the non-European tournaments? A golfer is only as good as his opponent. And while there were a few extremely good players on the non-white circuit, they too were curtailed in that they were forced to compete against the same pool of players over and over again.

So when the South African Golfers' Union informed FM that they could not accept Papwa's application unless he had prior government clearance, Papwa wasn't surprised. Disappointed yes, but not surprised. Reiterating government's stance, Minister of Planning, Carel de Wet, said that there would be no mixed sport regardless of the proficiency of those involved.

Perhaps this acceptance of government's decision and not getting his hopes up too high in the first place was because he was becoming wiser, Papwa thought. Perhaps it meant that he was preparing to let go of his dreams. A tiny, hidden part of him knew that no matter how he tried to paint it, for a while, he had once again allowed himself to become buffeted by seductive stratagems.

FORTY-FIVE

"Gary's disappointed that they're not letting you play," FM announced, bearing a rolled up newspaper under his arm. "Says they're putting their heads in a noose and that you meet the minimum requirements to play."

"But Gary won't do anything to convince government to let me play?" Papwa asked.

"No, brother, I'm afraid not, even though everyone knows he has Vorster's ear."

"Plays golf with Vorster too. I know," Papwa said, not sure where he was going with that line of thought.

"Funny thing is, they are putting their heads in a noose," FM mused aloud. "You must know what the press is saying about you –"

"No," Papwa answered. I try to avoid hearing what the press has to say about me. "Sometimes even I am tired of being 'poor Papwa'."

"But people are on your side, Papwa. You have to believe that. Morris Zimmerman, he was a Springbok rugby player you know, says that the average South African, I suppose he means white South African, is ashamed that the government banned you," FM said.

"What does it matter if people are on my side?" Papwa hated the petulance to his voice. "They still won't let me play!"

FM sighed. He had further bad news to break. "Actually, it is Gary I want to talk to you about. You know how the press picked up on the story about raising money for you to go overseas?"

"Yes, what does Gary have to do with it?"

"Well Gary says that the wealthy Indians of Natal are the ones who should be responsible for raising the money to send you overseas."

Papwa took a deep breath. He felt light-headed with rage. FM's oft-repeated phrase of keeping one's friends close teased him. He would no longer pretend that the passing acquaintance with Gary was anything more. Gary's manager hadn't responded to FM's letter either.

"To think that Gary sponsors a tournament for black players."

"Which you won," FM reminded him.

"Yes. Not like the prize money was anything like what I've had made in the white tournaments, but I suppose I have to grateful for every little bit. The bonus helped too," Papwa said, referring to the R250 he'd received from Gary's own pocket in recognition of his record-breaking score of five under par in addition to the R270 for first place. "What else did he say?"

"Nothing, just more of the same, but some good has come out of this at least. The South African Indian Council has come out in your defence. Listen to what the chairman had to say: 'When a European does well, he is always acclaimed by everybody in the country, including the Indians. Why should it be different for Papwa?' He also says that while he's sure that the Indian community can help raise the funds to send you overseas, there's no sense in calling you a South African golfer if others don't get involved."

"It's hard to consider myself a South African golfer," Papwa said softly. This insight, entertained only in his subconscious mind and unvoiced for so long, felt good to say aloud.

"That's not all," FM continued, choosing to ignore what Papwa said. "There's a Mr Naidoo, CK Naidoo, who's offered to set up a committee to handle the money donated and make all the arrangements for you. He says they want to see to all your needs so you can practise without any worries before you go overseas. That's good news, right?

"Yes, FM, that is good news." Papwa wondered why it did not feel so.

A few days later, Papwa understood why he had had such a deep sense of foreboding when he'd received the news of the Indian community's support. He'd come to FM's office to sort out the paperwork for the new fund.

"Ah, Papwa, there's something I must tell you." FM looked embarrassed. "It's about Louis, you see."

"What did Louis do now?" Louis had risen through the ranks of black golf administration and was now at the top of the pole as president of the South African Non-European Golf Association.

"He spoke to the press about you yesterday. I think it's best if I read what he said. It's in all the newspapers ... 'Papwa is not the only non-white golfer struggling in South Africa and should stop relying on public sympathy to raise money', is what Louis said."

Papwa's face paled and then flushed. He could not look at FM though the man was only reading what his former manager had said.

"It gets worse," FM said. Squinting at the cramped newsprint, he continued: "'Wealthy Indians have dug deeply in their pockets on three occasions to send Papwa overseas and have not got a thing back for it. It is about time he stopped complaining and did a day's work himself.'"

"But no one hoped to get anything out of my playing," Papwa said. "It's not like there was ever enough prize money to share."

"I know, brother, I know. Louis is resentful that the media is paying all this attention to one player – you – when there are other, younger players emerging. You know he wants to send those six youngsters to play in Britain and Europe in June. The association is already busy raising funds. If I remember correctly, Louis said that the plan was to carry on the tradition of non-white golfers taking part in international golf, 'following the breakthrough' you made."

"Would he even have known about sending players to Europe if it wasn't for Mr Wulff?" Papwa asked, for once failing to use the honorific he usually employed. "What have I ever done to Louis?" he added, looking at FM searchingly, as if the other man had all the answers.

FM glanced at the open newspaper spread out on his desk. Should he tell Papwa the rest, he wondered. How could he? Louis had gone on to say that Papwa's recent scores were not good enough when compared to international standards. Louis had not considered the restrictions placed on Papwa. Nor had he factored in the expense of international travel, which meant that the 1967 trips were the last Papwa had taken to date, only being able to afford to play in tournaments in South Africa and neighbouring countries. And Louis had not acknowledged Papwa's win of the Non-European Natal Open earlier that month with a score of nine under par, nor his subsequent victory at the Non-European South African Open – Papwa's eighth to date – in which he'd not only finished several strokes under par, but had also shot a round that equalled the course record. No, FM wouldn't mention that part of Louis's tirade to Papwa. Nor would he mention the part that he assumed was directed at him as Papwa's manager: that applying for permission to compete on the white circuit was a waste of time given the imminent elections.

FM smiled and turned his full attention on Papwa. "Forget about Louis, it's nothing but sour grapes, that's all. If we respond, we'll only be giving him the attention he craves. In this instance I think it's best to let lying dogs sleep."

But FM responded anyway, noting that Papwa had not asked for assistance. He added that he found Louis's comments shocking in that they came at the same time that Papwa was being denied a chance to earn a better living by playing on the white South African circuit. Although wealthy Indians had helped send Papwa overseas in the past without seeing a reward, FM implied that Louis himself had gloried in the reflection of Papwa's fame.

FM was not the only one to rush to Papwa's defence. Mr Naidoo, his new benefactor and fundraiser, told reporters: "The appeal started spontaneously after Gary Player suggested Natal's wealthy Indians should dip into their pockets to send Papwa overseas. I started the appeal on my own and nothing is going to stop me in achieving the object, even if I have to dig a bit deeper into my own pocket." Disagreeing with Louis's views on Papwa's fitness to play overseas and implied laziness, he said of Papwa: "He is a professional golfer. He can't work and play golf at the same time, and he shouldn't have to. His recent performances show that he is still good enough to play overseas."

FORTY-SIX

In May, several newspapers reported that Papwa had left for Europe where he planned to participate in a dozen or so European tournaments, including the German and Dutch Opens and the British Open to be played at St. Andrews, the home of golf. Papwa had not been too well and Suminthra was worried about him. As usual for his European tour, the British Open was one of the first events in which Papwa played. Joining him this time, were a number of black South African players, of whom only two made it through the qualifying stages – Papwa and Lawrence Buthelezi. Papwa had known Lawrence since his caddying days when Lawrence was the caddie master at Howick Golf Club in the Natal Midlands.

Papwa's promising form did not last. He shot 72-78 in the next two rounds and missed the cut by one stroke – this after scoring a record-breaking 64 during the qualifying rounds. Golfing friends on the tour would later claim that Papwa was feeling lonely and depressed, though he'd tried to hide it with his usual affability and charm. He was drinking more too, they said.

All Suminthra knew was that by the time he returned Papwa was not his usual self. Now Papwa was late to come home. He'd left the house early that morning and had taken nothing with him: no golf bag, no fishing pole, though she hadn't seen him leave. She'd been busy out back and couldn't tell whether he'd left alone or whether one of his friends had come to fetch him. Papwa was not one to stay out late without a word for her or one of the children. He knew she worried.

Suminthra knew that Papwa was disappointed. After days of

silences and moods, he'd begun to open up to her again, telling her about his trip to Europe. To think all those places her husband had travelled to, and she who'd never set a foot on an aeroplane. Before England, he'd gone to Rhodesia as usual. The children had insisted he tell them all about his trip. She remembered Papwa's face when Rajen, now seven years old and in school, had asked his father where the trophies were. Papwa's face had seemed to collapse into itself, like a balloon slowly leaking air as he'd informed the boy that this time Pa did not have a trophy to bring home. He'd finished eighteenth in the Dunlop Masters, fifteenth in the Bush Babes and seventh in the Flame Lily.

After the British Open where he'd done so well last time, but so poorly this year, Papwa had played in the Rest of the World against Britain, he'd explained to the children. In this tournament, he'd lost out to Brian Barnes by one shot. So close, Suminthra knew, and sometimes she thought that must be the biggest disappointment: to lose by so few points. In Europe Papwa had had to cut his trip short because of that old story: not enough money. FM had run around trying to raise funds. He'd even appealed to the Western Province Coloured Golf Union but they said they could not help, what with their new golf course costing so much money and all, FM had explained.

And if Papwa did not have enough to worry about, government kept on turning his applications down. Every time there was a new development in government, FM would excitedly come over to tell Papwa about it and how he was sure that this time they would not refuse him a permit to play. Suminthra was fond of FM and knew he meant well, not like others she might name, but sometimes she thought he raised Papwa's hopes for nothing. Like when people overseas started protesting against Gary, showing up at his games and causing a hullabaloo, FM had said he was certain that government would allow Papwa to play if it meant that Gary would get a better reception when he travelled. Or when the white South African team was banned from that tennis match and soon afterwards when that Vorster man said he was willing to meet the demands for mixed sport. The day after that, Suminthra remembered, the United Nations, the organisation that FM held so highly, called yet again for a boycott of apartheid sport and expressed support for the idea to exclude South Africa from the

Munich Olympics and the international sporting organisation itself. And when it happened, when South Africa was finally ejected from the International Olympic Committee later that year, FM had again come with his talk and his dreams of a South Africa where her Papwa could compete in whichever tournaments he desired.

It had been the same story when those countries in Africa threatened to walk out of the Commonwealth Games in Scotland if the South African cricket tour of Britain went ahead. According to FM, the British government itself had placed pressure on the English Cricket Council to cancel the all-white cricket tour, and when it happened, Papwa had once more held his breath. There'd be other times too, but Suminthra could not remember it all. Some big to do about rugby protests in Britain and Ireland and Wales, called Stop the Seventy tour or something like that. Nothing had come of any of it as far as Papwa's golfing career was concerned.

A neighbour's dog barked and Suminthra inched the curtain away from the wall to peer through the window. It was late; the night had darkened as it always did just before it turned light. The children would be up soon and she'd need to feed them and help the younger ones get ready for school. It would not do to be tired. Resigned, she gave up waiting and went to bed.

Suminthra was asleep when she heard the noise. The neighbour's dog had picked up its barking again, but the noise was closer. Frightened – there'd been a few burglaries in Chatsworth recently – Suminthra belted a thick cardigan over her nightgown. Ma was asleep and could sleep through any commotion. If there was someone out there, she'd have to investigate. Just to be safe, she snatched the bush-knife from under the bed where Papwa kept it.

The back door shook under a constant thudding. The dog's barking was louder, more frantic. Suminthra hoped the neighbours were awake and would hear her shouting if she had to.

"Who's there? What do you want?" Suminthra wished her voice did not sound so timid. Summoning her courage, she said with more vigour: "I have a knife, my husband's home and will sort you out!"

Someone or something bashed against the door. Suminthra thought she heard laughter, soft, almost indistinguishable as such. Her grip tightened on the handle of the long knife. Then she made out words.

"Suminthra, it's me my darling, your husband, open up my love!" It was Papwa's voice, but Suminthra was not used to hearing such endearments from him. Why had he come around the back? Where was his key? She opened the door quickly; it would not do for the children to wake and see their father like this. Papwa was drunk, he smelled like smoke and some sort of alcohol that smelled stronger than his usual cane.

Papwa lurched inside, laughing. "What are you doing with my bush-knife? You want to kill me?"

Her grip slackened, but she continued to hold the knife. Before she could release it, Papwa had grabbed it out of her hand, running callused fingers along the dulled blade. She followed him to their bedroom and closed the door.

Before she had time to react, Papwa had taken the knife to his golf bag propped against a corner of their room. She watched horrified as he began to slash ineffectually at the bag's thick fabric.

"What are you doing?" Suminthra demanded, surprising herself with the power in her voice.

Frustrated at his lack of success with the bag, which was merely gouged and still standing, Papwa threw the bag on their bed. Clubs and balls rolled out with a clamorous clatter made even louder in the slumbering silence of the household. She hoped that Ma and the children had not been woken by the disturbance.

Papwa began to hack at the clubs. "I might as well break these, for all the good they do me," he shouted.

"Papwa, give me the knife. *Kanna*, you're not yourself," Suminthra tried to reason with him. If she attempted to take the knife away from him, someone could get hurt.

But Papwa wasn't listening. Somehow, he succeeded in hacking the head off one of the clubs. He laughed, demented laughter, determined laughter. It was the kind of laughter that came before one broke down and cried.

"Papwa, the knife. Please, you're scaring me! Look at your hands!"

Papwa's hands were torn and bleeding. Mute now, he dropped the knife on the bed with the golfing gear. Then the tears came.

"Without golf, I am nothing. I am not a man," he said between sobs.

"No *Kanna*, you are a man, my man," she said, taking a wounded hand within her own.

"But I am not you see –" His eyes searched hers, held them.

Suminthra did not know what to say.

"Tell me Papwa; why do you want to play golf so badly?' she asked eventually. Theirs was not a marriage where they discussed such things, but she thought, maybe if she understood why playing was so important to him, she could support him better, perhaps even offer her husband some of her wisdom if he cared to listen.

"It's what I know," Papwa said hesitantly.

Suminthra waited for him to continue, knowing that he'd only talk once he was ready.

"How else am I to support our family?"

"There are other things you can do, Papwa. Maybe you can ask Mr Wulff for your job back; maybe even go back to Beachwood ..."

She watched as a range of emotions played across Papwa's face. His jowls quivered in agitation. When had his face begun to bloat so? His belly too, was flabby, this husband of hers who'd always been so vain about his fitness and his physique. He'd taken such painstaking care of himself in the days when he played regularly. "My practice," he'd joked and she'd not minded that the game he loved took him so often from her and their family. He was never without a cough or a cold these days. She blamed the cigarettes for that, but she knew that Papwa would not smoke so much if he was not stressed. She hated the government for what it was doing to him. Sometimes she blamed golf itself, but she would never say so.

She'd known about the golf when she married him. But then she was marrying a caddie boy. A poor caddie boy, and she'd been satisfied to be doing so. Would she have been as satisfied had she known of the fervour he felt for golf, guessed at the extent of his ambition? No, she could not blame Papwa. He'd been happy to merely play. Other people had filled his head with those dreams that now thwarted were breaking his heart and destroying his health.

"You don't understand *Kanna*," Papwa said, grabbing her hands, both now covered with his blood and stared straight into her eyes as if willing her to see what he saw. "When I'm on the golf course, playing of the golf course, I'm somebody. Somebody people want to know. Now

I'm nobody, I'm done; used up, just like my father was used up and his father before him!"

"Don't say that Papwa! You are somebody. You are my husband and my children's father, we are all so very proud of you. You are a good, good man."

"I have lost my heart, *Kanna*. I have nothing, Suminthra; you and the children deserve more. Maybe it would be better if I was dead."

"Don't say that, my love. Don't talk like that. Tomorrow will be better, you'll see. Go sleep now, my love. You'll feel better in the morning."

FORTY-SEVEN

Finally, in 1971, the changes that FM had predicted for so long began to come. It was Gopaul of all people who came to break the news to Papwa. Raj had left for overseas some years now; disgusted by the indignities of the Group Areas Act that saw his family lose the home and business they'd built up over generations, he'd taken his wife and children to England to start life anew. Jayendra had "gone underground," as Gopaul euphemistically called it, while his family remained behind in Durban. Fishy too had been moved to Chatsworth, but to an area some distance from Papwa's home in Mobeni Heights.

"So Vorster has a new sport policy now," Gopaul said without preamble. "He talks about multiracial sport and multinational sport. See, multiracial sport is still not allowed, that's where, say, a white South African team can't play against a black South African team, same as before, but then he also has this thing called multinational sport. Whites and blacks and *chār-ous* like us or what have you, can compete against each other in separate teams, or in an individual capacity like with golf, but only on an international level. So as long as you don't compete against whites on club, provincial or national level, they'll allow you to play in those tournaments they call multinational."

Nonplussed, Papwa stared at his friend. "So I can play on the white circuit again? I'm not banned anymore?" Papwa asked by rote rather than any sense of optimism. He was no longer by nature a hopeful man. He had days he conceded, when he was able to find joy on the few golf courses that still allowed him, like Circle Country Club in Pinetown, which allowed black people to play on their course on

Thursday afternoons, in much the same way other white clubs opened their courses to their caddies for a few hours every Monday morning. Playing with his friends for those few hours a week, Papwa felt almost happy. With the jewel-blue sky above him, the verdant green grass and the warmth of the sun on his neck, Papwa would bellow his favourite song, Louis Armstrong's *What a Wonderful World* at full strength until his partners were forced to join in. People still watched when he played, and Papwa was always willing to offer advice and tips to friends and strangers alike. Often he'd bet on the rounds, and like his caddying days, others would bet on him too, sharing in his exhilaration when he won. A bet on Papwa was a sure thing, so they bet on scores – by how many strokes Papwa would claim a round – or whether he would make certain shots. It was not the same as before, not like the days when he was playing on the white circuit, or travelling overseas regularly, but it was a life, a golfing life of sorts.

"No, it doesn't mean you're not banned anymore; nor does it mean that you suddenly have the freedom to play in all the tournaments of the white circuit unless they designate them all as multinationals and I'm not sure they will. But there will be a few other tournaments, which they'll call multinational tournaments, and those you can play in."

"What are the tournaments, do you know?" Papwa asked.

"It hasn't been decided yet as far as I know," Gopaul answered, "but I believe that the Golfer's Union and the PGA are going to ask the Minister of Sport to make all the events on the professional and amateur circuits multinationals."

"That's good," Papwa said hesitantly. "It will be good for the younger golfers, I think. My time is past. Sometimes I think my best golfing days are behind me."

"Don't say such a thing, *bru*. This year you're going to Australia and New Zealand. You wouldn't be invited if people didn't believe you still had it in you to win. Your sponsors, your supporters, the organisers –"

"I'm tired," Papwa began, but Gopaul did not want to hear.

"You are a good player, Papwa; the best I've ever seen play, or had the privilege to play against. You must believe in yourself!"

Papwa laughed inwardly, thinking of all those thwarted times when he had believed in himself; had possessed the confidence to take on the world's best. What had happened to his bravado? When he'd been younger, some people had thought his talent supernatural. "Bewitched," they'd said. Others said that it was his calm mind-set that had made him invincible. Papwa didn't know what to believe. There were tremors in his hands these days and his lungs were not that good either. No one wanted to believe that he was infallible; not when he was a symbol of what an Indian man could accomplish on the golf course.

He was about to tell Gopaul about his fears, tell him that he was not a young man anymore, but noting how his old friend looked at him, he knew that to Gopaul, he would always be Beachwood's undefeated caddie champion, three-time winner of the Dutch Open and the man who'd beaten Gary Player when he'd been playing at his best.

Sensing Papwa's sombre mood, Gopaul sobered too. "You know this is just window-dressing, don't you? Apartheid sport is virtually isolated. You know that last year Sally Little was turned away from the Women's Amateur Championship in Britain and this year Sweden wouldn't accept Bobby Cole's entry into the Volvo Open? And people have the nerve to talk about apartheid in reverse!"

Months later, Papwa travelled to Australia and New Zealand where he failed to impress. Upon his return to South Africa, he played in the South African Non-European Championships held at the Benoni Country Club in the Transvaal. Vincent Tshabala entered the third round with a four-shot lead over Papwa, but Papwa fought back until the final hole of the last round where he missed a relatively easy putt. Vincent holed the shot and in so doing, claimed the title that Papwa had dominated for so long by a one-stroke margin.

Papwa had missed the first of the "Open International Tournaments" – the PGA Championship and was conflicted about entering the remaining two: the South African Open and the General Motors Classic. He sought Gopaul out to discuss his trepidation. Gopaul believed that Papwa was concerned about the political implications. There'd already been calls for black players to boycott these events which did not offer true equality and were but mere concessions when compared to the enormity of apartheid sport. Papwa's fears were more elemental: that his playing was not good enough, but again he could not voice them as articulately as he'd hoped to.

"If Raj was here, he'd tell you not to play," Gopaul said. "But I won't. I know how much your golf means to you."

"If I win, the prize money would make a big difference to my family," Papwa agreed.

With this in mind, Papwa entered the South African Open and the General Motors Classic and both entries were accepted. The General Motors Classic was held at Port Elizabeth's Wedgwood Park Country Club. Papwa and the other newly admitted players could eat and socialise in the clubhouse, but were not allowed to use the same toilets as the white players and spectators. In this, his first tournament on the white circuit in six years, Papwa missed the cut in a stunning reversal of the prowess he'd displayed when he'd last appeared on the circuit. Four non-white players qualified for the final rounds of the GM Classic: Vincent Tshabalala, Ismail Chowglay, Bobby Anooplall and Richard Mogoerane, with Ismail finishing best on 301. It was in many ways a poignant time for Papwa, a dose of bitter with the sweet.

"Look at all the golfers, black and white, mixing freely. It's marvellous to be treated as a golfer for a change and not some sort of freak," Papwa told sportswriter Norman Canale after dropping out of the tournament.

"I'm very happy for the young non-whites who have their golf careers ahead of them. But it's come too late for me. I'm 43 now. There's no way for me to go but down in this tough game of nerves. I'm just about all washed up."

In September 1975, Piet Koornhof, the Minister of Sport in Vorster's cabinet, announced that the South African professional golfing tour would in future be open to all races. Golf was the first sport chosen for this complete breakthrough, a condition which many commentators ascribed to the fact that both Koornhof and Vorster were themselves keen golfers. Trumpeting the decision, Ted Partridge, the editor of *SA Golf* wrote: "By removing all barriers of race and making merit the strict yardstick by which a man's qualification is measured, golf has become the first major sport to win the battle of politics." The decision was a lucrative one; the changes had already seen South Africa hosting the World Cup of Golf and the South African PGA Tournament boasted new sponsorship highs.

Yet as Papwa had predicted four years earlier, these changes were indeed too late for him. He competed in as many of the former whites-only tournaments as he was able to, but though he'd make the cut, he'd routinely finish out of the top ten.

FORTY-EIGHT

Suminthra was worried. For days Papwa had not been himself. He was slimming, she noticed, first in the bagginess of his trousers and the looseness of his shirts, but it was there in the cast of his face too, reminding her of the lean caddie she had married. It was not hard to picture him as he'd looked on the day of their wedding. Wearing that bright orange suit and garlanded in marigolds, his face wreathed in a smile. He was always smiling then. "A happy chappy," her father had described her future groom all those years ago.

She'd had such modest hopes then, Suminthra thought. Then again, her hopes had always been modest: to marry a good man, to raise healthy children, to live in peace. Papwa and his big dreams had changed that, and for a while she too had dared to dream the impossible. Still, she had few complaints. Her Papwa was a gentleman. He'd never raised his voice to her or the children; never displayed any anger. The only time she'd ever seen him lose control was that time he'd taken the bush-knife to his clubs, and then it had been the drink's fault, not his. Even then, his rage had been directed inward, at the clubs that were as much part of him as his hands were. Papwa was not a man to lash out at others. Sometimes Suminthra thought it would be better if he was that kind of man, healthier to let some of the frustration out than keep it bottled so-so deep inside him.

But no, her husband was not a bitter man. She herself was always careful to hide her own feelings of bitterness from him, to tamp down her disappointments. Unlike Papwa, she was not afraid to apportion blame were blame was due. Call it a wife's prerogative.

When Papwa was playing well, he'd made good money. They'd led a comfortable life then. Look how the newspapers used to write about him then and the crowds! She could remember the people that gathered to meet him at the airport the first time he came back from overseas. Oh, how their lives had changed after that: the gifts, the money, the photographs in the newspapers. Funny, how that day had been the only time she'd been part of the celebrations around him. Would things have been different if she were the kind of woman to follow her man around a golf course? No, of course not! Who'd have looked after the children; stayed home with Ma?

She grimaced at the thought of her late mother-in-law. Ma had passed four years ago at a time when Papwa had been at his lowest ebb. Ma hadn't lived to see him being given his chance to play and make something of his talents once more – even if he wasn't winning as many competitions as in the old days, he still won. Non-European tournaments mainly, yes, but a win was a win after all – even if it was by one stroke only – as FM always reminded her husband.

Yes, Papwa was slimming now, becoming healthy again though he did not play as much golf as he had in the past, preferring to spend the day fishing at the nearby Umlazi River or travelling all the way to Durban North where he'd fished with his father as a boy.

Suminthra thought of all the changes that had come about in the past few years. FM had been so excited whenever government made a new announcement regarding its sporting policy. She knew that golf was not the only sport to be affected by the changes, but it was golf that Papwa was interested in, so she'd smiled with him last year when she heard what FM said: that non-white golfers would be able to play in the South African amateur tournament, under-23 and all provincial open championships from now on, and that white clubs and non-white clubs could play against each other in friendly matches and enter the same league.

"That is with government approval and all," FM had stressed, "but still subject to its permission."

Suminthra recalled thinking how good it would be if government was serious about the changes and Papwa could play in all those competitions. If that was the case, he would not have to travel abroad to play, for she knew how lonely he felt in a foreign country, away from his family for long stretches at a time. His last overseas trip had been two years ago, but Papwa had been saddened that he had not done too well then. It was his health, Suminthra knew, but if Papwa could play in all the big tournaments at home, everything would be better. And FM had agreed.

Funny how different Papwa's two managers were, Suminthra thought. FM was like a brother to her and Papwa; their children regarded the man as an uncle. And Louis? Well, Louis was Louis as Papwa liked to say. A few years ago, a new organisation had been formed to cater for the needs of the swelling numbers of non-white golfers – the South African Professional Players' Association, which aimed at addressing administrative issues and the problem of factions. As chairman of the Non-European Golf Association, Louis had been instrumental in setting up this new body. Papwa however, had a problem with one of the new organisation's dictates: in order to be considered for inclusion in the tournaments under its control, players had to first join the association.

"I refuse to be a political football," Papwa complained to whoever would listen. "I'm getting tired of non-white golf officials who put themselves above the game." In a further show of protest, Papwa chose to boycott a tournament in Houghton, while Daddy Naidoo, one of Papwa's young friends, along with sixteen other golfers refused to show for another tournament in which they'd already entered. Needless to say, Papwa also refused to join the South African Professional Players' Association as it was not affiliated to the white PGA and as such, ran the risk of being barred from the multinational tournaments. However, at the association's annual meeting, Papwa who'd since changed his mind about playing in the Houghton tournament with its purse of R1500, was given the option of paying a R50 fine, or being banned from the tournament. Papwa had no choice but to pay, but it rankled. And he blamed one man for the insistence that he pay the fine on the morning of the meeting. He saw one man's influence behind such punishment. Still, he counted himself lucky as eight golfers were given a two-year suspension for taking part in multinational events. Papwa went on to win several of the tournaments under the association's banner, but Suminthra knew that Papwa had found his treatment at the meeting humiliating. Suminthra did not know what Louis had against her husband. Perhaps she did not want to know, she reckoned.

Putting such heavy thoughts aside, Suminthra got out of bed. Papwa could lie in, she decided. She had always been rather protective over her morning solitude before Papwa and the children rose. She could do her devotions in private and prepare the family's breakfast in peace.

Staring out the kitchen window as she shaped the home-made bread into rounds, Suminthra sensed that it would be a lovely day. The weather was calm, the sun signalling its intent with orange-yellow streaks on the far side of the sky. Though Chatsworth was not as noisy as Riverside had been, Suminthra could make out the early dawn sounds: someone's rooster crowing in a nearby yard, the *adhan* in the distance waking the Muslim faithful for their first prayers of the day, the slow tick of a motor as a neighbour left for work or arrived home from the night shift. The rolling complete, she filled a pot for tea, adjusted her sari and checked her *sindhur*, the mark of a married woman, in the window's reflective surface.

It was nearly seven, but she decided to let the children sleep late. It was school holidays and they worked so hard the rest of the year. She began frying the home-made bread, and heated the pot containing the gravy from last night's fish curry. One by one her children trickled into the room, roused by the pungent smell of the masala and curry leaves she added to the pot.

The children were hungry. "Ma, when we can eat, Ma?" Dinesh, the youngest asked.

"Go wake your Pa, we can't start without him." When Papwa was home, they ate all meals together as a family. Ma used to say that that's the way it had been when her late husband had been alive, and so the younger family had kept the tradition.

"I can't wake my Pa, Ma!" Dinesh shouted from the bedroom.

Dishing the food onto plates, Suminthra gestured to Rajen. "See if you can wake your Pa, please boy."

"Ma!" Rajen's scream chilled Suminthra to her marrow, causing her to drop the spoon in the pot. Warm gravy spattered over her hands, burning like hot ghee, but she did not register the pain.

Steadily, she walked to the bedroom. Rajen was keening on the floor next to the bed where his father lay prone. There was a smile on Papwa's face, but Suminthra knew he was not asleep. She'd nursed Ma until the end; she'd lost her son when he was only a little boy. She knew what death looked like. Ushering Dinesh out of the room, she asked him to go next door and ask the neighbours to call a doctor. Walking to the other side of the bed, she placed a warm hand on Papwa's chilled brow.

"Wait with your brothers please, boy," she asked Rajen firmly, willing him out of his stupor. The boy tried and failed to compose himself, but he obeyed his mother.

Suminthra smoothed Papwa's hair from his face, stroked his beloved face and waited. After a while, it could have been minutes, it could have been an hour or more, the doctor came and pronounced Papwa's death.

"I think it's a heart attack, Mrs Sewgolum," the doctor tried to explain. "We can't know for certain yet, but it looks likely."

Had her husband's heart simply given in? And he so young? Suminthra knew that Papwa had been taking medication for his heart, but never once had she considered that what ailed him could be life-threatening. "My Papwa's suffering from stress," she'd told herself time and time again. "And who could blame him with the way government and others have treated him?"

"I have lost my heart, *Kanna*." Suminthra thought back to the words he'd spoken that terrible day when he'd taken a bush-knife to his golf kit.

In the end, golf had been everything and without it, Papwa had lost the will to carry on. As soon as Suminthra allowed this thought to cross her mind, she rescinded it immediately. It was the grief making her think that way, the shock. Her Papwa was a fighter. He would never have willingly given in. There was no such thing as dying of a broken heart and her husband's heart had been filled with other things besides golf. There was herself, the children – too young to be without a father, his brothers, his sisters, his nephews and nieces, his friends ... Papwa was a well-loved man, a man who'd loved broadly and deeply.

As the day progressed, the house filled with neighbours, family and Papwa's friends. It was easy for Suminthra to imagine that these men had come to drop her husband off after a day's golfing, or had come by to wish him well before a long trip, like the time he'd left for Holland, the first time, when he'd come back a winner and they'd all met him, gracing his neck with flowers and the crowds – so many people that at times the cars were forced to a halt. Her Papwa had been a hero, not only to their family, but to so many. They'd been so young then, she and Papwa both. She was not old now, and her husband, the same age as she, had been too young to die.

"My deepest condolences, Ma."

Sammy – one of Papwa's golfing friends had come in. Suminthra remembered to smile, even on this day, to be polite. Her Papwa would have wanted it that way, she knew.

Whenever Sammy or one of the others had dropped Papwa at home after the day's golfing, her husband would invite them in and she'd offer tea and snacks, *bel puri, chevra*, often a plate of curry and rice. Papwa had always been a generous man and she'd learnt over the years to be hospitable to his friends, often sitting with them as they told their stories Ma had not liked it, saying that it was not a woman's place to sit around chit-chatting with men.

It was from Papwa's friends that Suminthra had heard about Papwa's antics on the golf course. Papwa's tales had been more perfunctory, blow-by-blow accounts until she could imagine the game for herself, but it was his friends' talk that had made the great golfer her husband was, come alive for her.

"If you don't see the sun, create it," Farouk, a journalist said.

"He was a genius on the greens," another added.

"A true genius," the mourners agreed. "Couldn't read or write, but no one could cheat him on scores."

"Remember that time Gary Player tried to get him to agree to the wrong score?"

"It was during the '65 Natal Open," someone else added.

"Don't talk about the '65 Natal Open. I remember the day he won the '63 Natal Open. Now that was something. You had to be there, brother. The weather was so bad, but our Papwa shone that day."

"We were all there to see him play."

"Yes, he played exceptional golf under those conditions. He deserved to win."

"And don't forget what happened afterwards."

"Who can forget that? It was a shame, an outrage."

"Forced the world to take notice of how apartheid affected real people."

"Changed the way the rest of the world saw South Africa."

"Helped jumpstart the sport boycotts."

"Our boy changed history."

"We lost a great man today, a great golfer." Fishy said.

"A real gentlemen!" everyone agreed.

"But such a joker!" someone said.

"And the man could sing! Hear a song once, and know all the words."

"Oh, how he loved Satchmo's *What a Wonderful World*, even after they took everything away from him, he still sang it on the greens, still believed the world to be a place of wonder."

"And rock 'n roll," someone else mentioned. "Remember his rock 'n roll shot?"

The voices rolled into one, creating an intricate tapestry of Papwa, the man who'd been her husband and the father of her children, yet had belonged to them all. It saddened Suminthra anew to think of the man she had known and not known. But she was grateful that her children would hear the stories. She had always been able to talk about the man, but not the golfer. Yes, he'd been her man, a poor caddie boy when they married, but her man. He would be so to the end of her days.

EPILOGUE

"You hold the club just like *Aja* used to," the man says to his son.

The boy shrugs. "I don't mean to, it's just comfortable this way."

"*Aja* had an excuse. No one taught him to play or to hold a club. He taught himself."

"But he was the best anyway," the boy says, pre-empting his father. "The best of the best."

"Right," his father smiles, "still, you're right-handed. You should place your right hand below your left hand. It will give you more control and you won't have to bend your left arm over the back swing like you're doing. Just because it worked for *Aja*, doesn't mean you shouldn't learn the correct way of holding the club."

"They named the grip after him, Dad. Did he ever show you how to hold the club?"

"No," the father replies. "*Aja* never taught me how to play. None of us ever saw him play – not in person, at least."

The boy nods. This is a story he's heard many times before.

"I was twenty-five years old when I first learned to play golf," his father continues. "I was working then, a grown man. *Aja* wanted his children to get an education first and foremost. He was an intelligent man, your grandfather. Used to say education was the key to success. Not a learned man, but he was smart. He used to tell us to always try harder. If one of us brought home a good report card, he'd ask us if we came first in class. And if we hadn't, he'd encourage us to do better next time. Good wasn't good enough for him. We had to be the best."

The boy smiles. Does his father not realise that this is the way he's treated him and his sister? All his life he's heard his father's stories of his own father. He knows that his grandfather died when his father was only sixteen years old; just two years older than he is now. He wonders what it must have been like for his father to lose a parent at such a young age. He cannot bring himself to ask his father that question, cannot imagine a life without his father in it.

His grandfather had been taken so young, so unexpectedly. Few provisions had been made for the family's future. From his mother, the boy knows that despite winning all those tournaments, his grandfather had never been a wealthy man. At least some of his grandfather's friends had organised collections and benefit tournaments to help the family in the days and weeks after *Aja's* funeral where a guard of honour brandishing golf clubs above his coffin, had seen him off.

The money raised had helped to pay off the mortgage on the family home, but it only went so far. *Aji*, his grandmother, has told him stories of how she was forced to apply for a social grant to help raise her two children still living at home – his father and, *Kaka*, his youngest uncle, Dinesh. Mr Paul had helped out too, *Aji* said. But there was only so much the man could do. There are times that the boy thinks that his grandfather must have been terribly irresponsible, but he'd never say anything to his dad or *Aji*. They'd disagree with him, of course.

"Was it hard being *Aja's* son?" The boy asks, thinking back to his father's words.

"No, not at all. Everyone knew him, knew who he was, so there was that, but *Aja* was such a gentleman, he never had a harsh word to say about anyone. He was a generous man too, never was a miser. People admired him so. It meant a lot to be his son."

The boy smiles. Even today, more than twenty years after his grandfather's death, people still ask him whether he is related to the late Papwa upon learning his surname. It is a name that means something in Durban. So many people claim to have been his grandfather's friend that the boy doubts whether they can all be talking the truth. How many friends could his grandfather have had? Others mention how wonderful it was to see *Aja* in action on the golf course, recounting his feats with imagination and vigour.

"So you were proud to be *Aja's* son, Dad?" the boy asks. He's heard stories about his grandfather: the drinking, the smoking; the wasted years. Women too, though no one mentions that in front of *Aji*. No one can say a bad word about her husband.

"Always," his father replies. "Even with him being gone so long, perhaps more so ... because he'd been taken too soon ... especially since I'm a father."

The boy nods. He knows how seriously his father takes his role.

Then time for conversation is over as the two resume the serious business of playing golf. The day is overcast and cold by Durban standards, but the course is busy. It is a Saturday after all. The sea beyond the freeway is grey and flat, mirroring the sky, but the club's swimming pool sparkles with an azure glow. A match is being fiercely contested on the tennis court; the grunts and shouts of one of the players reach as far as the green. The boy wonders that the red-faced and perspiring man is allowed to make such a racket. Golf is after all supposed to be played in silence. "Must be an important member," the boy thinks aloud. His father says nothing; he is now a member too.

Eventually father and son reach the eighteenth hole.

"It was here that it happened, hey Dad? What did they call it? 'The prize-giving that shook the world?'"

The father tilts his head to nod, but reconsiders. "There was more to your *Aja* than receiving a trophy in the rain. Times were different then. You know that ... It was a tournament that defined *Aja* in the minds of many, but it was not the defining moment of his life, not by a long shot. There were too many to count, plus he always had a fondness for the time he won the Natal Amateur. Only sixteen years of age mind you – not much older than you, but he'd already been playing for many years. But yes, it was here where it happened."

The eighteenth hole is a par four. When the boy sinks the putt, he does so within the requisite number of strokes. This makes the father think that the boy is a natural since it is only the third time he's played.

"One of these days you're going to have a better handicap than me," the father tells his son.

"It was nothing, Dad." The boy shrugs a shoulder, but cannot hide his grin. Then, "Do you really think I can beat you one day, Dad? Even if I hold the club the wrong way?

The father shakes his head, his answering grin as wide as his son's. "If you continue to practise, I don't see why not."

They finish up the game and walk the short distance to the clubhouse built in the Cape Dutch style. After all this time, the edifice with its white walls and gleaming dark wood and brass fixtures remains imposing, but the father notes how his son takes their being there for granted. The boy is growing up in an era where there are no laws defining where a person may go or not go. He is not intimidated by a white skin, something the father recalls himself being once upon a time.

Before entering the clubhouse, they pause on the terrace, looking to see the plaque on the exterior wall facing the eighteenth green. It is to the right of the French doors, one needs to know where to look, but the boy and his father know where. The boy watches as his father traces each word, as if to slow down his reading rate.

> ***In Honour: Sewsunker "Papwa" Sewgolum***
> *This plaque was commissioned by the members of the Durban Country Club to commemorate local golfer Sewsunker "Papwa" Sewgolum's historic victories in the 1963 and 1965 Natal Open Championships, making him the first person of colour to win a professional golf tournament in South Africa. We salute the talent of this self–taught legend of the game.*

Once the reading is complete, the father ushers his son into the clubhouse without a word. His boy thinks nothing as he hurtles through the doors that still bring to mind snooty butlers and tacit warnings attendant to an era gone by. How must his father have felt coming here all those years ago? The man thinks. How intimidated he must have been even before they refused him entry inside!

They pair walk down the corridor towards the changing rooms, past pretty watercolours of prior incarnations of the clubhouse, framed photographs of previous prize-winners and mounted tables of fixtures, including its list of female champions dating back to 1948.

Amongst the trophies and photographs of former champions being awarded their prizes, is another photograph – Papwa in a group shot featuring the winner and runners up of the 1963 South African Open in which he came third. There is another framed picture: a hand-drawn caricature of Papwa. The father and son pause at each. Looking at the small picture, the boy thinks: "This is my grandfather," and is proud. But why, he wonders, is Papwa not more prominently profiled?

"One day your photo will be up there, hey?" the father says, noting the frown on his boy's face.

The boy looks up at his father and smiles. "I hope so, Dad. I hope so."

His father smiles, broadly and confidently, throwing an arm over his son's shoulder. "I know so son, I know so. One day you too will be a champion. It's in your blood. The world wasn't ready for your grandfather, but when your time comes it will be – ready to welcome the next golf champ with the name of Sewgolum! Mark my words, boy. One day, you'll see!"

GLOSSARY

Aarti	Hindu religious worship ritual in which light from ghee- or camphor oil soaked wicks is offered to one or more deities. An Aarti plate is therefore one that bears or contains these wicks.
Adhan	Muslim call to prayer
Aja	Hindu term for paternal grandfather
Aji	Hindu term for paternal grandmother
Arkatia	Recruiter
Arré	Exclamation derived from *hare*, the Hindu term for God.
Achar	Pickled fruit or vegetable preserved in spiced oil.
Bel Puri	Mixture of savoury titbits served as a snack.
Beta	Hindu term for son; when used by an older person to address a child, it can be used for boys and girls.
Bhai	Hindu term for brother
Bindhi	A (usually red) dot on a married Hindu woman's forehead that denotes her status; sometimes worn by unmarried women for decoration.
Birdie	A score of one stroke under par on a given hole.
Bogey	A score of one stroke above par on a given hole.
Bru	(sl.) Brother or friend

Budhape ka sahara	Only support of old age; this term refers to the traditional role of sons in Hindu culture, while daughters are seen as *Paraya Dhan*, see below.
Bush-knife	Large scythe
Chār-ou	(sl.) Indian person in South Africa
Chevra	Crisp snack comprising cereal grains, nuts, legumes and/or fried noodles made from chickpea flour (*sev*).
Choli	Short, often tight-fitting blouse worn under a sari.
Coolie	Indian person; often used derogatorily.
Coolie lines	(sl.) Housing rows where indentured Indians were accommodated; also known as barracks.
Dharma	Tenets and duties by which Hindu people live relating to faith, religion, charity, justice, and custom.
Dompas	(sl.) Official document that black people had to carry during South Africa's apartheid years to prove their identity and right to live and work in certain areas.
Dos	(sl.) Sleep
Eagle	A score of two under par for a given hole.
Ghee	Clarified butter
Gora	(sl.) White person, or someone with a pale skin.
Gulab Jamun	Popular sweet, made by soaking fried balls of dough or cheese in a rosewater syrup.
Itar	Fragrance applied to a Hindu bride.
Jalebi	Bright orange sweet made from a deep-fried batter soaked in syrup.
Kajal	Kohl
Kamarband	Cummerbund; waist sash
Kanna	Term of endearment used by Papwa's wife for her husband.
Karma	Destiny or fate; the outcome of good or evil actions in past of present lives.
Karwa Chauth	One-day fast undertaken by married Hindu women for the health and well-being of their husbands

Larney	(sl.) Boss or employer (noun) Opulent (adjective)
Lightie	(sl.) Young boy
Maang tikka	Jewelled hair accessory that hangs from a female's hair parting to her forehead.
Madumbi	Tropical plant of which the leaves and tubers can be eaten.
Mehndi	Application of patterns made from a paste made from the leaves of the henna tree.
Pallu	Extreme part of a sari used to cover the wearer's head.
Par	The score that perfect play would produce on a given hole or set of holes.
Paraya Dhan	Female children are regarded as the property or wealth of others as it is believed they will benefit the families they marry into, by bringing dowries for instance, and not their birth families (who will have to pay dowries by the same analogy).
Pattha	Rolled pastry snack filled with the leaves of the madumbi plant
Pattha-leaves	Leaves of the madumbi plant
Pekkie-ou	(sl.) A black man
Possie	(sl.) House or home
Puja	Acts of devotion that includes offerings and prayer.
Roti	Generic term for bread
Saptapad	Seven steps the bride and groom take around the sacred fire while reciting their vows during a Hindu wedding ceremony.
Shehnai	Double-reed oboe made from wood and with a metal bell at the bottom.
Sindhur	Red powder applied to the forehead of married Hindu women as a dot or to the parting of the hair; a widow does not wear a sindhur as a sign of her status.
Sirdar	Overseer during the indentured labour period.

Solah shringar	The sixteen adornments of a Hindu bride
Sona	Term of endearment used for children.
Tabla	Pair of small hand drums
Tickey	(sl.) Small South African silver coin, a three-penny piece, which was withdrawn from circulation in 1961.
Tickey-line	(sl.) Common, socially unacceptable
Tilak	Dot applied to a Hindu person's forehead as a symbolic mark.
Umfaan	Zulu word for boy; derogatory term for black male servant.

Printed in the United States
By Bookmasters